LEVINAS AND JAMES

T0339166

American Philosophy

John J. Stuhr, editor

LEVINAS AND JAMES

Toward a Pragmatic Phenomenology

Megan Craig

Indiana University Press
Bloomington & Indianapolis

This book is a publication of

Indiana University Press
601 North Morton Street
Bloomington, Indiana 47404-3797 USA

www.iupress.indiana.edu

Telephone orders   800-842-6796
Fax orders   812-855-7931
Orders by e-mail   iuporder@indiana.edu

♾ The paper used in this publication
meets the minimum requirements of the
American National Standard for Information Sciences—Permanence of Paper
for Printed Library Materials, ANSI
Z39.48-1992.

Manufactured in the United States of
America

Library of Congress Cataloging-in-Pub-
lication Data

Craig, Megan.
   Levinas and James : toward a pragmatic
phenomenology / Megan Craig.
      p. cm. — (American philosophy)
   Includes bibliographical references and
index.
   ISBN 978-0-253-35534-8 (cloth : alk.
paper)—ISBN 978-0-253-22238-1 (pbk. :
alk. paper) 1. Levinas, Emmanuel. 2.
James, William, 1842-1910. 3. Phenomenology. 4. Pragmatism. I. Title.
   B2430.L484C73 2010
   194—dc22
                                    2010008688

1 2 3 4 5 15 14 13 12 11 10

For Nick.
And in loving memory of Tom and Kay Ulmet,
&
Jean and Fred Craig.

TIME PASSES. LISTEN. TIME PASSES.
COME CLOSER NOW.

—Dylan Thomas, *Under Milk Wood*

CONTENTS

PREFACE

i

On first reading Emmanuel Levinas's *Totality and Infinity,* I felt I had found a book whose rhythms I could anticipate. It tapped into a semi-articulate but firm sense I grew up with, of the importance of another person's face and of looking someone in the eye. This was good manners. It was also a way of communicating—a kind of a verbal silence—familiar to me from growing up in a rural part of New England where the only crowds were trees. Anyone familiar with a New England winter knows this earnest, silent kind of speech. It's not that I believed at that time, or believe now, that a face guarantees goodness or some kind of instant ethics—but I did then, and do now, believe that bodily confrontation with another life provides a baseline experience. There is something about another person's face looking back at you that makes things feel more complicated, more full.

As it happened, my reading of *Totality and Infinity* coincided with the war in Bosnia. I was seeing images coming out of Sarajevo, and I attended a conference on human rights violations, women as victims of war crimes, and genocide. The conference was called "Challenging Boundaries" and was held at Yale University in the fall of 1996. Various speakers used images from the war, many of them projected alongside imagery from the liberated concentration camps at the end of World War II. Most of the pairs of photos—one from the present, the other from the past—were impossible to differentiate. At about the same time, I saw Michael Cimino's 1978 movie *The Deer Hunter* about soldiers trying to return home after Vietnam.

The images from Bosnia and *The Deer Hunter* were the backdrop against which I was reading *Totality and Infinity*. The idea of the "face to face" seemed suddenly naïve and idealistic, like an idea you have when you're young, but give up when you leave the woods, move to the city, and start to deal with the real, brutal world. War changes faces. The idea that a human face always looks recognizably human seemed newly complicated and opened a host of questions. What is a face? What does it look like and how will we recognize it? What is human? This was when I put *Totality and Infinity* aside and enrolled in a course called "The Problem of Evil," in hopes of finding a more rigorous, politically viable, problem-solving kind of ethics with principles and rules—leaving Levinas and looking for Kant.

ii

Today there are new wars with new faces, and it is against the backdrop of these wars that this book has taken shape. Therefore, some questions: Why read Levinas now? Why read Levinas in our own time of war? We might broaden these questions and ask, why read at all? Shouldn't we be *doing* something, getting up from our chairs and taking action? This question is acute with Levinas, since he is known as the preeminent philosopher of passivity in the twentieth century. He is also a philosopher who demanded a radical revision of ethics, asking whether we are duped by morality, following the Holocaust.[1] His starting points are passivity and skepticism, and we have to ask ourselves what this means, and how it might help.

There are several answers to the question, why read Levinas now? Most of them are answers I did not expect to find when this project started. I began, in fact, with the thought that Levinas did not have enough to say and would have to be supplemented by other writers and works (Aristotle's *Politics,* for instance). In particular, I doubted that Levinas provided an account of recovery or reparation that would allow us (his readers) to move beyond either memories of the Holocaust or a debilitating sense of insufficiency. I believed his account of ethical subjectivity was too dark. He brilliantly described trauma, but there didn't seem to be another side. It seemed like a bad idea to immerse myself in trauma for a prolonged period of time without there being *some* other side. My first plan was to open with Levinas and then move on. Part of the reason for my original plan was that I had written about Levinas before, and each time I found myself with a nightmarish pile of notes and pages that never seemed to gel. This time, I would dip in and out.

As I began writing, I realized that the more I tried to orient Levinas in the direction I wanted or to bill him as an opening act, the more opaque and impenetrable his texts became. This was the first lesson. Reading Levinas requires a suspension of disbelief, without which there is no point of entry. His texts seem rigged with a sensor, dropping a veil when opened by any reader who knows what she is looking for. There is no way of tricking the books. The draft of my first chapter attempted this, and for weeks my books sat on my desk, shrouded.

I started again, this time with genuine confusion and without knowing where things would lead, although still worried that I was heading toward something I wouldn't want to find—heading toward Kurtz, into the heart of darkness. That was when I learned a second lesson: *Totality and Infinity,* the book that won (and broke) my heart, was the wrong place to start. It was not only too charged for me, but also overly examined by commentators and critics. *Totality and Infinity* is a romantic, unwieldy, wild book. It is where many of Levinas's most recognizable themes first appear in their full, articulated forms. Commentators have a tendency to seize on the themes from *Totality and Infinity,* work on them, repeat them, and wear them out. The book is easy to love and easy to hate, and this also makes it a prime target for the most damning readings of Levinas.[2] I wanted to table some of the clichés that have become attached to Levinas and to see if his other books were more resistant to caricature. I found this resistance in several places, but above all in *Otherwise Than Being or Beyond Essence* and *Existence and Existents*—the former published in 1974 and the latter, his first book, published in 1947.

Although I have drawn from a variety of Levinas's texts, *Otherwise Than Being or Beyond Essence* and *Existence and Existents* are the two that helped me begin on solid ground and provided me with a subplot I had not expected. These are underrated texts that can help us move beyond some of the traditional Levinas scholarship, move in new directions.[3] Looking at Levinas's early work provides insight into the motivating forces of his ethics without the recognizable vocabulary that emerges in *Totality and Infinity.* Looking at his late work sheds light on his concerted effort to undermine the (self-initiated) slogans perpetuated by both his critics and his commentators following the publication of *Totality and Infinity.* Significant Levinas scholarship revolves around questions as to why Levinas bothered to write another major text on ethical subjectivity after *Totality and Infinity,* and whether his late work is an extension or radical revision of his earlier project.[4] I see *Otherwise Than Being or Beyond Essence* as both an extension and a careful recalibration of themes that emerge in *Totality and Infinity.*[5] But I also think that the later work can best be understood in light of writings that predate *Totality and Infinity.* In particular, *Existence and Existents* focuses on embodiment and art in ways that helpfully complicate both mystical and dogmatically anti-aesthetic interpretations of Levinas. Challenging such interpretations is one of the goals of the present work.

As I worked through *Existence and Existents,* I found the first answer to the question why we should read Levinas in this time of war. Very simply: he writes about hope. It is not just any variety of hope, but the kind of hope available in the midst of war, in the most hopeless times.[6] It is a hope found in other people and banal decencies, the hope inscribed in Levinas's description of ethics as these words: "After you."[7] There is a very real kind of promise he writes about that is not terribly complicated and certainly not mystical. It is the promise that, in the absence of any ethical guarantees and faced with the reality that things will, and do, fall apart, we retain a capacity to be decent and dignified. The possibility of saying "After you" remains open. This is not an account of love, friendship, trust, benevolence or justice. There is no big promise or full, exuberant hope. Rather, Levinas writes about the hope allowed by the repetition of the seemingly least significant gesture.

"After you." It's a decent thing to say. Often we say it without thinking about it. We even say it without saying it out loud—with a nod of the head or a sweep of the hand. Levinas pauses at this gesture, asking us to think about it so that, when it becomes less simple (as it inevitably will), we won't forget how uncomplicated it once felt.

It turned out that I was not heading into a consuming darkness but a shifting light, an ambiguity. Hope does not always come in the form in which you first expect it. Sometimes you find it in the least likely place—and if you find it, it's unlikely that you find it once and for all. As philosophers, we tend to gaze up looking for the peak we might climb for the best view. Levinas turns us around and brings us down to earth. He brings us all the way down to the closest, most dense things—to the people we live among, their expressions and faces. We have to give up the idea of a single peak with the best view. But we gain a new landscape of smaller and larger valleys and hills that look more like a place we could actually inhabit. We lose the overview but gain an infinite number of close-ups.

iii

We could use some realistic hope. This is the first reason for reading Levinas today. As a prisoner of war in a Nazi labor camp from 1940 to 1945, he has something to tell us about returning from isolation and picking up the pieces of a life broken by war. He writes from experience and through him we are repeatedly turned back to experience in a way that makes it impossible to separate thinking from life. In Levinas's terms, this is the impossibility of separating philosophy from a face. Faces are sites of hope but where hope *is* nothing but an interruption, a refusal of any last word. The fact that there is not just one face, not a *single* pivot, means that the turn toward a human being happens in an ever-new way: there is no way of simply turning around and finding *the* face. We are surrounded by faces; each is unique. Ethics is the ability to keep spinning, to stay awake to new faces. This is why Levinas describes ethics in terms of *insomnia*. Ethical insomnia is where I begin in chapter 1.

But can we say, "turned back to experience" (as I did above) with respect to Levinas, when he criticizes the language of "experience" as being the language of totality, and opts for "metaphysics" in his description of ethics? I think we can. There is an empiricism in Levinas, which he calls "a very new sort of empiricism" (PN 110).[8] To miss this is to let his philosophy hover without a ground—and he does not, indeed, have solid ground. There is no bedrock. But instead there is the ground provided by another person, a weight and density that moves. Without the embodied touchstones provided by human beings, Levinas's philosophy would be theology and his hope the utopian dream of a world yet to come.

Lived experience—emotion, fatigue, insomnia, and bodily weight—are central features of *Existence and Existents*. This is the text that led me to think about Levinas's "new sort of empiricism" and a link between Levinas and William James.[9] More specifically, it led me to investigate the parallels between Levinas's unique redeployment of the phenomenological method and the strand of pragmatism James identified as "radical empiricism." Holding Levinas next to James, and reading the letters between James and Bergson (who was profoundly influential for Levinas) opens uncharted areas in Levinas. What happened to the legacy of the relationship between Bergson and James, the intersection between two philosophers on two continents, from two traditions? This question was in the back of my mind as I thought about Levinas's strange breed of phenomenology. Levinas's phenomenology is resonant with James's radical empiricism, and hearing this resonance is one way of hearing them in a new key. Reading Levinas and James in concert helps draw out the ethical implications of James's radical empiricism, while seeing the influence of James on Levinas helps to recalibrate the language of excess and trauma that is central to Levinas's project. James brings Levinas down to earth, and Levinas discloses the ethics of James's pragmatic pluralism.

The link between Levinas and James informs the entirety of this book, but it requires some initial staging that may call for patience on the part of those who are primarily interested in the ethical import of James's pluralism. It was Levinas who first led me (back) to James, and I have followed this trajectory in my writing. The relationship between Levinas's phenomenology and James's radical empiricism is the guiding thread of chapters 2 through 4. Chapter 2 confronts the degree to which Levinas radicalizes the phenomenological method he inherits from Husserl and Heidegger by introducing the "face to face"—a situation that Levinas calls *l'expérience par excellence* (TeI 10) (and that Derrida identified as "a discreet but irreversible mutation" in the history of philosophy).[10] Chapter 3 looks at Levinas's concept of experience in *Existence and Existents* in conjunction with James's radical empiricism, comparing their notions of consciousness, sensibility, and religious experience. Chapter 4 centers on the centrality of emotion and feeling in both philosophers' descriptions of ethical subjectivity, highlighting the importance of the body, sensible *impact,* and responsivity in any viable account of ethics.

iv

In their introduction to *Pragmatism and Phenomenology: A Philosophic Encounter,* Sandra Rosenthal and Patrick Bourgeois warn: "A real philosophical encounter is an occasion not for the melting down of one framework to another, but rather for two traditions to be fed in such a way as to clarify for themselves their own positions and deepen their own insights."[11] This is important advice to remember when one undertakes a comparative study of any kind. The goal is not to level either thinker or tradition down, but to show the expansive space for new work that is generated by an encounter that reveals distinct strengths and weaknesses.

There are strengths and weaknesses to investigate in Levinas and James, particularly in light of the capacity for their work to inform and inspire future directions in philosophy. James is crucial in helping to draw out the minimalism of Levinas's ethics, the radically empirical aspects of his philosophy that are critically present but not always easy to see. Without these emphases emerging in their full force, one might be tempted to think that Levinas has nothing concrete or practical to contribute.[12] This is not at all the case. Seeing Levinasian ethics as urgent and timely entails appreciating the ways in which Levinas recalibrates and defuses expectations about what ethics is or can accomplish (his minimizing agenda)—and grasping how much more there is to do in light of more realistic expectations (his maximizing agenda). At the same time, the ethical implications of James's radical empiricism intensify when viewed against the foil of Levinas's concerns, and particularly his worries about the very possibility for ethics in the wake of the tragedies of the twentieth century. These are not ruptures James knew, but his commitments to plurality, sociality, nuance, and "vigilance" (TT 263) resound with increasing urgency. Levinas and James are thinkers who focus on the ordinary, minimal interval of the interpersonal, and who articulate ways in which we might become increasingly humane. In an age of globalization, fragmentation, and increasing alienation, we can return to them to help us find a method for attending to the particular and the personal—a method for tolerance, openness, and creative engagement with our world. This is vital for anyone working in the areas of ethics or creative expression broadly construed.

Suggesting that Levinas and James are not self-sufficient may dismay or dissuade readers who approach either philosopher entirely convinced by and committed to their positions in advance. Moreover, for those who are dead set against one of these philosophers, the conjoining of the two will likely seem gratuitous (why does the one need the other?) if not blasphemous (why would you contaminate the one with the other?). Their connection, however, is both historically and philosophically justified, and there is no good reason for insulating either of them from influences that were real in their time and extend into our own. The matrix of concerns they articulate should help further and deepen dialogue between the European and American traditions that have yet to overcome a polarizing divide that dates back to the 1920s. Levinas, in particular, has suffered a slow and cool reception in Anglo-American philosophy.[13] My work is weighted toward Levinas in an investigation that brings him into contact with sources outside the typically invoked canon of European influences, with James being foremost among the new additions.

This book is, therefore, intended for anyone interested in the interrelation of phenomenology and pragmatism as it impacts ongoing work in ethics and aesthetics. Together, Levinas and James represent the potential for forging a pragmatic phenomenology that retains a focus on sensibility and experience, embraces experimental forms of writing and creative expression, and propounds an ethics based on ongoing attention to particularly and plurality. Seeing Levinas in light of radical empiricism also allows for a deflationary reading that establishes distance from what Dominique Janicaud calls French phenomenology's "theological turn."[14] In the present climate of religious fundamentalism and widespread intolerance, this distance is critical.

This leads to the second reason for reading Levinas today: Levinas, following James, provides a philosophic alternative to broad universals and systematizing theories. Both refuse to establish an ethical principle, to give rules. This leaves things ambiguous and messy. Levinas and James (with different styles and philosophic resources) attend to ambiguity, resist the impulse to categorize things under sweeping themes, realize that new problems require new answers, and prioritize particularity over generality. In the present time, we badly need examples of and practice in this subtler, more modest variety of thinking. We live in a time when there is a crisis of subtlety, an allergy to ambiguity. We need some additional humanity to test our descriptions, more faces to challenge our politics.

The third reason for reading Levinas today is that his descriptions complicate philosophy. We should welcome this complication because it raises questions about how philosophy works, how it is written, and what relationship it has with other forms of expression, particularly with poetry and painting. Philosophy is not self-sufficient. It needs the human faces Levinas adds, but it also needs examples from other things that move us—examples from novels, poems, films, and paintings. We have to read these examples as well as the prose, and this means more than imagining them. We need practice reading in more expansive ways—in going out, looking, walking, running, working, and traveling—so that we can be better readers of our world and not only of books. This is one reason (among others) that I have added some pictures of paintings by Philip Guston in the last chapter. There is an aesthetic dimension to Levinas's ethics—a dimension that has been largely overlooked. Levinas has a tricky relationship with art that reflects his equally complicated relationship with a phrase that is ever-present in his writing: *il y a*. Chapters 5 and 6 confront these complications and the degree to which Levinasian ethics and Jamesian pluralism rely on art.

A dense and expanding literature has grown up around Levinas.[15] This work enters that dialogue, but my plan is to enter it with a new voice, establishing some distance from traditional Levinas scholarship. This distance will be notable foremost by the themes I do not take up, namely: "ethics as first philosophy," Levinas's Judaism, politics, and feminism (there are others but these are among the most contentious and continuous themes with respect to Levinas). Invoking three terms—the personal, the pragmatic, and the poetic—I am proposing a shift in emphasis in how we go about reading Levinas. He gives us, as Derrida notes, "very little—almost nothing" (VM 80). Yet in that dash interposed between "little" and "nothing," there is a narrow interval where what *is* there comes vividly to the fore. The first is another person's face and the inescapably personal meaning that registers at the abstract, bodily level Levinas associates with "sensibility." The second is the concrete, situated experience Levinas makes a touchstone for non-theoretical meaning and his pragmatic realism. The third is poetry, the poetry linked to Levinas's way of writing, but also the poetic density of ordinary life.

It is difficult to categorize Levinas, and this difficulty has its own value. Reading him forces one to give up certain expectations about what philosophy is and what it can or cannot accomplish. This may be experienced as a disappointment. His ethics operates in a narrow margin. Yet there is a lot to be done in this margin, and if, in this minimal space, we find something personal, pragmatic, and poetic, then perhaps we find enough to become increasingly humane, engaged, and moved.

ACKNOWLEDGMENTS

This book has developed over the course of many years, and in the process I've incurred many debts—both professional and personal.

I would like to thank everyone at Indiana University Press, particularly Dee Mortensen, as well as John Stuhr and my excellent copyeditor, David Dusenbury. Without their wisdom and enthusiasm, this work would never have seen the light of day. I would also like to thank my anonymous readers for the Press, whose comments and critiques were invaluable in the final stages of editing these chapters into a book. Thanks as well to Karyn Behnke at the McKee Gallery in New York, and to Berit Potter at the Whitney Museum of American Art, for facilitating copyright permissions and providing images of Philip Guston's paintings.

I am privileged to teach at Stony Brook University alongside colleagues whose work and presence are alike sources of inspiration. My thanks to Eduardo Mendieta for his mentorship, advice, and infectious energy. Special thanks to Ed Casey, who first introduced me to Dee, read my work in its initial stages, and provided extensive comments on chapter 2. Ed's work in phenomenology has been a crucial model and stimulus for my own work, and he figures more centrally in this book than might appear at first glance. My students at Stony Brook are among the most refreshing and brightest philosophers I know, and I feel lucky to work with them all. Particular gratitude goes to Rachel Tillman, my research assistant, for her organization of articles and astute comments on chapters 2 and 4. I also owe thanks to the remarkable members of my Levinas seminar in the fall of 2008 and the James and Bergson seminar in the spring of 2009.

My work on Levinas began at The New School for Social Research, and my deepest gratitude there goes to Richard J. Bernstein and Simon Critchley. The trajectory of my work surely owes something to these influential teachers, who each embody the crossing of boundaries and interdisciplinary spirit that fosters creative philosophical work. I owe special thanks to Richard Bernstein for his seminar on *Totality and Infinity* in the fall of 1999, and to the members of the Levinas reading group that semester—in which we barely got past the preface. I would also like to thank Jay Bernstein for his comments on an early version of chapter 6 and for his course on "Mourning and Melancholia," and Claudia Baracchi for her courses on Plato and Aristotle. There are too many friends at the New School for me to thank them individually, but all of the courses and conversations in my time there inform my work and have enriched my life. I am profoundly grateful to have studied philosophy in such a vibrant, public, and progressive department.

This book took shape in New Haven, Connecticut, where a circle of friends at our local coffee shop provided me with much-needed conversation, distraction, and tea. I am particularly indebted to Ralph W. Franklin, whose extensive copyediting, dialogue, and honest critique were crucial to this project in its early phases.

Thank you to my family for their love and support: to my parents, Susan and Peter Craig, to my sister, Jessica, and my brother, Derek. This book is partially dedicated to my grandparents, Kay and Tom Ulmet, and Jean and Fred Craig. They have left me with a lifetime of beautiful memories, and their goodness sheds a permanent light on my life. Finally, infinite gratitude is due to the two people closest to me. First, to Nick Lloyd, with whom my life is lovingly entwined. It would take another book to enumerate the ways in which Nick has supported me and made this work—and all of my work— possible. Suffice it to say that he is the sole person to have read every word I drafted, and that without him there would have been no dinner. Secondly, and finally, thank you to Cora Simone Lloyd, who was my constant companion through the last months of writing—and whose arrival has imbued our life with a previously unimagined joy.

ABBREVIATIONS

Works by Emmanuel Levinas

AE   *Autrement qu'être ou au-delà de l'essence* (The Hague: Martinus Nijhoff, 1974)

AT   *Alterity and Transcendence,* trans. Michael B. Smith (New York: Columbia University Press, 1999)

BPW   *Basic Philosophical Writings,* ed. Adriaan T. Peperzak, Simon Critchley, and Robert Bernasconi (Bloomington: Indiana University Press, 1996)

BV   *Beyond the Verse: Talmudic Readings and Lectures,* trans. Gary M. Mole (London: Athlone, 1994)

CPP   *Emmanuel Levinas: Collected Philosophical Papers,* trans. Alphonso Lingis (Dordrecht: Martinus Nijhoff, 1987)

DF   *Difficult Freedom, Essays on Judaism,* trans. Seán Hand (Baltimore: Johns Hopkins University Press, 1990)

EaE   *De l'existence à l'existant* (Paris: J. Vrin, 1963)

EDHH *En découvrant l'existence avec Husserl et Heidegger* (Paris: J. Vrin, 2006)

EE   *Existence and Existents,* trans. Alphonso Lingis (The Hague: Martinus Nijhoff, 1978)

EI   *Ethics and Infinity,* trans. Richard A. Cohen (Pittsburgh: Duquesne University Press, 1985)

EN   *Entre-Nous: Thinking of the Other,* trans. Michael B. Smith and Barbara Harshav (New York: Columbia University Press, 1998)

EP   "Enigma and Phenomenon," in BPW

GDT   *God, Death, and Time,* trans. Bettina Bergo (Stanford: Stanford University Press, 2000)

HO   *Humanism of the Other,* trans. Nidra Poller (Chicago: University of Illinois Press, 2006)

IRB   *Is It Righteous to Be? Interviews with Emmanuel Levinas,* ed. Jill Robbins (Stanford: Stanford University Press, 2001)

LB   "Lévy-Bruhl and Contemporary Philosophy," in EN

LR   *The Levinas Reader,* ed. Seán Hand (Oxford: Blackwell, 1989)

MS   "Meaning and Sense," in BPW

OB   *Otherwise Than Being or Beyond Essence,* trans. Alphonso Lingis (The Hague: Martinus Nijhoff, 1981)

OE   *On Escape,* trans. Bettina Bergo (Stanford: Stanford University Press, 2003)

OGM   *Of God Who Comes to Mind,* trans. Bettina Bergo (Stanford: Stanford University Press, 1998)

OS   *Outside the Subject,* trans. Michael B. Smith (Stanford: Stanford University Press, 1993)

PN   *Proper Names,* trans. Michael B. Smith (Stanford: Stanford University Press, 1996)

RS   "Reality and Its Shadow," in LR

TI   *Totality and Infinity,* trans. Alphonso Lingis (Pittsburgh: Duquesne University Press, 1969)

TeI   *Totalité et Infini: Essai sur l'exteriorité* (The Hague: Martinus Nijhoff, 1961)

Works by William James

ERE   *Essays in Radical Empiricism* (Lincoln: University of Nebraska Press, 1996)

LWJ   *Letters of William James: Two Volumes Combined,* ed. Henry James (New York: Cosimo Classics, 2008)

MT   *The Meaning of Truth* (Cambridge, Mass.: Harvard University Press, 1975)

P   *Pragmatism: A New Name for Some Old Ways of Thinking* (Cambridge, Mass.: Harvard University Press, 1975)

PP   *The Principles of Psychology,* 2 vols. (New York: Cosimo Classics, 2007)

PU   *A Pluralistic Universe* (Lincoln: University of Nebraska, 1996)

TT   *Talks to Teachers on Psychology; and to Students on Some of Life's Ideals* (New York: Henry Holt & Co., 1906)

VRE   *The Varieties of Religious Experience, A Study in Human Nature* (Cambridge, Mass.: Harvard University Press, 1985)

WWJ   *The Writings of William James, A Comprehensive Edition,* ed. John J. McDermott (Chicago: University of Chicago Press, 1977)

Other Works

BT   Martin Heidegger, *Being and Time,* trans. John Macquarrie and Edward Robinson (San Francisco: Harper, 1962)

CE   Henri Bergson, *Creative Evolution,* trans. Arthur Mitchell (Mineola: Dover, 1998)

KW   Henri Bergson, *Key Writings,* ed. Keith Ansell Pearson and John Mullarkey, trans. Melissa McMahon (London and New York: Continuum, 2002)

TFW   Henri Bergson, *Time and Free Will,* trans. F. L. Pogson (Mineola: Dover, 2001)

VM   Jacques Derrida, "Violence and Metaphysics," in *Writing and Difference,* trans. Alan Bass (Chicago: University of Chicago Press, 1978)

WD   Maurice Blanchot, *The Writing of the Disaster,* trans. Ann Smock (Lincoln: University of Nebraska Press, 1995)

LEVINAS AND JAMES

ONE

INSOMNIA

Time is living me.
More silent than my shadow, I pass through the loftily covetous multitude.
They are indispensable, singular, worthy of tomorrow.
My name is someone and anyone.
I walk slowly, like one who comes from so far away he doesn't expect to
arrive.

—JORGE LUIS BORGES, "BOAST OF QUIETNESS"

1. The Split Subject

In the preface to *Totality and Infinity,* Levinas describes his work as a "defense of subjectivity," explaining: "[This book] will apprehend subjectivity
not at the level of its purely egoist protestation against totality, nor in its
anguish before death, but as founded on the idea of infinity" (TI 26). In these
opening lines Levinas parts ways with Hegel's dialectic, Husserl's transcendental ego, and Heidegger's being-toward-death, three attempts to describe
the constitutive structures of selfhood. Levinas unites Hegel, Husserl, and
Heidegger in their fixation on an autonomous, self-conscious subject intent
on being free, even if, as Heidegger showed, freedom itself is "finite" (BT 436)
and inseparable from "death, guilt, conscience . . . and finitude" (BT 437).[1]

Critiquing dominant models of subjectivity, Levinas warns: "We have been accustomed to reason in the name of the autonomy of the ego—as though I had witnessed the creation of the world, and as though I could only have been in charge of a world that would have issued out of my free will" (OB 122). Autonomy, consciousness, and freedom are the privileged terms of subjectivity in the history of Western philosophy, beginning with Plato's vision of the philosopher freeing herself from bondage in the cave in order to individuate herself from the crowd, overcome her own clumsy physicality, and ascend to the light of reason. The subject Levinas conceives begins otherwise and elsewhere—in the dark, bound and off-center, tied to others who refuse to leave her alone.

The Levinasian subject has her center of gravity outside of herself. Orbiting against her will, she is caught, like a planet, in the gravitational pull of a distant star. In 1514 Copernicus scandalously threatened the geocentric theory of the universe by suggesting the sun, not the earth, occupies the center of the universe. Similarly (and also scandalously), Levinas dethrones the "I," the "ego," and "consciousness" from their privileged positions in the center of subjectivity. Unseating the "self" and replacing it with the "other," Levinas replaces *freedom* and the subject/object relation with *responsibility* and the intersubjective relation as the problems driving philosophy, making ethics the preeminent philosophical domain.

Unlike Copernicus's revolution, Levinas's universe entails infinite suns, infinite centers of gravity pulling each other off center, none fixed in any place. Every de-centered subject exists in concert with other subjects in a populated world. Levinas draws significant inspiration from the dispersed and average world Heidegger's Dasein inhabits as it tries to differentiate itself from the faceless crowd of *das Man*. But Levinas also shows the limits and dangers of Dasein's project of individuation, describing a tensely interpersonal world where subjects incessantly impact one another, even when they ignore each other. In such a world, ethics entails a capacity for exposure. Keats invoked a power he called "negative capability" to indicate an openness to the world free from the anxious quest for knowledge, information, or clarification.[2] Levinas describes a distinctively human aptitude for weakness, passivity, or "susceptiveness" (*susception pré-originaire*) (OB 122 / AE 195) and defines ethics as "the calling into question of my spontaneity by the presence of the Other" (TI 43). In this account, ethics is not a set of rules or maxims one might internalize and subsequently enact. Instead, ethics is the interruption of freedom and its attendant powers by the visceral exposure to the vulnerability of another person, a vulnerability begetting vulnerability.

The Levinasian subject, never solitary, finds herself inherently plural and entangled in a multifaceted world. No individual ego crystallizes into a self-sufficient core of identity that one might claim as definitive or finally one's own. Every subject is multiple—split and plural all the way down. Levinas discovers a philosophical model of inner multiplicity in Descartes' Third Meditation, in the moment when Descartes, alone in his room, discovers the thought of infinity—a thought exceeding his capacity to think and proof of his inability to be perfectly self-sufficient or entirely abandoned. Levinas takes Descartes' revelation of infinity as the structural model for ethical subjectivity, describing the psyche as both touched and activated by something beyond one's own power or control. Descartes attributes infinity to God, but Levinas locates infinity in the other who "remains terrestrial" (TI 172), in the face of another human being.

Plurality, in the form of a diverse, social world *and* the plural, social psyche, is the infinity interrupting the subject's steady and indifferent biological pulse, "dephasing" (*déphasage*) (OB 68 / AE 111) subjectivity. "The identity of the subject," Levinas explains, "is . . . brought out, not by a rest on itself, but by a restlessness that drives me outside of the nucleus of my substantiality" (OB 142). The negative consequence of being founded on infinity is that the subject is never pulled together, never *whole,* self-identical, nameable, recognizable, or knowable.[3] The subject, deeply enigmatic even to herself, yields no *authentic* self. Instead, a population inhabits consciousness, as if the psyche were composed of the "folds" Deleuze describes in the curvature of every body, "dividing endlessly. . . . an infinitely porous, spongy, or cavernous texture without emptiness, caverns endlessly contained in other caverns, no matter how small."[4] This may sound like a personality disorder. It is not a consoling picture of subjectivity, and in spite of Levinas's emphases on passivity, his is not a tranquil model of the psyche. Levinas offers a context-specific account of subjectivity and substitutes the ancient question *what am I?* for a more ambiguous set of questions demanding different answers at different times, namely: *when, how, where, and who am I now?*

Prone to fracture, the Levinasian subject lives at risk of being torn apart. And yet, for the same reason, she also lives with a unique potential for transformation and reconfiguration. The positive consequence of being non-identical and subject to infinite interruption is that the subject is constitutionally open to excess. Never statically fixed in one place, she revolves in increasingly complicated ways, called further off center by faces all around. Levinas insists on the difference between the priority of the other in his ethics, and the existentialists' championing of the individual expressing its own freedom, rising above the crowd. Yet late in life, even Sartre acknowledged the priority of the other, offering a Levinasian admission: "I was looking for ethics in a consciousness that had no . . . other. Today I think everything that takes place for a consciousness at any given moment is necessarily linked to, and often is even engendered by, the presence of another—or even momentarily by the absence of that other—but, in all events, by the existence of another."[5] Sartre, who famously identified hell as other people, ends up describing human beings as irrevocably tied together and ethics as "one person's relationship to another."[6] Levinas would not use the term "relationship," but prior to Sartre, he articulates humanity as fundamentally intersubjective and ethics as the repetitive, never-complete actualization of an inherent potential for interaction. The Levinasian subject is psychically structured and internally organized for openness, prefabricated for ethical experience. Her vulnerability puts her at risk of being hurt or wounded, but it also allows her to become increasingly open, responsive, and humane. This is the beginning of Levinas's ethical philosophy and his critical, first insight: subjectivity *is* ethical subjectivity.

Ethical subjectivity dominates Levinas's thought. There will be much more to say about his account of subjectivity in what follows. This opening chapter focuses on subjectivity insofar as it lays the groundwork for Levinas's notion of ethics and brings into focus the "radical multiplicity" (TI 220) that serves as an initial point of contact with James's pragmatic pluralism. But this chapter also attempts to defuse some of the anxiety surrounding Levinas's dethroning of the ego (*le Moi*) and destabilizing of the self (*le soi*), an anxiety that is not without cause. One might well ask, given Levinas's claims about the split subject, how his philosophy qualifies as a "defense of subjectivity." It might be seen instead as the destruction of the "self"—a permanently damaging loss of stability with disastrous consequences.[7] Levinas exacerbates this anxiety by delivering the news in language that is itself traumatic and becomes increasingly so over the course of his work. By 1974 when he writes *Otherwise Than Being or Beyond Essence*, he describes ethical subjectivity as "persecution," "substitution," "trauma," and "insomnia."[8]

The last of these descriptions, *insomnia*, dominates Levinas's early *and* late work and serves as the guiding figure of this chapter.[9] Levinas uses insomnia to describe a radical wakefulness and an alternative subjectivity to that based on presence, consciousness, or ego. In his 1976 address, "Philosophy and Awakening," he attributes his philosophical interest in waking to Husserl's Intersubjective Reduction, in which Levinas reads "the awakening, beyond knowledge, to an insomnia or watchfulness (*Wachen*) of which knowledge is but one modality" (EN 87). Elsewhere, wondering whether the analysis of waking must be "pushed . . . beyond the letter of Husserl's text," Levinas insists upon the "irreducible, categorical character of insomnia,"[10] calling insomnia "a scission of identity" and "an irreducible category of the difference *at the heart* of the Same, which pierces the structure of being, in animating or inspiring it."[11] What began as a suggestive intimation of non-epistemic vigilance inspired by Husserl's phenomenology becomes the dominant image of ethical responsibility across Levinas's work. Husserl's "awakening" to ever deeper, expansive levels of apperception turns, in Levinas, into a pre-reflective, permanent interruption constitutive of subjectivity, intensifying from *theoretical* vivification into visceral realization.[12] Insomnia highlights the bodily, lived experience underpinning Levinas's conception of the self—a deeply physical core. Illustrative of the radical vigilance of ethical subjectivity, insomnia also describes an effect of Levinas's prose, the interruption and disruption characteristic of his unconventional syntax and jarring imagery. Reading his traumatic descriptions requires advancing at a place that is slow enough to follow the "spiral" in his text, as Simon Critchley describes it.[13] The difficulty of reading Levinas thereby becomes a preparation for the stamina, creativity, and receptivity necessary for the work of ethics.

2. Interruptive Prose

Traumatic imagery dominates Levinas's texts. On a basic level, Levinas contests classic philosophical hierarchies—same/other, autonomy/heteronomy, mind/body, light/dark—in each case showing the value of the underrated term. He is above all a philosopher who questions the priority of light and vision, arguing that ethics takes place in the dark. His writing contests the privileging of clarity and illumination through deliberately interruptive prose and an arsenal of images that are decidedly dark. The literary disruption extends to the grammatical acrobatics Levinas performs in his late work to avoid totalizing constructions, most significantly in his obsessive avoidance of the copula.

Alphonso Lingis emphasizes the difficulties inherent in translating Levinas, whose "thought succeeds in formulating itself without being set forth in predicative assertions" (OB xxxviii). Lingis admits that English is less amenable than French to the experimental constructions Levinas employs, making the English translation significantly more structured and rigid than the original. Jean-François Lyotard, one of Levinas's most sensitive readers, describes his prose as "a discourse that sets a trap for commentary, attracting it and deceiving it."[14] Basing his ethics on trauma and interruption, Levinas employs both of these as stylistic devices. But prose characterized by trauma and interruption can be both traumatic and disorienting to read.[15] I will say more about the critical importance of Levinas's style to the delivery of his ethical message in chapter 5, alongside the distinct, but equally important aesthetics of James's writing. To begin, however, it seems crucial to acknowledge that, for readers unreceptive to or unprepared for "tropes of excess" (to use Edith Wyschograd's phrase), the initial encounter with Levinas's prose might be alienating and frustrating.[16]

One upshot of feeling frustrated is that readers turn away from Levinas's own texts in search of commentaries or summaries employing more familiar language and based in a traditional philosophical model of definitions, facts, and arguments. When—if—one finds such things, they may be helpful in getting oriented in Levinas's work, but they can also fuel increasingly simplistic and clichéd characterizations. Commentaries and succinct overviews can give readers a false sense that separating style from content is a necessary step in shoring up the *philosophical* content of Levinas's thought. Without doubt, Levinas has benefited from a host of talented interpreters, Derrida being first and foremost among them (from his 1961 essay, "Violence and Metaphysics," to "Adieu," his 1993 eulogy). Yet Levinas (and one could say the same of Derrida) has also suffered from the discomfort his prose inspires and the difficulty of writing *about* him without writing *like* him. His prose can seem repellent, alienating one group of readers altogether, or infectious, making disciples and mimics of another group.

Levinas's early work is dominated by a style of writing characterized by repetitions, stutters, fragments, and compounding descriptions. In later work, he makes language and his method of writing philosophy explicit issues. His rhetorical devices intensify, culminating in *Otherwise Than Being or Beyond Essence*, where the syntax and grammar of language itself mirrors Levinas's claim that ethics entails infinite responsibility. Levinas argues there is no way to exhaust or fulfill responsibility in a populated world where there is always yet another face, one more opening or interruption.

His method of writing is the literary enactment of infinite opening: a rejection of closure, a never-ending story. Comprised of multiple voices— passive and active, present and absent—interruption becomes the dominant feature of Levinas's writing, disrupting progress in a simple forward trajectory (right to left, top to bottom).[17] Although he does not dwell on style when discussing his own work, Levinas describes his method of writing near the end of *Otherwise Than Being or Beyond Essence* as:

> An incessant unsaying of the said, a reduction to the saying always betrayed by the said, whose words are defined by non-defined words; it is a movement going from said to unsaid in which the meaning shows itself, eclipses and shows itself . . . (*un incessant dédit du Dit, au Dire toujours trahi par le Dit dont les mots se définissent par des mots non définis, mouvement allant de dit en dédit où le sens se montre, périclite et se montre . . .*) (OB 181 / AE 278)[18]

The "saying" (*le Dire*) and the "said" (*le Dit*) are technical terms in Levinas's late work—terms I will say more about later in this chapter. For now, it is enough to grasp Levinas's concern with disrupting definitive meanings. A hide and seek dynamic animates Levinas's writing. There is a rhythmic refusal of disclosure or sedimentation that Derrida aptly describes as "the infinite insistence of waves on a beach: return and repetition, always, of the same wave against the same shore, in which, however, as each return recapitulates itself, it also infinitely renews and enriches itself" (VM 312, n. 7). Writing about the essential openness of the Talmud, Levinas invokes a similar image, citing "an unceasing back and forth" definitive of the Talmud's "oceanic rhythm" (NTR 8). The problem is that words (and particularly *written* words) have a tendency to solidify into familiar terms, closing into the "said." The challenge of linguistic closure is acute in philosophy, where entrenched, repetitive terminology loses its animating sense and words become jargon, flattened and mute. Concerned with counteracting the deadening of language and bringing philosophy back to life, Levinas couples entrenched philosophical terms with "non-defined words" (OB 181), pulling words out of their usual contexts and juxtaposing them against something surprising and new. The hybrid, jarring, disrupts the familiar tropes of spoken language and the comfortable rhythms of reading.

The effort required for reading Levinas differs from the focus needed to follow an intricate argument or the stamina needed to plow through an epic

story. Reading Levinas demands a suspension of expectation and a medita-
tive openness to the sometimes murky feel of his prose. Silencing the internal voice that rushes to complete a sentence before it has fully unfurled, one
needs to proceed slowly, to read without skipping ahead, to acclimate to a
lack of closure, and to relinquish the expectation of transparently clear and
distinct ideas. For some this will feel only laborious and negative, as words
that once seemed familiar—supposedly simple words like "experience,"
"face," and "understanding"—become ambiguous and strange; for others,
the same estrangement will reanimate bits of language thought to have long
since expired.

In either case, language becomes "gluey" in Levinas's hands, an effect
Georges Bataille noticed, isolated, and applauded in his review of Levinas's
first book.[19] His prose renders words foreign, as if one were encountering language for the first time and sounding it out with the awkward effort of a first-
time speaker who has yet to find the right cadence and accent. Levinas returns
us to the labor entailed in the advent of speaking—to the work that is largely
forgotten once one learns to maneuver with confidence in a native language.
It is, however, an experience of strain that recurs in moments when words seem
to fail or when the mere act of speaking becomes suddenly difficult, perhaps
impossible. In such times (Levinas calls them "moments of human density"
[EE 7]), even the simplest words get caught in one's throat.

Levinas's style is integral to his ethics. Attempting to separate form from
content will not clarify his thought or distill the rigorously philosophical
from the ambiguously poetic components of his texts. Such an attempt
would be futile from the start and would risk silencing the unique sense, or
voice, of his prose. To confront, rather than evade, the coincidence between
trauma and ethics, between *how* Levinas writes and *what* he says, one might
begin by focusing on Levinas's distinctive imagery, approaching his texts
with an openness typically reserved for a poem or a story that contains
enigmatic, recurring motifs which require careful and ongoing analysis.
Levinas's verbal images are the footholds of his thought, the places where
his thinking breaks with traditional philosophic language and becomes
strikingly unique. As such, they offer a place to get some traction.

Levinas avoids using the word "image" in descriptions of his own writing, evading a term that has such powerful visual implications. And yet, his
texts are vivid in their imagery and distinctive in their descriptive power.
In the concluding section of *Otherwise Than Being or Beyond Essence,* titled

"In Other Words" (*Autrement Dit*), Levinas explains and defends the need for an alternative philosophical vocabulary, admitting that he is "introducing some barbarisms into the language of philosophy" (OB 178). Although he does not specify the terms himself, one could compile an instructive list of Levinas's "barbarisms," which might include the now-familiar "face" and "other," but also the more evocative "neighbor," "desert," "trauma," and "insomnia." Such terms live, as Levinas says, in the "margins" (OB 178) of a Western tradition that has privileged knowledge, essence, and light. Levinas's particular obsession with insomnia relates to Husserl's emphasis on awakening but also, as we will see in chapter 3, to James's analysis of fatigue and various complications of the will considered in *The Principles of Psychology*. "Barbarisms" like insomnia differentiate Levinas's texts from traditional philosophical work, inject his prose with an aesthetic dimension atypical of traditional philosophic language, and become sites of "unsaying" that ultimately erode and transfigure the meaning of surrounding words. Beginning with his "barbarisms" is one way of beginning in the thick of it with Levinas. Each one leads almost immediately into a dense tangle of terminology and a host of negations but also serves as a lifeline back to the concrete.

3. Insomnia

You can't get to sleep. You've been up all night—for nights. It's the horrible scene in the movie *Insomnia* (the American remake) where Al Pacino looks like hell, driving his car and gazing vacantly at a road that warps in and out of focus, losing his mind, black crescents hollowed out under his eyes.[20] Insomnia is not a trivial restlessness, boredom, or ambivalence. Perhaps most especially, it is not anxiety, although anxiety may be one of its symptoms. Insomnia is the physical realization of an anxiety that has gripped you and won't let go. Against the idea of a subject coming to terms with being essentially anxious, Levinas introduces insomnia. It's worse than we thought, more pervasive, consuming and depleting, more serious, concrete, elemental, and physical. You can't sleep. You wear this on your face for everyone to read, and insomnia gives you away. I imagine Levinas turning to Heidegger to ask, "How did you sleep?" He would say it in the unassuming way one might ask a guest who has spent the night. And I imagine Heidegger responding as if he were that guest, "I slept well, thank you."

Through the figure of insomnia, Levinas questions the authenticity and severity of an anxiety that leaves room for sleep. Heidegger stands at the forefront of Levinas's critique, a significant presence in part because it is Heidegger who first dazzled the young Levinas with his existential phenomenology in *Being and Time*. Recollecting his year of study with Heidegger in Freiburg, in 1928–1929, Levinas recalled: "The work of Heidegger, the way in which he practiced phenomenology in *Being and Time*—I knew immediately that this was one of the greatest philosophers in history" (IRB 32). Levinas seizes on the emotional affectivity of Heidegger's account of anxiety and being-toward-death but wants to describe a full-time, whole-bodied restlessness and how that rends a person. In particular, Levinas questions the adequacy of Heidegger's description of angst in light of what he calls a uniquely "modern intelligence"—intelligence, that is, "after Auschwitz."[21] What Heidegger conceives philosophically, Levinas tests in life, and the difference between the known and the lived provokes a visceral change in the concept of anxiety. To make this difference perfectly clear, Levinas's first book, *Existence and Existents,* appeared in France in 1948 wrapped in a red band imprinted with the words: "Where it is not a question of anxiety" (*où il ne s'agit pas d'angoisse*).

Anxiety might be described as the privileged mood of the modern subject. Kierkegaard, Freud, and Sartre (among others) recognized the centrality of anxiety in the psychological tension of human beings, but perhaps above all it is Heidegger who elevated anxiety to a paradigmatically instructive mood. In division I, § 39 of *Being and Time,* Heidegger describes anxiety as one of Dasein's fundamental moods, calling it "one of the most *far-reaching* and most *primordial* possibilities of disclosure" (BT 226). Anxiety reveals Dasein in a distinctive light, illuminating the possibility for Dasein to awaken to a deep-seated insecurity and sense of alienation from the world. Interpreted negatively, anxiety ruptures the self's ability to carry on with its day-to-day activities, but Heidegger sees this interruption as positive insofar as it signals a newly sensitized, reflective attitude. Anxiety "individualizes" (BT 235) the self and becomes a threshold to the self's potential for standing out from the anonymous crowd of the "they" in order to authentically arrive "face to face with itself" (BT 229).

In division II, § 50, Heidegger provides the temporal horizon of anxiety, linking it with a presentiment of the future, looming catastrophe of death that will eradicate every possibility for Dasein, stripping the -*sein* (my *being*) from its *Da* (my *there*). In Heidegger's analysis, anxiety in the face of death signals a productive (if unsettling) refusal of the usual "tranquilizing" (BT 298) account of death perpetuated by the idle talk of the "they," chatter that attempts to rationalize death and blunt its sting. Anxiety indicates "courage" (BT 298) insofar as it signals a readiness to face up to the fact of mortality, "the disclosedness of the fact that Dasein exists as thrown Being *towards* its end" (BT 295). Facing death, Dasein clarifies its life, becoming newly attuned to the present through the sober glimpse into its unchosen but inevitable future. In Heidegger's account, the anxious attunement provoked by realizing that one is destined to die registers audibly as an internal voice calling Dasein back to the potentiality of its own life. In § 60, Heidegger names this voice "*the anxiety of conscience*" (BT 342). Conscience "summons Dasein's Self from its lostness in the 'they'" (BT 319), individualizing the subject and signifying an acute, if inarticulate, sense of purpose and possibility. Despite the certainty of death, life remains unresolved, leaving open *how* Dasein will live out its particular life, what its life will mean, and what its dying will thereby end.

Why is Heidegger's account of anxiety so unsatisfactory for Levinas? At first glance, it might seem that Heidegger's description of "conscience" as an interruptive voice "calling us forth" (BT 326) dovetails with Levinas's description of the split subject out of phase with herself. Both philosophers agree that the subject is internally divided. Yet they disagree regarding what occasions this divide, and whether the fissure can be (or should be) mitigated so that the subject might be made whole. In large part, their difference revolves around competing interpretations of the significance of death. Heidegger fixates on the anxiety of knowing *I* will die. He dismisses the possibility that death might take on a unique significance in the deaths of others, explaining "the dying of others is not something which we experience in a genuine sense; at most we are always just 'there alongside'" (BT 282). For Heidegger, the lateral (fallen) position of being-alongside, *attending* death, precludes the possibility of *facing* death authentically. Insofar as death provokes genuine anxiety (as opposed to the derivative emotion that Heidegger calls "fear"), death must be singularly one's own. Levinas grants Heidegger the insight into the mood attending the *thought* of mortality, but he considers a more personal and traumatic relationship with death. Death takes shape personally when someone dies, an experience of death that is relegated to survivors. A reversal of terms underpins Levinas's entire critique of

Heideggerian anxiety: not the *thought* of death but the *fact* of dying, not anxiety but *horror,* not *my* death but the death of the *other.*

Such reversals have ethical implications. Levinas's critique of the Heideggerian emphasis on *my* death is the cornerstone of the priority of the other that animates his philosophy. The anxious subject who responds to an inner voice of conscience remains dangerously solipsistic. Rather than a call emanating from the internal depths of the psyche, Levinas describes a call that originates outside the subject and that remains irreducible to any aspect of her consciousness. The Levinasian subject is not called back to her authentic self but called forth toward an other, furthering the displacement of the ego. Levinas interprets Heidegger's own involvement with Nazism as a warning that anxiety may indeed awaken one to one's "ownmost potentiality-for-being" (BT 346) without thereby awakening one to anyone else in the world. Asked about Heidegger's relationship with National Socialism in a 1986 interview with François Poirié, Levinas responded: "I don't know; it's the blackest of my thoughts about Heidegger and no forgetting is possible. Maybe Heidegger had the feeling of a world that was decomposing, but he believed in Hitler for a moment in any case. How is this possible?" (IRB 36). In the figure of Heidegger after 1933, Levinas saw an incarnation of anxiety's insufficiency. Anxiety might be a mood that signals a clarifying self-awareness and individuation, but insofar as it wrenches the self from the "they," it is also a mood that risks insulating the subject and justifying her withdrawal or inertia. For Levinas, Heideggerian anxiety remains tied to an inner resolution that need not manifest itself externally, becoming symptomatic of a stubbornly *self*-centered philosophy.

The ethical subject Levinas conceives is literally torn up inside. Anxiety is insufficient for expressing the rupture at the core insofar as the anxious subject retains reflective power, and anxiety itself remains a mode of thought.[22] Levinas situates the ethical subject prior to the thinking subject, arguing that ethical subjectivity emerges before reflective consciousness, at a deeper, indistinct level of the psyche. In *Totality and Infinity* he describes a disorganized pulsation at the heart of the psyche in terms of *memory,* "an inversion of historical time" (TI 56) and a radical interior dimension of "personal time free from common time" (TI 57). The psyche refuses to organize around a linear progression, and memory, "a spasm of time" (TI 170), already sketches a revolutionary orbit in the heart of the self. Thirteen years later, in *Otherwise Than Being or Beyond Essence,* Levinas refines this point and explains: "The psyche is the form of a peculiar dephasing, a loosening or unclamping of identity: the same prevented from coinciding with itself, at odds, torn up from rest, between sleep and insomnia, panting, shivering" (OB 68). The psyche that pulses chaotically in the earlier text pants and shivers in the later text, as if it has become a fully embodied, affective cacophony.

Levinas introduces insomnia as a foil to anxiety, beginning a life's work of intensifying Heideggerian moods with fully embodied alternatives. Insomnia becomes Levinas's description of the dissolution of a subject's physical and mental grip on herself. The self-conscious, knowing subject supposedly anchoring subjectivity (Descartes' *cogito*, Kant's *unity of apperception*, Husserl's *transcendental ego*) disappears. *Who* then remains? Posing this question, Levinas critiques accounts of subjectivity in which "manifestation remains the privileged and ultimate sense of the subjective" (OB 68). Unlike anxiety, a revelatory mood bringing Dasein "face to face with its own uncanniness" (BT 342), insomnia dismantles the subject, distancing her from her sense of self. Heideggerian anxiety results in the subject's finding herself more decisively situated. Insomnia culminates in the subject losing her base, *exposing* her and rendering her radically vulnerable. Ethical subjectivity begins with a weakening of identity and an inescapable contact with the impinging world. The insomniac, impacted beyond consolation, becomes a frayed nerve at the mercy of everything.

Levinas's emphasis on the subject's vulnerability coincides with his effort to re-dignify sensibility and to articulate a distinction between the significance derived from sensibility and the *knowledge* derived from experience. Unlike the early empiricists who championed sensibility, Levinas does not value sense-impressions as atomic building blocks of ideas but as wholly unique occasions of meaning irreducible to knowledge or understanding. In the history of Western philosophy, sensibility has been largely relegated to the lowest level of human existence. In the *Symposium*, Diotima places sense-perception on the first step of a stairway leading from the chaotic and shadowy temptations of the senses to the bright light of reason. The philosopher is meant to ascend those steps, moving onward from the visible realm of the body toward the intelligible realm of the mind. In Plato's picture, the senses are helplessly tied to the body, which is itself an awkward, mutable container for the immortal soul. Aristotle describes sensibility in terms of passive synthesis and growth, features he identifies with a "nutritive" part of the soul human beings share with all living things, all plant and animal life.[23] Descartes compares the body to a piece of wax to explain how impressionable it is and to show the instability and insufficiency of sense-impressions as sources of clear and distinct ideas. In the history of philosophy, having a body seems to be an unfortunate, if necessary, upshot to being a finite, living organism. The body is a source of ambiguity, error, and confusion, indignantly exposed to stimuli beyond its control. Sensibility—the body's vulnerability—is therefore relegated to an inarticulate, immature, or animal aspect of living experience to be overcome by the progressive acquisition of knowledge and reason. Sense-perception is conceived as the passive bodily threshold to something more distinctively *human*—something more noble, if not eternal.

The Levinasian notion of subjectivity stands in stark opposition to conceptions of being human that valorize an aptitude for thickening one's skin and insulating oneself from exposure. Levinas (in the company of Merleau-Ponty and others) contests the philosophical priority of the mind over the body, a hierarchy of consciousness over sensibility dominating Western philosophy into the twenty-first century. It is not a question of simply reversing the order of these terms—insisting that a human being is essentially more body than mind. Such a reversal would only perpetuate the either/or structure fueling the myth that the human subject can be reduced to an essential core or resolved into a theme. Committed to the "ambiguity of subjectivity" (OB 165), Levinas considers a being who is incessantly subjected by his exposure to the world. Sometimes a person seems exposed more dominantly in his physical vulnerability. In section III, part C of *Totality and Infinity*, Levinas focuses on torture and pain as extreme cases of bodily exposure.[24] But physical exposure also lays bare the subject's psychological vulnerability, revealing the degree to which impact compounds and complicates every attempt to distinguish between mind and body, between intellect and sensibility. Rather than mind *or* body, the subject Levinas describes is an ambiguous zone of vulnerability—a sensitive skin from the inside out.

To make vulnerability vivid, Levinas forgoes the language of sense-impression associated with empiricists like Hume and invokes bodily states that radicalize the intermingling of the physical and the psychological. This is one reason Levinas so often invokes trauma, a term that could mean (equally) a blunt blow to the body and a shock to the mind.[25] In addition to insomnia, other examples include "indolence," "hunger," "fatigue," and "labor," each bringing a subject to the brink of physical/psychological breakdown, wearing a person down and laying bare his incoherence. Such states—commonplace experiences of discomfort, weakness, or incapacity—reveal that "consciousness, and our mastery of reality through consciousness, do not exhaust our relationship with reality, in which we are present with all the density of our being."[26] An embodied ambiguity unravels the epistemic subject and reveals her human susceptibility: her whole-bodied immersion in life. Throughout *Otherwise Than Being or Beyond Essence,* Levinas's imagery for subjectivity remains tied to incarnate sensibility, and in particular, tied to moments when one finds oneself at the edge of a dissolving consciousness—burning out.[27]

Insomnia blurs the orienting distinction between night and day and exposes the precarious hold of consciousness. Denied the possibility of sleep, the insomniac's life mutates into newly visceral, painful terms, while lucid thought becomes an interminable burden and effort. Insomnia renders consciousness painfully sensible, engaging the whole body. The simplest acts— keeping one's eyes open—become impossible feats. This signals a strange intensification and reversal of the normal course of things, as actions that should be unproblematic or automatic suddenly require focus and labor. The more the insomniac struggles to sleep, the more she wakes. The body itself becomes highly sensitized to impact of all kinds. Every light is too bright, every noise too loud. The more she thinks about it, the worse it gets, until everything seems to slip out of her control and every stimuli becomes a trigger for a catastrophe.

For all these reasons, insomnia, a non-intellectual, affective, bodily loss of stability, stands in stark relief against a concept of anxiety that bears a special relation to the thinking subject, to the subject who no doubt *feels* anxious, but for whom anxiety is nonetheless a threshold to self-understanding and a way of coming into one's own. Levinas underscores the *subjection* in subjectivity, the subject's "susceptibility, its vulnerability . . . [and] its sensibility" (OB 14). When he describes subjectivity as "a subjection to everything, as a supporting everything and supporting the whole" (OB 164), the insomniac comes to mind—the one at the mercy of everything, who cannot rest, the one for whom there is no inward or outward escape, no chance for sleep. It remains to be seen how "subjection" becomes "a supporting everything," how insomnia turns into ethical wakefulness.

From the outside, it looks like the insomniac is unraveling. Insomnia gives a person away, giving her up so that there is nowhere to hide and no possibility of putting on a good face but also distancing a person from herself, wrenching the "subject" from subjectivity. Levinas explains that "consciousness is depersonalized" in insomnia, and he adds, "I do not stay awake: 'it' stays awake" (EI 49). The insomniac becomes a vigilant, open-eyed gazer without a person attending behind the gaze. An embodied vacancy introduces a margin into life and signals the terrifying possibility of an absence that is nonetheless present—of the walking dead, zombies. And this should remind us, in turn, of the human-seeming automata Descartes worried he might see out his window, and of Shakespeare's ghosts—both of which Levinas dwells on explicitly.

4. *il y a*

There is both a pedestrian and an extraordinary significance to insomnia. Depending on the severity and length of the condition, it might indicate a transient inability to get enough sleep, or a radically debilitating loss of sanity. For Levinas the mere and the extreme are coincident—the holding open of a door to let another pass is coextensive with not killing or crushing another person. Insomnia illustrates the same compounding of a seemingly insignificant gesture into a terribly meaningful condition. The first night that passes without sleep is uncomfortable, but the string of nights and the subsequent dissolution of any distinction between waking and sleeping show the terrifying slippage between sleep, madness, and death. At an extreme, insomnia indicates the trace of an ambiguous death inhabiting life, a "mute, absolutely indeterminate menace" (EE 54). Not surprisingly, "horror" ultimately bears the full weight of Levinas's alternative to anxiety in his earliest writings. Levinas names the horror of the insomniac's suspension between waking and sleeping, life and death, *il y a*.

Describing *il y a* in 1946, Levinas explained: "The disappearance of all things and of the I leaves what cannot disappear, the sheer fact of being in which *one* participates, whether one wants to or not, without having taken the initiative, anonymously" (EE 53). Intimately related to insomnia, *il y a* indicates a non-intentional persistence overflowing the bounds of the subject, rendering her anonymous. Levinas made explicit the link between *il y a* and insomnia in a conversation with Philippe Nemo in 1985, as he remembered: "My reflection on this subject [*il y a*] starts with childhood memories. One sleeps alone, the adults continue life; the child feels the silence of his bedroom as 'rumbling.'"[28] He continued: "It is something resembling what one hears when one puts an empty shell close to the ear, as if the emptiness were full, as if the silence were a noise" (EI 48). This is a rare but instructive mention of childhood by Levinas. The child tries to sleep but is kept awake feeling his room inhabited by the sensible absence of the adults, whose lives continue without him, downstairs. He hears the silence "rumbling." For the child, this coincides with the frightening realization that when he closes his eyes to sleep, the world does not therefore sleep with him. The night is inhabited by other lives going on without him. The night, which should be the dead time, is intensely alive.

The feeling of life persisting anonymously and impersonally through the dark is the feeling of *il y a*.[29] "There is" not something and yet not nothing, but a sensible presence beneath the surface refusing exposure or closure. Interminable, *il y a* is Levinas's description for the density of anonymous existence, "being in general" (EE 52), traversing like a current, as if life were suspended in a liquid membrane capable of seeping in "like bubbles of the earth" (EE 57). "A swarming of points" (EE 53), "an atmosphere, a field" (EE 59), "the existential density of the void itself" (EE 59): these are the expressions Levinas uses to describe a pervasive invisible presence that continues to "rustle" (EE 55) in spite of every effort to go to sleep or turn away. In the section of *Existence and Existents* titled "Existence without Existents," Levinas asks us to imagine everything "reverting to nothingness" (EE 51). He continues, "what of this nothingness itself? Something would happen, if only night and the silence of nothingness" (EE 52). The mind begins to race; images rush in. One is faced with an insubstantial, impersonal something— vague and indistinct. Nothingness is something after all.

Life resists stark division between neat dualities: waking and sleeping, light and dark, something and nothing. These are contaminated, unstable categories. *Il y a* signifies the haunted feeling of the insomniac's night, remaining intensely awake and inhabited despite the fact that the day has come to a close.

There is something nightmarish in all of this. *Il y a* invades a subject and awakens her to an ambiguous existence—an impersonal presence and a faceless life. Levinas asks us to sense the horror of depersonalization and the emergence of featureless shadows in the night: ghosts, lack of closure, the impossibility of nothingness. His favorite examples of insomniacs touched by the invisible presence of *il y a* come from Shakespeare: Hamlet and Macbeth, who each find, in their own ways, that dead is never dead enough. It is also John Marcher's revelation in Henry James's short story *The Beast in the Jungle,* beginning with his youthful, *hopeful* anxiety that there will be *something:* "To see suddenly break out in my life; possibly destroying all further consciousness, possibly annihilating me; possibly on the other hand, only altering everything, striking at the root of all my world and leaving me to the consequences."[30] Marcher confides these thoughts to the woman who later becomes his lifelong companion, May Bartram. But he remains consumed with the egoist thought of some future, heroic, devastating event that might render his life meaningful—all the while missing May, the love of his life so constant and present he never sees her at all. Years later, too late, standing at May's grave, Marcher realizes "this horror of waking"[31] in the face of a stranger passing him in the graveyard, whose "raw glare of . . . grief remained, making our friend wonder in pity what wrong, what wound it expressed, what injury not to be healed. What had the man *had,* to make him by the loss of it so bleed and yet live?"[32]

Death escapes being entirely meaningful or entirely meaningless. It doesn't accomplish a reversion to nothingness, and it doesn't leave its survivors alone untouched. Marcher, hoping for an unambiguous, decisive signal in his life, waits for a stunning catastrophe that never comes. In the process he misses the subtler, more real, meaning in his midst—he misses May's love and her life, even missing her death. No end is final. There is a haunting after every end expressed by James's formula, "so bleed and yet live." *Il y a* stands for this "yet," and insomnia is one way one is sometimes unwillingly subjected to the "horror of waking," touched by the disturbance or interruption of every attempt to end or turn away. Something keeps you up. You don't have the power to turn your back, to turn around, to roll over and go to sleep. These are steps toward the coring-out of the ethical subject who finds herself thrown into question and no longer at the center of her world. They are also like the steps Rilke described in Orpheus's journey out of the "deep uncanny mine of souls," ahead of Eurydice, "filled with her vast death, which was so new, she could not understand that it had happened."[33] Rilke's poem culminates in Eurydice's devastating word "Who?"—her inability to hear or recognize Orpheus calling out her name—and her silent retreat. After everything has been lost, after the descent into the world of the dead, who comes back? "That is in fact our problem," Levinas writes, "what does 'who?' mean?" (*que signifie* qui?) (OB 28 / AE 50).

5. *Se Passer*

Levinas begins with insomnia in *Existence and Existents* to illustrate an inter-rupted identity and a traumatic sense of vertigo that leaves the subject devoid of her usual footholds. If Levinas ended here, we would be left with a subject so deeply exhausted she would simply collapse. It would be a brilliant phenom-enology of fatigue, but without any articulate ethical implications. Instead, insomnia marks an initial step on a trajectory that leads from the abandoned, isolated, subject toward the "subject par excellence" (IRB 46), toward the other. Levinas explained the structure of *Existence and Existents* in very simple terms: "The first half of the book revolves around the subject, and toward the end, the other appears" (IRB 46). In the first half of his analysis, insomnia stands for the subject who can't sleep, but in the second half, insomnia becomes descriptive of the subject who, never solitary, awakens to another person.

A transition out of solitary confinement structures all of Levinas's writing. The subject finds herself called outside, touched by something she did not initi-ate. In *Otherwise Than Being or Beyond Essence* Levinas intensifies his descrip-tions of what it means to be vulnerable and exposed, placing additional em-phasis on *sensibility* and *passivity*—two terms critical to the subject's corporeality and her ethical subjection. In chapter III, "Sensibility and Prox-imity," Levinas invokes "the pure passivity of the sensible" (OB 61) to indicate a "subjective movement" (OB 61) distinct from the anxious, grasping activity of cognition. The Levinasian subject is animated by multiple currents ("a cross-roads of physical forces" [TI 164]). The opening of this chapter explains the different directionality and dynamism of two subjective tendencies: knowing (*le savoir*) and sensing (*le sentir*). Knowledge works on things, taking an active role in "stripping itself of the halo of sensibility" (*ceci se dépouillant du limbe de la sensibilité*) (OB 61 / AE 100) to establish a symbol, an image, or a claim. Insofar as knowing indicates a certain completion and finality, it corresponds to what Levinas calls the "said" (*le Dit*). When language is exercised in the dimension of the "said," words are used to set things up and pin them down. Naming, objectifying, predicting or making predicates, the "said" and knowl-edge are where Levinas situates "the birthplace of ontology" (OB 42). Ontology is born through language that finalizes meaning, closing the circle.

In comparison to the rigidity and apparent resiliency of knowledge, sen-sibility might appear pathetically insubstantial. Its distinctive characteristics include passivity, openness, and transience. It has no way of showing itself since it is always still undergoing and premature. And yet, Levinas insists that sensing is not a second-rate or under-developed way of knowing. Sensibility has "its own meaning" (OB 63) that leads in another direction entirely, re-opening and deepening the subject. As he did with knowledge and the said, Levinas finds a linguistic analog to sensibility in "saying" (*le Dire*), the disrup-tive, verbal countercurrent to the said. Saying remains tied to the pre-articu-late, bare expressive thrust of language. While the temporality of knowledge and the said is always the past (recorded history), sensibility and saying are distinctively present and in the midst, as if "out of time or in two times without entering into either of them" (OB 44). Sensibility disrupts the closure of the past by subjecting the subject to ambiguity and indeterminacy—strata of feel-ing and modes of experience that do not yet have descriptions and that cannot function as facts. The saying and the said fall over one another in an incessant cycle of openness and closure, fluidity and paralysis. Saying disrupts the said, and the said "anaesthetizes" (OB 64) the saying, moving according to a rhythm that parallels the inhalation and exhalation definitive of breathing. This is all to say that language mirrors the tension and complexity of the human subject, who is not single-minded or merely cognitive, but also "flesh and blood" (OB 74). Supremely susceptible, she is at the mercy of the "whole gravity of the body extirpated from its *conatus*" (OB 72).

The drive toward closure that is definitive of cognition and the said is a natural, inevitable part of the dynamic tension of language and subjectivity. Such a drive coincides with the relentless march of historical time through which everything eventually organizes around a story or theme, the time Hegel privileged in his epic dialectic. Yet another kind of temporality runs counter to closure, progressive overcoming, manifestation, and common sense. An alternative description of temporality mirrors Levinas's insistence that the human subject cannot be exhaustively described in terms of know-ing and willing—in terms of freedom and its seizure of the moment. Taking a cue from Bergson's analysis of the internal "process of organization or interpenetration of conscious states ... which constitutes true duration" (TFW 108), Levinas seeks to "unravel other intrigues of time than that of the simple succession of presents" (OB 10). Bergson described disorganized, non-discreet time as a living *durée*, indivisible and impossible to spatialize in terms of single points moving along a line or seconds marked by a clock. James, independently and several years earlier, offered the "stream of thought" as a metaphor for the ambiguous merging of psychic states, "tinged with emotions" (PP 1: 269). He later made the "compounding of conscious-ness" a central feature of his radical empiricism, as he noted: "in the real concrete sensible flux of life experiences compenetrate each other so that it is not easy to know just what is excluded and what is not" (PU 253–54). Levi-nas often relates non-spatial, living temporality to the time of trauma, which, refusing to reconcile into a stable past, erupts in unexpected ways repeatedly through the course of life. In less charged passages, he also characterizes such anarchic temporality as the time of aging, a corrosive time transpiring despite one's intentions, tending toward chaos.

Levinas links the time of aging with pre-reflective passivity, explicitly invoking Bergsonian *durée* to describe non-chronological time: "There ex-ists a *durée* removed from all will of the I, absolutely outside the activity of the I, and that, as aging, is probably the actual carrying out of the *passive* synthesis on the basis of the passivity of the *lapse* whose irreversibility no act of memory, reconstituting the past, can reverse."[34] The subject is subject to time against her will. In *Otherwise Than Being or Beyond Essence*, Levinas insists that "there must be signaled a lapse of time that does not return, a diachrony refractory to all synchronization" (*un laps de temps sans retour, une diachronie réfractaire à tout synchronisation*) (OB 9 / AE 23). The "lapse" cannot be recalled in memory to be worked over and incorporated (however minimally or problematically) into the present. In *The Writing of the Disas-ter*, Blanchot follows Levinas in describing a lapse in time connected with the "passive synthesis" of old age, explaining the lapse as "the dying which is in play in every living being and which removes each (ceaselessly, little by little, and every time all at once) from itself as identity, as unity, and as vital becoming" (WD 34). This is the time Levinas describes as "com[ing] to pass as a passivity more passive than all passivity" (OB 14). He continues, "'*Se passer*'—to come to pass—is for us a precious expression in which the self (*le soi*) figures as in a past that bypasses itself (*se passer*), as in aging without 'active synthesis'" (OB 14 / AE 30). Aging takes place without the subject's consent or initiation. Against the time of history, against the powers of the will, against the *conatus essendi* and the Darwinian struggle for survival, there runs a non-cumulative, unpredictable time undercutting progress and eroding everything in its wake.

The subject discovers the instability of the ego in the very structure of living time. To be in time is to experience the interruptive a-circularity of many kinds of time: the long slow time of labor, a quick explosive joy. In his chapter on the perception of time in *The Principles of Psychology,* James recalls "that interminable first week of an ocean voyage," and a "terribly long" night of pain in which "we keep looking forward to a moment which never comes— the moment when it shall cease" (PP 1: 626). Bergson's classic example involves the time spent waiting for a sugar cube to fully dissolve in a glass of water; an eternity lived in the space of a few minutes.[35] Subjectivity entails this temporal unraveling that refuses organization, a chaotic mixture of progress, regress, and lapse. *Se passer* is "a precious expression" (*expression précieuse*) (OB 14 / AE 30) for Levinas, because it is in time that comes to pass that the self loses its place, finds itself displaced, or passed over, non-identical—older against any will, passive. The *subjection* in subjectivity grounds Levinas's insistence on the primacy of sensibility over consciousness. In sensibility the "I" comes into contact with something outside itself and permanently out of reach. Levinas describes such contact as "proximity," noting that "in contact itself the touching and the touched separate, as though the touched moved off, was always already other, did not have anything in common with me" (OB 86). Contact is the sensible undergoing of a separation out of which one and another stand uniquely together and infinitely apart. The subject issues out of a subjection to this sensible distancing.

Levinas insists there is an *other* time that breaks up historical time, breaking up being's perseverance in being and the perfectly syncopated cycle of the self. In *Totality and Infinity,* he writes about "dead time" (*temps mort*) (TI 58 / TeI 51), as if there are times inhabiting time like the lost object that inhabits and deadens the soul of Freud's melancholiac. "Dead time" indicates moments of rupture refusing the incessant, one-way flow of historical temporality, creating eddies of discontinuity that attest to "the very dispersion and plurality of created being" (TI 58). In his 1956 essay on Blanchot, "The Poet's Vision," Levinas intimates a link between the irreducible plurality signaled by "dead time" and the "authenticity that is not truth" (PN 135) heralded by Blanchot's literature. Levinas describes Blanchot's writing as "being touched by what one sees—being touched from a distance" and describes "poetic language" in terms of a distant meaning that is "not the impersonal of eternity, but the incessant, the interminable, recommencing below whatever negation of it may be undertaken" (PN 132). The wearing away toward negation also resists negation. *Il y a,* which Levinas characterizes as "essence" in *Otherwise Than Being or Beyond Essence,* returns with its indifferent neutrality: "Essence stretching on indefinitely, without any possible halt or interruption . . . without respite, without any possible suspension, is the horrifying *there is* behind all finality proper to the thematizing ego ..." (OB 63). When Levinas insists, "the task is to conceive of the possibility of a break out of essence" (OB 8), he is framing the possibility of a resistance to the neutrality of historical time through which the personal retains meaning—through which a person's own and particular time is not reducible to an impersonal universal time, the neutral beat of *il y a*. He follows this a few pages later with "the breakup of essence is ethics" (*la rupture de l'essence est éthique*) (OB 14 / AE 30). Ethics entails a break out of essence and a rupture of subjectivity, both the rupture of traditional models of subjectivity (Kantian, Hegelian, and Heideggerian in particular), and a rupture definitive of subjectivity itself—Descartes' thought of infinity breaking through his solipsistic meditation. Near the end of *Otherwise Than Being or Beyond Essence*, Levinas explains: "Essence, the being of entities, weaves between the incomparables, between me and the others, a unity, a community ... and drags us off and assembles us on the same side, chaining us to one another like galley slaves, emptying proximity of its meaning. Every attempt to disjoin the conjunction and the conjuncture would be only a clashing of the chains" (OB 182). In the universality of essence everyone looks the same. The break with essence will be like a prison break out of which the "I" will become irreplaceable and unique. From the even light of being, individuals emerge one at a time. Levinas describes this transition in terms of a break with totalizing explanatory structures of subjectivity (consciousness, essence, being), and a grammatical shift from the nominative to the accusative case, from *le Moi* (the ego) to the *soi-même* or the *se* (the reflexive self). The subject, evading description, "cannot be generalized, is not a subject in general; we have moved from the ego [*du Moi*] to the me who am me and no one else [*á moi qui suis moi et pas un autre*]" (OB 13–14 / AE 29).

Essence, being, absorbs everything. I am nothing in the service of being. Everything is covered over and filled in. "I" stand between the deadening essence that blankets the world (like the snow at the end of Joyce's *Dubliners*, "falling faintly through the universe and faintly falling, like the descent of their last end, upon all the living and the dead") and life that burns through essence.[36] As a particular self, as the subject anchoring subjectivity, life flares up in the face of insignificance. Life flares up significantly in a face. Life entails what Levinas calls "an undergoing more passive than any passivity, leaving behind it not even a cinder. Yet it is an undergoing out of which meaning emerges."[37] The meaning that dawns after the disappearance of everything, emerges in its own time, against one's will. In *Totality and Infin-*

ity, Levinas describes the face as an interruption, an upsurge providing "the first signification" (TI 218). Some*one* absolutely new breaks onto the scene. Irreducible to any theme, a face injects essence with a living infinity—with a living time irreducible to one's own time or the impersonal time of essence. It is as if there are multiple infinities, inclining in multiple directions but above all, the infinite complexity of the other person, "whose mortality—and consequently whose life—regards me" (OB 36).

Nothing adds up to something after all. Subject to the erosion at play in essence's impersonal return, the "self" comes back without ever coming back the same. Older, different, changed, Levinas writes: "All my inwardness is invested in the form of a despite-me, for-another. Despite-me, for-another, is signification par excellence" (*Tout mon intimité s'investit en contre-mon-gré—pour-un-autre. Malgré moi, pour-un-autre—voilà la signification par excellence*) (OB 11 / AE 26). In sensibility Levinas sees the trace of this signifying structure—in aging—despite oneself, *se passer.* The ethical turn lies in the coincidence of the "despite-me" with the "*for*-another." Life comes to pass outside my willing, eager living. Life flares up. You pass me by.

The gaping of a subject who can't come back the same indicates a positive, though ambiguous possibility, a responsibility awakening the subject prior to consciousness. At the moment I thought I would be enclosed, cut off, safe—when I thought I knew it all or had it all or had lost it all—there is more life. The dull pulse of *il y a* and the flash of a face—life on all sides. It plays out in its horrors and joys, its light and sadness, its boredom and drama—it plays out in the living impossibility of solidifying around any single time or theme, "by recalling that what took place humanly has never been able to remain closed up in its site" (OB 184). There are multiple lives within life, multiple times. The impossibility of petrifying into any one time for all time indicates the possibility of a turning that is not a return, but a revolution. Ethics is inscribed in an anarchic subject capable of being revolutionary and bearing revolutions—capable of being turned, despite herself, inside out and all the way around.

6. Ethics in the Desert

Subjectivity is a precarious and temporary achievement that involves the incessant flaring up and burning out of the subject attached to being-in-the-world. The subject of subjectivity disappears, over and over. Insomnia: the riveting that wears away and dismantles consciousness points to a gap or abyss under-riding every intentional effort. Aging, the years piling up and wearing away, indicates an accumulation undoing being and time, an impacting, deforming exposure. The subject's erosion indicates a disappearance that makes no appearance as a stage of life, but that leaves a residue of "the restlessness of respiration, the exile in oneself, the in itself without rest" (OB 180). Blanchot expressed such restlessness as "the infiniteness of our destruction" (WD 30). Levinas calls it the "'further still' of the undergoing of the closure of oneself" (le 'plus loin encore' de la dé-claustration du 'soi-même') (OB 180 / AE 277) and, a few lines later, "the self as fissibility" (OB 180). An infinite, yawning space in the heart of subjectivity perpetually tries to close yet finds itself again pried open. Levinas names this opening "the wound that cannot heal over of the self in the ego" (OB 126), insisting that living includes a deepening despite oneself into a place still deeper than one imagined bearable, "a further deep breathing" (une respiration profonde) (OB 180 / AE 277).[38] Humanity is measured by this ambiguous and unlit space in reserve, a gap nothing ever fills.

Ethics, the break with essence, is inscribed in one's capacity to be turned or to pivot on a point always just outside the focus of one's last circle. This is a capacity Emerson described as "an apprenticeship to the truth that around every circle another can be drawn; that there is no end in nature, but every end is a beginning; that there is always another dawn risen at mid-noon, and under every deep a lower deep opens."[39] Echoing an Emersonian sense of openness, James insisted on the dynamic plurality of truths ("the panting struggle of men's live ideas for verification" [MT 110]) and later emphasized the "layer after layer" of untapped energy, a "third and fourth wind," and "deeper and deeper strata of combustible or explosible material" definitive of human beings and critical to ethical aptitude.[40] Describing "the self as fissibility" (fission de soi, ou soi comme fissibilité) (OB 180 / AE 277), and insisting that "truth is in several times" (OB 183), Levinas defines the self as breakable, capable of fracturing and splitting repeatedly, each crack a new circle widening its borders. Aristotle likened the human soul to a surface made of wax, a malleable material that is sometimes hard, sometimes soft—a structure with the distinctive characteristic James called "plasticity" (PP 1: 105). Levinas's "self" is also formed of something impressionable, flexible, and resistant, which he attributes not to the soul or the brain, but to the "living human corporeality . . . a self uncovered, exposed and suffering in its skin" (OB 51). Every effort to reclaim one's first skin is defeated in the de-phasing definitive of being in-time-out-of-time, too late for going back and already on the way forward despite oneself, already confronted with another face, another dazzling interruption. In Aristotle, new experiences leave imprints on the soul, like signet rings in sealing wax. In Levinas, each face leaves an impression on the skin of the self, contributing to the inevitability of "a face that is weighted down with a skin" (*un visage qui s'alourdit d'une peau*) (OB 85 / AE 135), a physical history of wrinkles and scars.

Insomnia describes what it feels like to live in a plural, social world peopled with faces, subject to interruptions and lapses, prone to the "infinite destruction" detaching and distancing beings from being. But the negative space hollowing out subjectivity has, in its openness, a positive possibility without having any positive content. The human subject Levinas describes as "a lung at the bottom of its substance" (OB 180), contains an immeasurable space in reserve. Openness leaves space for a human potential to forget being in general and one's own effort to be in order to remember a being in particular—another person. In the distance from being, from an impersonal essence rebounding from every defeat, one discovers the heartening or heart-rending proximity to another, personal being who is unique and irreplaceable.

Dazzling—ethics is the excessive, blinding flash of a face lighting its own way and calling one back to the "further deep breathing" (OB 180) coring-out even further the hollow space of subjectivity. But isn't this flash also the glaring light and infinitely empty space of the desert? Levinas recalled in his 1966 meditation "Nameless" (*Honneur sans Drapeau*): "We returned to the desert, a space without countryside, or to a space made to measure—like a tomb—to contain us; we returned to a space-receptacle. The ghetto is this too, and not just separation away from the world" (PN 121). Here, without mentioning the face, Levinas invokes "the screaming and howling of ruthless crowds" (PN 123), an effaced mob, humanity displaced and deserted. Dazzling might also be the "brilliance" Blanchot described when "dull, extinguished eyes burn suddenly with a savage gleam for a shred of bread, 'even if one is perfectly aware that death is a few minutes away,' and that there is no longer any point in nourishment" (WD 84). The gleam of animal hunger. A face, a desert, "extinguished eyes"—they all burn with the intensity of something that illuminates from within with its own blinding light. Humanity burns through life in multiple ways. Should we distinguish between the dazzling that is blinding, the oppressive heat and "high noon without shadows" (OB 133, 137, 145) of the desert, the searing flash of animal hunger, and something else?—Someone leaning out of her window, the mysterious way a stranger suddenly enters one's life, the burning warmth of life all around (life on the subway, life in the streets), something closer to Heidegger's beauty shining in the clearing, a face operating like the dazzling openness in "The Origin of the Work of Art"?

Why does Levinas envision ethics as the *ambiguous opening* of a human face? Why this optimism that the ambiguity at work in subjectivity is an opening and not a black hole? Why does he insist on humanity's hope and return? What about faces arising all at once, a sea of faces becoming a faceless sea?

In the five short pages of "Nameless," Levinas returns to "the end of the war" (PN 119) and notes, "what was unique between 1940 and 1945 was the abandonment" (PN 119). Modernity has seen—and continues to see—humanity raging in multiple guises: the burning out and collapse, the impossibility of "any measure to contain monstrosities" (PN 120). And yet Levinas comes back to the heart-rending *il y a* and a dazzling face. In the midst of the darkest chapters of human history, he emphasizes the failure of violence to be total, recalling the minimal "resistance of the *maquis* [rural French resistance groups], that is, a resistance having no other source but one's own certainty and inner self" (PN 121). Such resistance, without recourse to any externally condoned organization, does not guarantee the reversal or reconciliation of anything; but single, individual moments of refusal to bow to the tide of history signify the possibility of being otherwise than a spectator to, or an actor in, violence that has grown so universal that it ceases to appear. Singular stands testify to a certainty that Hannah Arendt articulated:

> That even in the darkest times we have the right to expect some illumination, and that such illumination might well come less from theories and concepts than from the uncertain, flickering, and often weak light that some men and women, in their lives and their works, will kindle under almost any circumstances and shed over the time span that was given to them on earth.[41]

Levinas also attests to the "weak light" and the indeterminate but nonetheless significant value of small, incremental gestures, "simple politeness and the pure polish of manners" (OB 185). Elsewhere he writes about a return: "values are being restored, and all the words we thought belonged to dead languages are reappearing in newspapers and books, and many lost rights are again finding institutions and public force to protect them" (PN

120). Levinas, though he insists that he separates autobiographical writings from philosophical writings, writes from the point of view of a return from incomprehensible loss.[42] Nothing comes back, and yet—even from the places where there were no ashes, survivors return. The survival of "a deafening trauma" (OB 111) is the "unjustified privilege" (PN 120) underpinning *Otherwise Than Being or Beyond Essence* and Levinas's work as a whole.[43]

Trauma remains un-thinkable, un-measurable. The impossibility of coming home, or coming back the same, in which Levinas sees an ethical openness is at the same time the impossibility of any full recovery and the weighty infinitude of grief and mourning—their endless, non-linear course. Blanchot explained: "In the work of mourning, it is not grief that works: grief keeps watch" (WD 52). Freud theorized mourning as a work of detachment and redirection of the energy expended in grief. Blanchot, and Levinas following him, has a less clinical, less neat conception of mourning and grief, arguing that grief keeps watch over mourning like Hegel's master over his slave, keeping mourning at work, disallowing closure, sending one back to the desert and the desertion. Something does come back, in some way, or for some, but Levinas also concludes, "when one has that tumor in the memory, twenty years can do nothing to change it . . . nothing has been able to fill, or even cover, the gaping pit. We still turn back to it from our daily occupations almost as frequently, and the vertigo that grips us at the edge is always the same" (PN 120).

Sometimes things become mere things again. They revert. It's useless. There is nothing—only the interminable desert and ruin of everything that has passed away or fallen down. The temple Heidegger envisions in "The Origin of the Work of Art" makes sensible the slant of light, the vault of the sky, and the trace of the long-departed gods; but there is also the abandonment and the blunt desertion of an uninhabited, uninhabitable place—a darkness that doesn't come to light, "as in a desert, [where] one can find no place to reside" (PN 136). Sometimes the long desert of grief, with its blinding clarity, looms—uninhabitable, impossible. Yet Levinas remembers Diogenes seeking "man among the rubble of things," his "lantern shin[ing] on the clutter of our closets, libraries, attics and museums" (PN 117). Out of the rubbish and rubble there emerges a sensible trace of humanity and a pulse of something refusing closure. Something comes of nothing. There is a raw humanness to a particular variety of devastation: the unmistakable mark and trace of what has passed and the strange shudder at the sense of what, irreplaceable and forever gone, weighs so heavily. A persistent absence and its sensible nonsense—above all the feeling of life all around taking hold the most in the very places wherein and times when life swells up incomprehensibly or has passed away before—the mereness of things (". . . a calm darkens among water lights. The pungent oranges and bright, green wings / Seem things in some procession of the dead, / Winding across wide water, without sound. / The day is like wide water, without sound . . .")[44] and the human touch they bear as a trace—this is where Levinas finds the decoupling of beings with being and their submission to a weakness indicative of an originary, ethical willingness.

In the end, the horror of *il y a* and the dazzling interruption of a human face fall on the heels of one another, displacing one another without any replacement. *Il y a* and faces sit disturbingly close, both of them infinite, both incoherent. They each have their own strange coincidence of saving and devastating grace. *Il y a* and essence take shape in institutions, laws, and justice seeking neutrality—seeking the stability of the "said." Then the face of someone rises up, defiantly reforming everything personal and close, infinitely defying every category and every theme, trembling in the "saying." Life unfurls and occasionally time stops all at once, as if nothing will ever get started again. There are actual interruptions, genuine lapses, and real faces interrupting the desert of essence consuming everything in its endless, even light. Ethics—nothing but these interruptions—anarchically deconstructs the systems erected to ward off anarchy. But in its disturbance ethics simultaneously knits us, one by one, together. We're always seeking something stable and permanent, something for all time. We try to make sense of everything. This is human. But nothing is for all time. Levinas shows that ethics can have no description but gaps that refuse closure, weakening the walls and opening us to being infinitely more vulnerable.

Weakening the walls may not seem good enough. In "Violence and Metaphysics" Derrida carefully identifies a Levinasian minimalism, describing Levinas as founding ". . . a community of the question about the possibility of the question. This is very little—almost nothing" (VM 80). Ten pages later he details the compounding impact of this breed of minimalism, writing: "This unthinkable truth of living experience, to which Levinas returns ceaselessly, cannot possibly be encompassed by philosophical speech without immediately revealing, by philosophy's own light, that philosophy's surface is severely cracked, and that what was taken for its solidity is its rigidity" (VM 90). The "almost nothing" is enough to tremble the walls of an entire tradition. The breath at the end of *Otherwise Than Being or Beyond Essence* is also this "almost nothing" that is so importantly something, a pulse indicating more life. In an interview with Richard Kearney, Levinas talked about the opportunity presented by philosophy's rigidity and the cracks in its walls: "The best thing about philosophy is that it fails. It is better that philosophy fail to totalize meaning—even though, as ontology, it has attempted just this—for it thereby remains open to the irreducible otherness of transcendence."[45] There's a "very little" opening in the edifice of philosophy—a crack providing some room for air.[46] Levinas writes to preserve this gap and enact the failure of philosophy that will ensure the openness of transcendence.

Undergoing without will, or against one's will, whether in the figure of aging, insomnia, trauma, love—all of these point to a possibility that takes shape concretely in the human. Levinas thinks about what it feels like to be human in "the twilight of a world" (EE 7), in moments when one is "weary of everything and everyone, and above all, [weary] of oneself" (EE 11). These are moments when things seem hopeless, moments Levinas finds "singularly instructive" (EE 8). James also thought about such moments in *The Varieties of Religious Experience*, defending his selection of "extremer examples" by pointing out that they "yield the profounder information" (VRE 476). Levinas's examples are even more extreme than James's, and they often rely on "hyperbole" and "superlatives" (OB 183). Yet we should not forget the minimal gestures he underscores: a bodily turn, a step aside, saying "welcome," taking a breath, waking up. These are actions that are equal parts easy (requiring nominal effort) and hard (requiring infinite repetition). In the extremer moments of one's life, when the simplest things seem impossible, one can be reminded of the importance of incremental steps. Levinas's insomniac cannot think straight, and yet, in her intensified susceptibility and sensitivity to everything around her, she discovers that thinking is only one aspect of her humanity and that the world she cannot escape is also the world that refuses to abandon her. Insomnia signifies both a risk and a hope: the risk of being subject to a day that never ends, and the hope of awakening to a world of faces that never close.

At the end we might return to the significance of Levinas's tortured imagery in *Otherwise Than Being or Beyond Essence* (but really through all of his writing) and the way it breaks with traditional philosophical language—the way, as Derrida says, it "cannot be encompassed by philosophical speech" (VM 151). There is a literary significance to Levinas's imagery. Recognizing it as such might help to defuse an over-reactive reading of Levinas that can't get past a sense of outrage at the dethroning of the ego, or (more fanatic and therefore more dangerous) a sense of awestruck fervor and reverence for self-sacrifice. I'd like to de-emphasize both extremes. Levinas writes between the poles of skepticism and faith, resisting both. He invites us toward the temptation to overcome ambiguity, to resolve everything, but at the outer edge of the temptation, he reminds us that ultimate resolution is not only an innocent daydream of another world, but equally a nightmare that tries to realize itself in the world in concretely de-humanizing, oppressive forms. Even death resists total resolution. In prose that breaks with the philosophical tradition, Levinas's imagery throws us toward a form of writing that tries to defeat expectations about what is concretely possible or impossible—that is, outside philosophical discourse toward something closer to literature or poetry. In this sense, when one asks where Levinas leaves us, it might be helpful to rethink what it means to end, to reconsider the multiple ways things might close, finish, end or aim, and to think of the end of a book, a play, a poem. At the end, we might think about how writing that defeats expectations can orient us in a new direction. We might think again about what it means to be left at or led to the end—to the edge, the pit, the hole, the interruption, the opening, the beginning.

TWO

FACES

What is more subtle than this which ties me to the woman or man who looks in my face?

—WALT WHITMAN, "CROSSING BROOKLYN FERRY"

Levinas writes about radical passivity, but he does not suggest we should do less or do nothing. Passivity is not a simple antithesis of action. Offering concrete examples of passivity as *patience, welcoming,* and letting the other go ahead of oneself, Levinas emphasizes the productive tension of a subject who is able to withhold impulsive powers in order to exhibit another, non-egoistic, potential. Passivity remains intensely active, even though the outward manifestation may be difficult to discern and will have nothing of the heroism or grandeur associated with more traditionally paradigmatic *actions.* Levinas admits that a subtler variety of action "does not tackle the Whole in a global and magical way, but grapples with the particular."[1] Emphasizing the discreet and the incremental, Levinas reminds us of a micro-level of potentiality, a level of nuance and ambiguity devoid of flagrant indicators. In the process, he provides no decisive markers and issues no set of rules for ethical activity, no code that might guarantee any specific results.

James also refused the idea of an ethical system, advancing an "anti-moralistic method" that included "passivity," "relaxation," and "surrender" (VRE 108). Linking these ideas with his pragmatic pluralism, James explained that pluralism entails admitting that the "world is always vulnerable, for some part of it may go astray; and having no 'eternal' edition of it to draw comfort from, its partisans must always feel to some degree insecure" (MT 124). Neither Levinas nor James provide a consoling picture or subscribe to a Panglossian optimism that all things work out in the end, that "all is for the best." Levinas, like James, argues that the meaning of ethics is ambiguous and always at risk. There are no guarantees. The minimal is also the maximal—the easiest and the hardest, the closest and the most distant. Ethics is the more and less of things—the close, the personal, the personality of the person in front of you, the particularity of the place and time that require you. Incessant, it will keep you up at night. All things will change and pass. The meaning will shift and collapse and perhaps reappear to haunt you or the world again, but in the meantime ethics stands against this shift and collapse, not by setting up a distant universal where something stands immobile for all time, but by individuals who stand in time, despite time, able to say that things matter even though nothing is for all time. Ethics is one name for this ambiguous, relentless, personalizing meaning—a meaning that James recognized as "provisional" (MT 55) and that Levinas called a "unique and one-way sense."[2]

1. A Descriptive Method

In 1928, at the age of twenty-three, Levinas arrived in Freiberg to study with Edmund Husserl, the grand founder of phenomenology. Levinas unwittingly arrived at a critical moment of transition. It would be the last year of Husserl's teaching and the first year of courses offered at Freiberg by Husserl's former student, a young and rapidly rising star named Martin Heidegger. Heidegger's *Being and Time* appeared like an explosion in the philosophical world in 1927. It was all anyone was talking about in Freiberg when Levinas arrived, and he found himself suddenly immersed in Heidegger's descriptions of anxiety, care, and being-toward-death—Dasein's self-illuminating moods. Thinking back on that critical year of study, Levinas remembered: "I came for Husserl but found Heidegger. It was Husserl who founded the entire procedure—the high art—of phenomenology. Heidegger took it up and made it sparkle" (IRB 156).

Levinas was immersed in the tradition of phenomenology from a young age, but the transition from Husserlian transcendental phenomenology to

Heideggerian ontology represented a shift that would reverberate through-out his life. For both Husserl and Heidegger, phenomenology represented a distinctive *method* of philosophizing. Rather than the systematic construc-tion of a theory that might solve any number of traditional philosophic problems (the mind/body problem, the problem of other minds, the problem of freedom, the problem of knowledge, etc.), phenomenology sought merely to describe what appears to consciousness in the most unprejudiced, naïve way possible. It was something Husserl called a "philosophy for beginners" insofar as phenomenological description requires a "phenomenological re-duction," a bracketing of everything one knows—every theory, system, cat-egory, and name—in order to reflect on the originating sources of cognition and experience. Phenomenology consists in descriptively capturing those sources in their nascent states. The goal is to return to the living emergence of phenomena as they dawn for consciousness in order to discern *how* this dawning takes place. Husserl admitted that in the process of reflecting on consciousness, "abysmal difficulties arise [and] cognition, the thing most taken for granted in natural thinking, suddenly emerges as a mystery."[3]

If Heidegger took up Husserl's descriptive method and made it sparkle, it was because he unleashed his immense descriptive powers on the world in which consciousness finds itself embedded. Levinas breathlessly described his excitement in finding Heidegger's trove of descriptions in *Being and Time*: "Every page was absolutely new . . . the marvels of his accounts of affectivity, the new access to the everyday, the difference between being and beings . . . the rigor with which all that was thought in the brilliance of the formulations, absolutely impressive" (IRB 33). Husserl's descriptions focused on the inten-tional life of consciousness, but Heidegger's descriptions focused on the exis-tential life of human beings: their being-in-the-world. This transition did not impress Husserl, who saw it as a betrayal of the pure phenomenological method and criticized *Being and Time* as a kind of anthropology. But it was precisely the transition from the inner life of consciousness to the inhabited landscapes of the world that, in 1928, attracted Levinas away from Husserl toward Heidegger.

The phenomenological method changes as it changes hands. This chapter considers what happens to phenomenology in Levinas's hands, paving the way toward Levinas's intersection with William James. Just as Heidegger breaks with Husserl, Levinas breaks with Heidegger.[4] These are not clean breaks. Considering why and how Levinas's departure from traditional models of phenomenology takes place, one begins to see the difficulty of situating his philosophy in any single tradition and to sense the prospects for a more pluralistic and radical phenomenology latent in Levinas's thought. On the one hand, Levinas follows in a tradition, and particularly a Heideggerian tradition, of prioritizing language in the form of the audible, expressive, and potentially poetic word. But on the other hand, Levinas breaks with this tradition by criticizing as disembodied the picture of a bare language or expression—that is, expression without a face. There is, therefore, a double gesture at work in Levinas: a gesture toward the ideality of ethical expressivity, and at the same time an undercutting of ideality through an insistence on the plurality of individual, incomparable faces. Ultimately, his focus on pluralism and his quest for a more vital phenomenology positions Levinas farther from Husserl and Heidegger and closer to James's radical empiricism. Before jumping ahead to that critical juncture, this chapter investigates the motivating factors and terms of Levinas's increasingly transgressive phenomenology.

2. Urban Phenomenology

In his 1984 lecture, "Transcendence and Intelligibility," Levinas articulates his divergence from the themes he saw dominating European philosophy in the years leading up to and following the publication of *Totality and Infinity*. In particular, Levinas contests the phenomenological focus on knowledge and the privileging of "presence."[5] He describes his version of phenomenology as "another phenomenology, even if it [is] the destruction of the phenomenology of appearance and knowledge."[6] What is other about Levinas's phenomenology is his emphasis on the "Other"—an ethical emphasis that Levinas sees as concretely at odds with Husserl's transcendental phenomenology and Heidegger's ontology. Levinas looks for a third way between being-for-consciousness and being-in-the-world by articulating an event and a meaning that is neither ideal nor futural. Ultimately he calls this "event" ethics, and makes the person the site of the meaning of meaning—a shift that is made possible by the living face.

In many ways Levinas has an easier time disentangling himself from Husserl than from Heidegger, whose analysis in *Being and Time* is emblematic of something Levinas thinks is "essential to phenomenology," namely: "approaching an idea by asserting the concreteness of a situation in which it originally assumes a meaning."[7] Phenomenology returns to the things themselves, and Heidegger in particular finds a way of describing "the concreteness of a situation" without bracketing the world in which it takes shape. With his unique attention to moods, his focus on time and language, and his compounding descriptions, Heidegger is the obvious inspiration for Levinas's sense of "another phenomenology." Levinas credits Heidegger with bringing the "concrete" back to life insofar as he restores a verbal sense to "Being" and describes the empirical events and accompanying moods of being in time. In his 1987 lecture "Dying For . . ." Levinas described the most significant upshot of *Being and Time* as: "The suspension of quiddity in the being of man in order to conceive of this *being* as *existence,* as the adverbial modality of the event of being . . . which constitutes a new approach to the meaningful."[8] Suspending the *what* in order to focus on the *when, how,* and *where* of beings, Heidegger finds a way of describing a moving, living meaningfulness that is simultaneously concrete and animated—real and alive.

Like Heidegger, Levinas seeks "a new approach to the meaningful." But parting ways with Heidegger, Levinas asks whether ontology provides the privileged site of meaning and whether the future defines the privileged horizon of understanding. Levinas ultimately accuses Heidegger of failing to make the full phenomenological turn, since the relationship with *being in general* is, in the end, an abstract relationship with "a bare fact" (EE 3) and not a relationship with anything or any*one* in the world. Restoring the "adverbial modality of the event of being," Heidegger gets things moving, but in the direction of a mysterious clearing that is essentially unpopulated. The absence of others in Heidegger's world fuels Levinas's critique, despite Heidegger's attention to *Mitsein* in division I, part IV of *Being and Time:* "Being-in-the-world as Being-with and Being-one's-self. The They."[9] Considering this crucial aspect of *Being and Time,* Levinas conceded that "Heideggerian being-with-one-another [*das Miteinandersein*] appears to me always like marching-together. That is not for me; there is no face there" (IRB 137). Levinas radicalizes the phenomenological turn by showing that a "bare fact" is never bare. There is never an empty clearing, even when a place looks like the emptiest place on earth. The fact of something rather than nothing is *il y a*—which is not really a fact but the erosion of facts, the contamination of the clearing, or the populating of every opening, however bare, with another face.

This is why, if Heidegger is right in his characterization of metaphysics as the attempt to replace the clearing with a particular being or group of beings, then Levinas is emphatically metaphysical.[10] But there is something misleading in this characterization, since what ends up being metaphysical in Levinas is just the face of another human being, a face never static or clear but always particular, moving, and out of reach. "Face" is not a "solving name."[11] The face is the site of a crossroads in Levinas's philosophy. Neither phenomenon nor form, the face falls between the cracks of traditional phenomenology and traditional metaphysics, landing somewhere ambiguously between the two in an intensely real, up close, and empirical ideality—the flashes of faces in a crowd, each one unique. This is not a neat picture. It is certainly not the pastoral picture conjured up by Heidegger's imagery: the plowed and sown fields and tree-lined clearings. Levinas's metaphysics returns to the crowds, to the streets and noise, of a more urban landscape.[12] It is as if Heidegger has a poetic counterpart in Wordsworth, walking in the meadow among the "dews, vapors, and the melody of birds, / And laborers going forth to till the fields."[13] Levinas's poetic counterpart is more like Whitman, crossing Brooklyn ferry:

> Flood-tide below me! I see you face to face!
> Clouds of the west—sun there half an hour high—I see you also face to
> face.
> Crowds of men and women attired in the usual costumes, how curious
> you are to me!
> On the ferry-boats, the hundreds and hundred that cross, returning
> home, are more curious to me than you suppose,
> And you that shall cross from shore to shore years hence are more to me,
> and more in my meditations, than you might suppose.[14]

Imagining Heidegger alongside Wordsworth and Levinas alongside Whitman helps differentiate their respective emphases and limitations, and aids in visualizing their different brands of humanism. Both of them sought to renew a humanism they feared had degenerated beyond repair: Heidegger advocated an "open resistance to 'humanism'" in order genuinely to question the "*humanitas* of *homo humanus*," while Levinas identified a "crisis of humanism in our times" and lamented "a preachiness that befell Western humanism."[15] Yet what the renewal of humanism means is different for each philosopher. In many ways it is just a difference of setting, a difference between landscapes and cityscapes, each of them with their own dignity and humanity. If one could stage Heidegger's *Being and Time,* it might be set outside, in an amphitheater with a few objects—Heideggerian things: a rock, a jug, a hammer, a radio, a pair of shoes—strewn amid unmown grass without any demarcation between the stage and the trees beyond. Perhaps it would not be a play at all, but a sound installation left in the woods ("in a grove where no light penetrates") so that we could happen upon it like "wanderers on the way into the neighborhood of Being."[16] Alternatively, one could imagine Levinas's *Totality and Infinity* taking place in a dimly lit subway car. It would not be staged as a play, but filmed: the whole of the action comprised of a series of close-ups, like an animated version of Walker Evans's candid subway portraits.

Heidegger and Levinas might thus be described as representatives of the difference between a rural and an urban phenomenology. Places and things dominate the former, while people dominate the latter.[17] Levinas sees Heidegger's descriptions as a critical step in setting the stage for any meaningful phenomenological description, but also expresses his anxiety over the setting of *Being and Time*: "The poetry of peaceful paths that run through the fields do not simply reflect the splendor of Being beyond beings. That splendor brings with it more somber and pitiless images."[18] The "somber and pitiless images" Levinas remembers include the images dominating Europe after the air raids in the final days of the war—piles of rubble, the haunting remnants of a peopled world.

Acutely aware of Heidegger's anxiety about cities and his devotion to the mountains, Levinas remembers his first impressions of Heidegger as: "Not very tall, walking around in a skiing outfit" (IRB 36). In another interview, he describes Heidegger's phenomenology itself in terms of a mountain, explaining, "Phenomenology—'to the things themselves'— . . . requires some kind of staging, a mise-en-scène. In this sense, *Being and Time* is a 'Himalaya,' a truly lofty landscape of the concrete" (IRB 151). Throughout his life (and despite Heidegger's politics) Levinas returned to *Being and Time* and ranked it among the greatest works of philosophy, the pinnacle of phenomenology.[19] Yet Levinas's entire philosophy could be described in terms of a descent from there. Like Heidegger, Levinas remains devoted to a phenomenological "staging." Both *Being and Time* and Levinas's *Totality and Infinity* describe and analyze the underlying structures of everyday experience, our being-in-the-world. But unlike Heidegger, Levinas conceives of a much less lofty and pristine place for being human. Coming down the mountain into the streets, Levinas's *mise-en-scène* entails re-populating Heidegger's world, showing that Heidegger's mountain towers above, and rises from, a ground dense with human faces.

3. Faces

Returning to populated landscapes of human existence, Levinas begins, not with the solitary subject looking for a way of reconciling her inner reality with an external world, and not with an inauthentic subject trying to individualize herself from the anonymous crowd of *das Man,* but with subjects immersed together in a bustling field of activity, inherently intersubjective. This is patently at odds with a traditional conception of phenomenology as issuing from a first-person perspective, from an "I" who reflects on the underlying structures of its own experiences. As we saw in the previous chapter, Levinas calls into question the identity of the "I" in his account of subjectivity as essentially plural and displaced. The Levinasian subject is populated from the inside out.[20] This means that Levinas's phenomenology will have to begin from a point other than the solitary viewing-deck of reflective consciousness. This will not be simple to describe or achieve. Levinas's phenomenology attempts to break with an egoism he reads in both Husserl and Heidegger. Rather than beginning with the "I," Levinas locates the first upsurge of meaning *outside* the ego in the interpersonal situation of the "face to face."

Levinas adds faces to Heidegger's world. Neither this description, however, nor Whitman's imagery ("Sauntering the pavement or riding the country byroad here then are faces"), clarifies what Levinas means when he speaks of the face. Whitman himself presents us with endless possibilities, among them the "faces of friendship, precision, caution," "the face of a dream," of a "rock," and "a face of bitter herbs."[21]

What then is a face? This question has plagued and baffled Levinas's interpreters since his introduction of the term and his conjoining of "face" with "the idea of the Infinite" in the preface of *Totality and Infinity:* "the gleam of exteriority or of transcendence in the face of the Other [*le visage d'autrui*]" (TI 24). In recent work, Diane Perpich examines both the possibilities and the limitations of Levinas's invocation of the face, presciently warning that "the paradoxes generated by Levinas's discourse on the face are permanent and intractable."[22] Just as *subjectivity,* a critical term across Levinas's work, takes on a radically new meaning in his hands, so does the seemingly simple word "face" (*visage*). Alongside *others* (*autrui*) and ethics, "face" is among *the* critical terms in Levinas, and remains the one most closely associated with his thought. Even those unfamiliar with Levinas might recognize the phrase "face to face" as paradigmatically belonging to him. At the same time, "face" is among the most difficult words to understand in his texts, rendering the concept of the "face to face" doubly enigmatic.

Levinas preys on the fact that "face" is such an ordinary, seemingly elementary word, free from the complexity of philosophically specific terminology, words like *ontology* and *metaphysics*. Yet it is precisely the ubiquity of the word in spoken and written language that renders it particularly difficult to situate, allowing Levinas to let it resound ambiguously.[23] Bernhard Waldenfels pays careful attention to this strategy in his essay, "Levinas and the Face of the Other," describing Levinas's method of philosophizing as "a *dérangement* which puts us out of our common tracks."[24] Waldenfels goes on to provide illuminating examples of the meanings and uses of "face" in several languages, arguing that we can distinguish a "narrow, rather common meaning from a wider, more emphatic meaning."[25] "Face" commonly indicates both the sensible area on the front of the head from the forehead to the chin and the exposed *surface* or façade of something inanimate (a "facing page," "face value," the "face of a cliff"). As a verb, and in its more "emphatic" manifestations, "face" could mean to turn in a certain direction or adopt a decisive psychological orientation ("facing up" to a problem, "facing down" a threat, "saving face"). Due to its widespread, shifting usage, there occurs a persistent temptation when reading Levinas to assume that "face" denotes something apparent and identifiable—something not that difficult or deep. As with the seemingly inconsequential expression *il y a*, "face" renders Levinas's work familiar (we know these words by heart) and deeply enigmatic (they are so familiar we have ceased to hear them at all). Both *il y a* and "face" work as reminders of the banality of everyday speech and as "barbarisms" (OB 178), deconstructing philosophical language (and the very possibility of phenomenological description) from within.

As with many of Levinas's terms, it is much easier to give a negative description of what the "face" is *not* than to provide a positive description. Foremost, the face is not reducible to the physical configuration of eyes, nose, and mouth. The face is not the face of someone we recognize, the features we know by heart or that we might paint in a portrait. In characteristically opaque language, Levinas explained in a 1988 interview: "All the naked and disarmed mortality of the other can be read from [the back] . . . The face, then, is not the color of the eyes, the shape of the nose or the ruddiness of the cheeks, etc." (EN 232). As Levinas describes it, the face is not even tied to the front of the head, which means we cannot determine its physical location relative to the human body. It might be "the nape of the neck" (EN 232), an image Levinas draws from Vassily Grossman's *Life and Fate* and invokes repeatedly.[26] If the face is not tied to the eyes, nose, and mouth, then the "face to face" cannot be the physical facing of individuals who look one another in the eye. Standing face to face *might* signify this configuration, but it might equally be the facing of eye to neck, arm to back, or the bare interface of "flesh" Merleau-Ponty described as a touch that feels itself touching.[27]

In the broadest way possible, "face" is a term for the way one is touched by the human: "the epiphany of the face qua face opens humanity" (*l'épiphanie du visage comme visage, ouvre l'humanité*) (TI 213 / TeT 234). For many, Levinas's linkage of the face with "humanity" signals a dangerous anthropocentrism that precludes other animals (specifically) and the environment (more broadly) from ethical responsibility.[28] This remains a particularly fraught topic given the urgency of contemporary crises: the human impact on global warming, worldwide food shortages and their relation to environmentally unsustainable and frequently inhumane farming methods and the treatment of animals, and the ongoing depletion of water, soil, forests, and other natural resources for sake of human "development." The list could go on. Levinas's philosophy engenders anxiety over who or what counts as ethically relevant and just how far responsibility extends. These issues fall outside the scope of the present work, but the fact that they arise as pressing questions as a result of Levinas's invocation of the "face" indicates the complexity and ambiguity built into a term that remains stubbornly non-defined. "Face" resists questions framed by quiddity. Such resistance results in a destabilization of the meaning of "face," but also, by virtue of Levinas's own coupling, in a disruption of the meaning of "humanity" and the concept of the "human." Levinas complicates his own lack of specificity about what constitutes a face with an insistence that a face, whatever it is, is paradigmatically human. Yet he also writes, "the human face is the face of the world itself, and the individual of the human race, like all things, arises already within the humanity of the world" (EP 73). Moments later he compares the transient expression of a face to "a ridge of sand on the earth" (EP 73). Such lines leave open the possibility of a more expansive notion of the face and of humanity, recalling Bergson's sense of radical novelty: "not only something new, but something unforeseeable."[29] Judith Butler, seizing on the positive potential for the ambiguity of faces, explains the distinctive impact of a face in the following way: "To respond to the face, to understand its meaning, is to be awake to what is precarious in another life or, rather, the precariousness of life itself."[30] Levinas links such an awakening to the essential vulnerability underlying intentionality, as if a subject assembles herself around a fluid core permanently at risk of puncture or eruption by exposure to another vulnerability—subjection via faces.

The broadening of possibilities for being faced with another "precarious life" coincides with Levinas's insistence that ethics takes place in the dark. We never fully see the lives that face us; they are deep with a significance that never comes to light. This is Levinas's reminder that one is never granted a clear or comprehensive view of what is taking placing or who is calling out, even when one feels most self-assured of grasping the whole picture. The world in its plurality defies global comprehension, just as each individual, herself a plurality of selves, defies identification. As we will see more fully in the next chapter, this is a point that James also emphasized, one that re-lates to the ethical implications of his radical empiricism. Stressing the dan-gers of conceiving ethics as a completed system, James concluded: "the *high-est* ethical life—however few may be called to bear its burdens—consists at all times in the breaking of rules which have grown too narrow for the actual case. . . . For every real dilemma is in literal strictness a unique situation."[31] Put in more Levinasian terms, this amounts to the claim that every real dilemma requires an ability to navigate in the dark.

Levinas critiques the philosophical privileging of light and the celebrated transparency of space, and this critique remains in full force in his lengthy exposition of the face in *Totality and Infinity* through his notably brief discus-sion of the face, "Phenomenon and Face," in *Otherwise Than Being or Beyond Essence* (OB 89–93). In *Totality and Infinity*, Levinas associates light and vision with power and knowledge, insisting: "Light conditions the relations between data; it makes possible the signification of objects that border on one another. It does not enable one to approach them face to face" (TI 191). In the light, we see things in their broader contexts, within horizons that inform them and help us glean their "*lateral* signification" (TI 191). One being illuminates an-other, making relative sense of things positioned side by side and occluding the dimensions of depth (and height) so critical to Levinas's descriptions of responsibility. The "face to face" breaks free from lateral relation, the *Mitsein* or being *alongside* that Levinas fears dominates Heidegger's world. Arriving "face to face" entails giving up the horizon, as if one were to step suddenly out of line and turn around to something directly behind one's back. The possibility of being "face to face"—ethics—does not depend on the broad light of day or the light of several witnesses. Even when no one is watching, faces persistently intervene, calling out for attention. Responsibility therefore extends beyond the scope of the visible world to the faces of those who cannot, or do not appear, to those who have been kept out of view or those one has simply ceased to see or to consider.

The face makes itself felt in multiple ways, appealing to more than the eye. The priority of light in the history of philosophy entails a privileging of vision as the most significant sense. Levinas structures his discussion of the face around an investigation of sensibility, accusing traditional accounts of reducing sensation to vision and touch.[32] He explains, "the object disclosed, discovered, appearing, a phenomenon, is the visible or touched object. . . . we use the term vision indifferently for every experience, even when it involves other senses than sight" (TI 188). James, like Levinas, defended the dignity of sensation as an essential threshold to awareness of "*bare immediate natures*" (PP 2: 3)—an awareness that is irreducible to subsequent knowledge *about* things. "Sensations," James insists, "first make us acquainted with innumerable things, and then are replaced by thoughts which know the same things in altogether other ways" (PP 2: 6). Noting the tendency to overlook, underplay, and reduce the complexity of sensation, James explained:

> We are constantly selecting certain of our sensations as *realities* and degrading others to the status of *signs* of these. When we get one of the signs we think of the reality signified; and the strange thing is that then the reality (which need not be itself a sensation at all at the time, but only an idea) is so interesting that it acquires an hallucinatory strength, which may even eclipse that of the relatively uninteresting sign and entirely divert our attention to the latter. (PP 2: 41)

Ideas *about* sensation have a way of occluding sensation. The intellectual individuating of sensations results from an act of reflection and distillation in which certain aspects of sensation are seen (retrospectively) as emblematic and given prominence. James sees this as an inevitable feature of conscious life, which is always moving ahead of and processing experiences into increasingly manageable, thinkable chunks. Yet he warns of the "hallucinatory strength" of an idea that has replaced the living flux of sensational experience. Such a substitution entails a transfiguration of sensation, a forced clarification, a deadening of "sensational *tang*" (PP 2: 7) and, as Levinas, worries, a reduction. Once the reduction takes place, we are likely to count as significant only those objects we classify as *real* (James's word) or those we can see and hold (following Levinas)—objects that are clear and distinct (in Descartes' language) or ready-to-hand (in Heidegger's terminology).

To counter ocular/haptic-centric accounts of sensibility, Levinas focuses most of his attention on the sense of hearing in *Totality and Infinity*, providing an account of the face as invisible but singularly expressive and *audible:* "the face speaks" (TI 66). Levinas adds to hearing the sense of taste in *Otherwise Than Being or Beyond Essence,* through the invocation of *hunger* and an insistence on "thermal, gustative, olfactory sensation" (OB 65).[33] The transition from the earlier to the later text shows that Levinas expands and complicates his own account of sensibility, even as he remains (regrettably) tied to a traditional model of five discernible senses. Given the radicalism of his notion of ethics and his strategically erosive use of the term "face," one might expect a more radical rethinking of sensibility, a more complex picture of embodiment, and a more synaesthetic notion of vulnerability that refuses to take any single sense as leading or emblematic. There are resources for this train of thought in Levinas, but they remain primarily suggestive for work others might pursue.

Just as the face might indicate any aspect of a body that exposes humanity, the face also engages and grips the whole body of the one who is facing. It radicalizes the receptivity and vulnerability of the skin, as if in the act of facing the entire body transfigures into pulsing, trembling organs or a bundle of nerves.[34] Separating the face from its superficial features, Levinas insists on an impact that prefigures and complicates any subsequent judgment about identity or the categorization of human beings into different *types* (Jew, Arab, black, white, female, male, etc.) according to which one might count another as either more or less one's own responsibility.[35]

Not the source of recognition but of infinite ambiguity, the face, contrary to any intuitive understanding, turns out to be the least identifiable aspect of another person. In *Totality and Infinity,* Levinas insists that the face, which is "neither seen nor touched" (TI 194), does not appear. In *Otherwise Than Being or Beyond Essence,* this claim intensifies into a more pointed account of the non-phenomenality of the face, rendering more urgent the question whether and how Levinas practices phenomenology. The face, Levinas offers, "is the very collapse of phenomenality. Not because it is too brutal to appear, but because [it is] in a sense too weak, non-phenomenon because less than a phenomenon. The disclosing of a face is nudity, non-form . . ." ([*Le visage*] *est la défection même de la phénoménalité. Non pas parce que trop brutal pour l'apparaître, mais parce que, en un sens, trop faible, non-phénomène parce que 'moins' que le phénomène. La dévoilement du visage est nudité—non-forme . . .*) (OB 88 / AE 141). In a later interview with Philippe Nemo, Levinas refuses to acquiesce to Nemo's description of his philosophy as a "phenomenology of the face." "I do not know," Levinas responds, "if one can speak of a 'phenomenology of the face,' since phenomenology describes what appears" (EI 85). With an increased focus on hunger and "flesh and blood," *Otherwise Than Being or Beyond Essence* also deploys a new vocabulary of "non-place," "desert," and "homelessness," as if the exile of the face from the realm of phenomena coincides with a global, terrestrial expulsion, an essential nomadism that comes to dominate much of Levinas's work after 1974. In *Totality and Infinity* the face refuses representation and appearance in the light, but in *Otherwise Than Being or Beyond Essence,* Levinas links the face with a more thoroughgoing and traumatic displacement—desertion to an uninhabitable no-place: "non-world, non-habitation, layout without security" (OB 179).

In a rare and surprisingly *positive* description of the face, Levinas tells us: "The shock of the divine, the rupture of the immanent order, of the order that I can embrace, or the order which I can hold in my thought, of the order which can become mine, that is the face of the other" (IRB 48). The face scrambles every category. This small term that seems to bring Levinas's philosophy all the way down into the streets and crowds, is also the term that introduces an immeasurable height into the world: "the shock of the divine." Just as insomnia upsets subjectivity with a unique temporal dimension (an eternity in the present), faces interrupt subjectivity with a unique spatial dimension, a height (and a depth) that cannot be measured by any overview or surveyed by any topographical instrument.[36] "Face" is Levinas's description of something that interrupts every order and reconfigures every space, producing an opening in the closely knit fabric of experience—a jolt of something entirely unforeseen, "the shock of the real" (OGM 24) that ignites the initial spark of sensibility, "an insomnia or a throbbing in the ultimate recess of the subjective atom" (OGM 24). Far from sinking back into the tangible, physical features one might recognize in a glance, the face resists every description, overflowing every horizon.

Levinas's goal, therefore, is not to describe the essence of the face, reducing it to a definitive set of features or characteristics. He provides no ethical checklist one might take out into the streets to better identify faces when one meets them. Unlike theories that define the human in terms of rationality, speech, empathy, or any number of definitive distinguishing capacities or physical traits, Levinas gives us nothing to help us identify *who* or *what* is human. His steadfast refusal to offer a straightforward definition of one of his key terms might be seen as a lack of specificity that only renders things more confusing— or worse, mystical to the point of meaninglessness, as Dominique Janicaud fears.[37] But the lack of definition might also be interpreted as an invitation to remain open and receptive to an incessant reconfiguration of the very notion of identity and the essential instability of every name. By not providing circumscription of *what* a face is, Levinas points us beyond his texts toward the risks of experiential, embodied confrontation with and exposure to (and by) facings we cannot recall, imagine, or anticipate. One can find precursors to Levinas's insistence on the priority of living exposure and the derivative, always partial and inferior, place of *theory* in the final imperative line of Rosenzweig's *The Star of Redemption,* "INTO LIFE"; in Bergson's concept of *élan vital* and his critique of intellect in *Creative Evolution;* and (as I will elaborate in the next chapter) in James's notion of "radical empiricism." Each of these thinkers, crucial to the development of Levinas's work, warns that thought divorced from living immersion suffers a dangerous transmutation. James in particular insists: "knowledge about life is one thing; effective occupation of a place in life, with its dynamic currents passing through your being, is another" (VRE 479). Levinas's ethics is tied to a vitalism and a distinctively Jamesian empiricism that is the subject of the next chapter. We will always be taken by surprise and unprepared when humanity breaks out in the world in a new face. When such ruptures occur, they reconfigure the sense of the human, expanding humanity in ever more novel, unexpected directions.

4. Traces

Faces push phenomenological description to its outer limits, to the point where words begin to fail. Rather than seeing this failure as a sign of defeat, or a reason to abandon phenomenology altogether, Levinas adopts a Beckett-like attitude toward the phenomenological method: "Fail again. Fail better."[38] Running phenomenology up against insomnia, *il y a,* and the face, Levinas demonstrates the insufficiency of any method to capture or explain life in its living complexity. Such is the impasse between life and reflection, the former forever outrunning the latter. In a revealing exchange with Theodor de Boer, Levinas details his philosophical activity as the description of "mutation," goes on to suggest "Exasperation as a method of philosophy!" (OGM 88), and offers the following analysis of the very notion of a philosophical method: "I do not believe that there is a transparency possible in method. Nor that philosophy might be possible as transparency" (OGM 89). These last lines underscore Levinas's refusal of clarity and bringing to light as the ultimate philosophical ends. Giving up the expectation that phenomenology could be rigorous, scientific, final, or definitive—giving up the quest for a last word—Levinas instead exercises phenomenology in directions he knows it resists, testing to find the places of weakness and breakage where failure becomes instructive.

Resisting the powers of vision, theory and knowledge, faces remain enigmatic and quasi-phenomenal. Ed Casey coins the term *"periphenomena"* to describe "appearances whose paradigm is neither perception (with its emphasis on the directly given and robustly materialized object) nor thought (a cognitive operation with tenuous ties to bodily expression)."[39] These indistinct phenomena make up a disproportionately large part of experience, yet they are not the sources of any definite information or knowledge. Faces, perhaps *the* paradigmatic "periphenomena," occupy an ambiguous middle ground between perceptual objects and cognitive thought. This means the very starting point for Levinas's investigation is at odds with his method—a method traditionally based in the painstaking description of *phenomena* as they arise for consciousness. If Levinas practices phenomenology, then it is a version that relegates phenomena to a second tier. Along with phenomena go light, theory, knowledge, intention, intuition, consciousness, and subjectivity. If anything remains for phenomenological investigation, it is not clear what.

Everything central to traditional transcendental or descriptive phenomenology occupies a level separate from a primary plane, something Levinas associates with corporeal vulnerability and "a preoriginary susceptibility," where vision has not yet usurped sensibility and nothing truly appears.[40] Concerned with an ambiguity characterized by the failure of pure appearance and the failure of pure disappearance, Levinas isolates events resistant to the either/or structure of presence and absence as the subject matter for his alternative phenomenology, insisting that the ubiquity of such *"epiphenomena"*[41] proves the insufficiency of traditional phenomenology. Whole swaths of the world fall outside of traditional modes of description. Phenomenology's insufficiency becomes increasingly apparent as Levinas accumulates an arsenal of examples of things that fail to reconcile as either present or absent. These include subjectivity itself, dreaming, trauma, memory, emotion, insomnia, and—above all—faces and *il y a*. In some places Levinas also includes poetry, literature, and certain examples of visual art and music in this list. All of these necessarily remain blind spots in a phenomenology that is enslaved to a duality between presence and absence and is focused on intentionality, on how phenomena appear to consciousness. Life contains more than one sees in a glance or measures relative to any horizon—life includes shadows and incoherent chapters. Levinas becomes a periphenomenologist of this daybreak or twilight—of what remains barely visible and inarticulable, and yet infinitely significant.

Levinas fixates on phenomena that resist appearing and on experiences that, resisting objectification, indicate a hesitation between one state and another. Therefore, neither the word "phenomenon" nor "experience" is quite right here. Making this explicit, Levinas explains, "I prefer the word 'ordeal' (*épreuve*) over 'experience' (*experiénce*), because the word 'experience' expresses always a knowledge of which the I is the master" (IRB 97). He describes the movement toward experience before any solidification into a definite state or event occurs, before experience becomes *mine*. "Ordeal" retains a sense of continuance or a lack of closure, expressing an undergoing that mirrors the open-in-the-midst quality of the "saying" as opposed to the finality of the "said." Elsewhere, Levinas explains that "the 'great experiences' of our life have properly speaking never been lived. . . . Their grandeur is due to this exorbitance exceeding the capacity of phenomena, of the present and of memory" (EP 72). Worried that the word "phenomenon" expresses something overly decisive and articulate, Levinas introduces the terms "enigma" and "trace" to describe a flickering hesitation between disclosure and dissimulation.

In two essays, "Meaning and Sense" (*La Signification et le sens*) from 1964 and "Enigma and Phenomenon" (*Enigme et phénomène*) from 1965, Levinas provides a sustained discussion of his philosophical method and its relationship to other forms of phenomenology. Both of these essays appeared in the years between *Totality and Infinity* and *Otherwise Than Being or Beyond Essence*, sketching out the transition to Levinas's intensified "flesh and blood" vocabulary, his focus on "saying" and "trace," and his increasingly irreverent, experimental phenomenology. As Richard Cohen explains, "Meaning and Sense" centers principally on "the origin and nature of meaning," but Cohen also argues that the essay refers (without explicit reference) to the infamous Cassirer–Heidegger debate, which Levinas attended at Heidegger's invitation in Davos in the summer of 1929.[42] Cassirer taught that human culture and the generation of symbolic forms are the source of meaning, while Heidegger countered that "Being is . . . nearer to man than every being, be it a rock, a beast, a work of art, a machine, be it an angel or a God."[43] Although Levinas sided with Heidegger in 1929 (and regretted his own treatment of Cassirer for the rest of his life, confessing, "during the Hitler years I reproached myself for having preferred Heidegger at Davos" [IRB 36], and more emphatically admitting, "I did not even pity Cassirer. For years afterward, the scene haunted me" [IRB 189]), by 1964 he was concerned with breaking both molds—Cassirer's significance of culture and Heidegger's significance of Being—in order to differentiate an embodied *sens* and to situate it in the a-contextual expression of a living face.[44]

The titles of the essays from 1964–1965 stage alternatives between privileged phenomenological language ("meaning" and "phenomenon") and Levinas's alternative terms ("sense" and "enigma"). Throughout these essays, Levinas largely avoids the Saussurian terminology of "sign" and "signified." As he explains in the 1972 foreword to *Humanism of the Other,* he has in mind an account of a *unique* significance that ruptures "synchrony and its reversible terms" (HO 6). The non-reciprocity or irreversibility of terms is a crucial aspect of Levinas's ethics. An enigma has a sense, despite its lack of meaning and failure to show itself as a distinct phenomenon. Because Levinas seeks material and events that have traditionally evaded philosophical reflection, he abandons or actively deforms the dominant language of Western philosophy that he sees as complicit in this evasion. He finds new words to move phenomenology in new directions, and his readers have to learn a new language if they are to follow him. This transition has to do with the ethics of language—with the ways in which word-choices and habits of speaking reflect attitudes and biases, both conscious and unconscious; with the ways in which, as Wittgenstein remarked, "to imagine a language means to imagine a form of life."[45]

"Speech" and "discourse" are dominant topics of *Totality and Infinity* (and of work from the 1930s to the 1950s, pre-dating Levinas's first major text), but the description and use of language becomes even more central and complicated in Levinas's later work. This is in part due to Derrida's hugely influential deconstructive reading of *Totality and Infinity* in "Violence and Metaphysics" and his critique that, despite Levinas's heroic efforts and beautifully original analyses of the expressive utterance of a face, "discourse is originally violent" (VM 116). In reaction to this critique, Levinas embarks on a quest to write a text that eludes violent totalization, a text that is itself "periphenomenal." "Meaning and Sense" begins with a discussion of metaphorical language to illustrate one of the ways in which language becomes uniquely expressive and potentially transcendent. Levinas argues that metaphors animate meaning "beyond the given" (MS 34). This "beyond" is critical. One of Levinas's central criticisms of Heidegger's phenomenology in *Being and Time* is that it remains tied to *presence* and to the given, tied to *es gibt*.[46] Levinas is concerned with a transcendent meaning that cannot be reconciled into any single word or definition. It is meaning that extends beyond the sum of any parts. Metaphorical language gestures toward such excess, indicating the possibility of a cacophonous pluralism resistant to closure and irreducible to any definitive sign.

A metaphor, nonetheless, can be explained. Language may scintillate in its metaphorical, poetic dimension, but it can also become the object of investigation, interpretation, translation, and etymological history. None of this lessens the value of metaphor for widening the scope of meaning, showing the arbitrary rigidity (and false pretension) of denotative language, and illuminating the enmeshment of words, but Levinas worries that language, while potentially transcendent, remains subject to reduction and re-inscription in the *"this as that"* (MS 38) economy of linguistic identity. Pinning down the metaphor, "deflating it" (MS 35), is a way of reducing meaning to data—a move Levinas associates with intellectualism in all its varieties, and particularly with empirical positivism in its emphasis on the verification and truth-value of sentences. Empirical positivism privileges a scientific method for discerning meaning, running language through a series of reductions to determine a sentence's fundamental, essential components. The focus lies in analyzing language into atomistic constituents. Levinas finds phenomenology promising because, unlike empirical positivism, it sees meaning more holistically and fluidly, attending to the compounding emergence of simultaneous meanings that are irreducible to static facts. Phenomenology seems poised to accommodate multiple types of truths and variable meanings.

Concerned with making a radical and decisive break with positivism, Levinas accuses first Husserl, then Heidegger, and ultimately Merleau-Ponty (whose book *Signes* appeared in 1960 and whom Levinas credits with "guiding the present analysis" [MS 39]) of not having gone far enough. Levinas in fact calls Husserl's phenomenology "a sort of positivism" insofar as Husserl locates meaning in "the transcendental inventory . . . as though one were dealing with an investment portfolio" (MS 36). Meaning remains the "given," even if it is given to intuition as an "investment"—as a promissory note or a check that has yet to be cashed. Elsewhere, Levinas critiques phenomenology more broadly as "the phenomenology of immanence," insisting that "seizure, appropriation, and satisfaction" remain the dominant practices of any phenomenology that gives temporal and spatial priority to presence: *le maintenant* (the now) and *le main* (the hand).[47]

There is certainly progress through Husserl's intentional analysis and Heidegger's hermeneutic phenomenology toward increasingly open and flexible accounts of meaning. Levinas credits Heidegger in particular with going further than anyone else, emphasizing that it was Heidegger who first awakened *verbs*: he "accustomed us to this verbal sonority," and "reeducated our ear" (EI 38). He also applauds Merleau-Ponty for bringing meaning to bear "in a body which is also a hand and phonetic organ, a creative activity in gestures and language" (MS 38–39). Levinas's concern, however, is not with the meaning of language considered abstractly, nor with uncovering the "threads of silence that speech is mixed together with."[48] Levinas turns instead to the place where language issues both enigmatically and personally—the pre-linguistic expression voiced in a living face.

The kind of meaning Levinas attributes to the face is called "the trace." One of the striking differences between *Totality and Infinity* and *Otherwise Than Being or Beyond Essence* is Levinas's restrained use of "face" in the later text, and the new prominence given to "trace" and "saying." This shift seems to reflect an awareness of the danger that the "face to face" could (or inevitably would) become a slogan. Firmly associated with *Totality and Infinity*, "face" risked losing its power as a disruptive, a-philosophical term, and functioning as a readymade symbol of Levinas's philosophy as a whole. Levinas never abandons invoking the face, but his later work reflects an active attempt to keep the term alive by further displacing and delaying its definition.

In "Meaning and Sense," Levinas devotes the final section to "the trace," describing it in the following way:

> The signifying of the trace consists in signifying without making appear . . . it establishes an obligation and does not disclose, and if, consequently, the trace does not belong to phenomenology, to the comprehension of *appearing* and *dissimulating*, we can at least approach the signifyingness

in another way by situating it with respect to the phenomenology it interrupts. (MS 61)[49]

A trace signifies "as a disturbance," without bringing anything to light. In
Otherwise Than Being or Beyond Essence, Levinas insists, "a face is trace of
itself" (OB 91), the "trace of a passage which never became present, and
which is possibly nothingness" (OB 91). In "Enigma and Phenomenon," he
calls the trace "this primal desolation" (EP 69). True to his habit, Levinas
isolates a commonplace understanding of what a trace might be, using as
examples the fingerprints left by a thief and the tracks of an animal that is
followed by a hunter. In these cases, a trace works as a sign, pointing to
something or someone who, while no longer present, was once there. These
traces, however dimly or vaguely, disclose; they can be followed or unraveled
to reveal their sources. Just as a face could be experienced as a phenomenon,
a trace could be taken as a clue. But these are not the distinctive meanings
of faces and traces that Levinas has in mind. The real trace for Levinas is the
trace that "is not just a sign like any other" (MS 60). In its less common,
more radical sense, a trace entails what Jill Robbins calls "the mark of an
effacement of a mark,"[50] and which Levinas names "a trace lost in a trace"
(OB 93). This is a doubling up of erasure, a residue made non-residual by a
second gesture that no longer aims at obliterating or covering over any sign,
but that cancels the very gesture of erasing. If the first trace signifies a disappearance, the second trace signifies the disappearance of disappearance. The
radical trace belongs to a past more ancient than anything that is accessible
to memory or recalled in any history.[51]

There is no way of pointing to a Levinasian trace, no way of capturing
it for closer examination. Traces, neither present nor absent, remain suspended in a margin outside the substantiality of being and the insubstantial-
ity of nothingness. Nonetheless a trace, without appearing on the scene, calls
for—and even demands—attention, like something left unspoken that overwhelms a conversation. The refusal of disclosure makes the trace enigmatic
and points to a realm of "signifyingness" which is elusive to theory and
knowledge and irreducible to anything given. Traces are not blocks that
could be foundational or assembled into a structure; they are even less than
the depressions left in a ground after the removal or disappearance of something solid. Levinas frequently uses the imagery of shadows cast in advance
of things, an echo preceding its sound, or footprints preceding their steps,
to describe the disturbing sense and non-appearance of a trace. In a way, the

trace is nonsense, or defies sense, and yet the enigmatic nonsense of a trace points to an intermingling of sense and nonsense that cannot be reduced to one or the other or be synthesized into a neutral third term.

5. Close-Ups

Traces indicate a different kind of meaning than universal, cultural, linguistic or historical meaning—meaning conferred by reference to an overarching horizon, totality, or ideality. However, just as "experience" and "phenomenon" already say too much, the word "meaning" is also misleading. Levinas is careful in his own texts to differentiate between the German *Sinn*, which he translates as *sens* (sense), and *Bedeutung* or *Meinung*, which he translates into French as *importance* (signification) and *signification* (meaning), respectively.[52] Insisting on the difference between sense, signification, and meaning, Levinas is only concerned with the first of these options, since sense retains an openness that John Drabinksi, in a book devoted to Levinas's unique enactment of a phenomenological method, describes in terms of a "more pluralistic or fluid structural item than meaning."[53] Meaning is too fixed in the ego—too much "mine"—and signification is both too rigid and overly dependent on something sensible. *Sens* (which also connotes direction in the French) offers the best possibility for a non-egoistic, independent, and original impact. Focusing on sense allows Levinas to work at the level of sensible impact—sensibility—prior to consciousness, a level he defines as "a layer of the psyche that is deeper than consciousness" (GDT 114).

Sensible impact defines the narrow band of life on which Levinas plans to focus. Refusing organization into a horizon, it is a part of life that has been overlooked or obscured by phenomenological reduction. In the central chapter of *Existence and Existents,* Levinas considers "a worldless reality" (EE 49) and uses the example of cinema close-ups to illustrate a poignant sense of reality uncoupled from a horizon and without definitive edges, a fragment occupying the whole screen. Explaining the *sens* of close-ups, he elaborates:

> Their interest does not only lie in that they can show details, they stop the action in which a particular is bound up with a whole, and let it exist apart. They let it manifest its particular and absurd nature which the camera discovers in a normally unexpected perspective—in a shoulder line to which the close-up gives hallucinatory dimensions, laying bare what the visible universe and the play of its normal proportions tone down and conceal. (EE 49)

These lines prefigure Levinas's later association of the face with Grossman's "nape of the neck," but they demonstrate his early and ongoing interest in ambiguous and irreconcilable instances of finding oneself captivated by the particular's "absurd nature," a sense of feeling intensely alive to something in its strange uniqueness. Although he never makes film an explicit topic of investigation in his work, the cinematic close-up Levinas envisions in 1947 foreshadows his focus on "proximity" and "obsession" in *Otherwise Than Being or Beyond Essence*. Notably, Levinas does not specify the close-up associated with a human face in *Existence and Existents*. Deleuze, seizing on the philosophical significance of film, describes such cinematic close-ups as revealing the essence of the face, "this organ-carrying plate of nerves which has sacrificed most of its global mobility and which gathers or expresses in a free way all kind of tiny local movements which the rest of the body usually keeps hidden."[54] According to Deleuze, the tension of surface and movement characteristic of close-ups renders all kinds of things "facified" (*visagéifiée*).[55] Bergman's ordinary objects, for instance—clocks, shoes, strawberries— thereby register in his motion pictures as faces, looming larger than life. Deleuze, following Bergson, finds even the most seemingly inert matter animated by forces and micro-movements: vital properties and "moving zones" (CE 5). Without making as explicit or expansive a claim, Levinas suggests a similar convergence of "face" with a dynamic, cinematic tension that troubles and transfigures one's expectations of stillness and mobility, a tension that renders things suddenly, and strangely, alive.

In a close-up, a face loses its world and setting in a horizon, crossing from the realm of light ("the visible universe and the play of its normal proportions" [EE 49]) into the obscure realm of *il y a*. A close-up interrupts the movement that constitutes a moving picture as such: it is a "still" that "stops the action in which a particular is bound up with a whole" (EE 49). But in stopping one variety of action, the close-up signals a different kind of activity. Things are happening minutely, closely. Occupying the whole screen, a face loses its edges and becomes increasingly obscure as the camera zooms beyond its focus.

The close-up represents a privileged, cinematic possibility for Levinas, since it illustrates the dramatized experience of a face overflowing every frame that tries to contain it. Even when a literal human face appears still, asleep even, a close-up reveals the subtle, continual animation of a living body, its breath and pulse. The capacity for endless withdrawal, opening or deepening, saves the face from the paralysis Levinas associates with "manifestation" (a paralysis he associates with both art and death). Infinitely open-ing, faces are impenetrable by virtue of being infinitely deep, bottomless wells. A face expresses an un-fixed, living sense that resists appearing as a petrified, mute phenomenon, resisting every effort of reflective conscious-ness to disclose, critique, deduce, or analyze it.

Its originary vitality keeps the face from settling into any single form and is definitive of the face's unique expressive potential. Unlike a static image, a face constantly shifts and changes, meaning multiple things in different ways. This *movement* is the face's expressivity, or what Levinas calls the face's ability to "speak." He elaborates: "Speaking is before anything else this way of coming from behind one's appearance, behind one's form, an openness in the open-ness" (MS 53). A face speaks without having to say anything, without uttering any actual expression. "Speaking" is therefore not tied to a capacity to speak a particular language or articulate specific words. The face's speech is a bare expression of openness and vulnerability, a source of inarticulate, poignant fluidity.[56] As sources of pre-verbal meaning, faces provide access to a meaning that is not an atomic fact or a static sensation, but a fluctuating and irreiterable expressivity that remains utterly complex, unique, and abstractly poignant. Without saying anything that communicates information or denotes specific content, the face speaks with a sheer performativity, an expression of expres-sion, invisible but nonetheless audible. Accordingly, a hierarchy of the ear over the eye is one upshot of Levinas's transgressive phenomenology, the audible expressivity of the face leading him toward a phenomenology of acoustic space and giving him the basis for describing the ethical importance of a distinctive passivity—the ethical importance of listening.

6. Sensibility

Describing the inarticulate sense of a face, Levinas tests the limit of descrip-tive phenomenology. It is a limit he makes explicit in the 1964–1965 essays we discussed, but one he also anticipates much earlier. Phenomenology is his starting point and testing ground, but in the section devoted to insomnia in the last chapter of *Existence and Existents,* he admits his departure from the tradition: "Our affirmation of an anonymous vigilance goes beyond the *phenomena,* which already presupposes an ego, and thus eludes descriptive phenomenology. Here description would make use of terms while striving to go beyond their consistency; it stages *personages,* while the [*il y a*] is the dissipation of personages" (EE 63). Here *il y a* works as an alternative to phenomena and the compounding "descriptions" characteristic of phenomenology. The centrality of *il y a* in *Existence and Existents* differs from Levinas's focus on the face in later work, but there remains a similarity in how Levinas describes both terms that points to a disconcerting similarity between *il y a* and a face. Both have a capacity to dissolve incompletely or hover between dissolution and solution. In *Existence and Existents* Levinas personifies this hovering in the figure of insomnia, which works as a unique crossroad between the face—on which one can read the insomniac's insomnia—and *il y a*—through which the insomniac senses a horrific anonymity. The insomniac's face reads like a place where someone present is, at the same time, absent—unable to be there.

Overwhelming, insomnia detaches the subject from subjectivity. The loss of a distinct subject compounds into a loss of distinct objects, rendering everything unstable and uncertain. Blurring categories and decoupling stark alternatives, insomnia is a paradigmatically destabilizing condition where nothing registers or qualifies as evidence. Descriptive phenomenology emphasizes a reflective, evidential, and descriptive approach to encounters with objects as they emerge for consciousness, but Levinas approaches a situation that eludes reflection and for which there is no evidence. He focuses on the advent of subjectivity prior to its foothold—how subjection precedes a subject, and this takes place in a marginal non-experience of being affected and impacted that only later (as a thinking subject) becomes reflected and understood as *happening* or *having happened to me.* Following Husserl in his "return to the things themselves," Levinas asks whether the *Erlebnis* of lived *experience* might be captured before it solidifies in any reflection as *my* experience. In *Totality and Infinity* he describes this as a return to "a forgotten experience from which [objectifying thought] lives" (TI 28).

A sense for things—sensibility—is a gesture toward the unintentional receptivity that prefigures intentionality. As I noted earlier, James also defended sensibility, claiming "the trouble is that most, if not all, of those who admit [sensation], admit it as a fractional *part* of the thought, in the old-fashioned atomistic sense which we have so often criticized" (PP 2: 5). In James, sensibility stands for a primary "acquaintance" with things that have not yet reconciled into decisive objects or facts. Notably, James stresses that such intimate and ambiguous acquaintance is not (for adults) a sustainable way to encounter the world, since perception always falls on the heels of sensibility in much the way that Levinas describes the "said" as solidifying the "saying." In Levinas, sensibility indicates an essential passivity that, without being decisively meaningful, is nonetheless essential and has meaning: "Sensibility does not simply register the facts: it sketches out something like the 'vital statistics' and metaphysical density of the being experienced. The senses make sense" (PN 110). Levinas finds traces of this thought in Husserl, particularly in the "living present" described as *the primal impression* from *The Phenomenology of Internal Time Consciousness*.[57] In a late essay entitled "God and Philosophy" (1975), Levinas defines insomnia in precisely these terms, as a "living present" and "a wakefulness without intentionality."[58]

Levinas also finds a source for the unique import of sensibility in Lucien Lévy-Bruhl's descriptions of emotion and sensation, detailed in his 1922 text *Primitive Mentality*.[59] In a section titled "The Metaphysics of Anonymity," from his paper "Lévy-Bruhl and Contemporary Philosophy" (1957), Levinas describes the "desubstantialization" of substance ushered in by Lévy-Bruhl's disruption of classical categories of experience. In his studies of the role of emotion in the psychic life of native peoples, Lévy-Bruhl recounts a "mystical experience" prefiguring any logical or rational order. In this first level of experience everything swims together in "a mysterious and inexplicable fusion of things that lose and preserve their identity simultaneously."[60] One can hear unmistakable echoes of these lines and of Lévy-Bruhl's vocabulary in Levinas's later descriptions of *il y a* and of the face.[61]

Levinas transcribes Lévy-Bruhl's idea of things swimming together as a "contact with being" (LB 42) and a direct, immediate "poignancy of feeling" (LB 42). Levinas also borrows terminology from Jean Wahl to give an account of sensation as "blind bare contact," "a jolt, a shiver, a spasm" (PN 114). He finds in Lévy-Bruhl and Wahl the suggestion of a more ancient, primordial subject than that of the rational, thinking subject—be that *animal rationale* or *ego cogitans*. Both Lévy-Bruhl and Wahl provide Levinas with alternative descriptions in which sensation is no longer something irrational, simply animal, or inherently private, "shutting us up within ourselves" (LB 43). Instead, sensation punctures a subject, exposing her to the outside. The body's sensible openness to the world is not an indistinct, confused way of knowing something but an altogether different way of coming into contact with things, a contact Lévy-Bruhl calls *sensing*: "not an empty form of knowledge, but a magic spell . . . confronting us face to face" (LB 47).

Levinas captures something significant from these descriptions of an original sensibility that is not an inarticulate, underdeveloped variety of reason or knowledge. Following Lévy-Bruhl, he describes sensibility as "the very narrowness of life, the naïveté of the unreflective I, beyond instinct, beneath reason" (TI 138). He keeps his distance, however, from some of the language Lévy-Bruhl employs. In particular, he hopes to retain the ambiguous sense of things swimming together and the idea of a transcendent emotional subjection without narrowing himself to the realm of anthropology, the "primitive" character of a form of mindedness or describing the face to face as a "magic spell." Levinas criticizes Lévy-Bruhl's language of mysticism and magic for "nourishing a nostalgia for outdated and retrograde forms" (LB 51). This is the same nostalgia Levinas criticizes in the late, increasingly poetic Heidegger—nostalgia for the ruined temple and the departed gods, a dangerous paganism and sense of fate that Levinas found reflected in National Socialism. Instead, he is looking for ambiguity without mysticism. Levinas in fact warns of the "horrors of myths, the confusion of thought they produce, and the acts of cruelty they perpetuate" (LB 51). This warning is crucial, since he is so close to Lévy-Bruhl in his descriptions of a sensible impact prefiguring rationality.

7. The Infinite in Person

What could such non-mystical ambiguity be? Sensible, powerful, unthinkable, and immediate, it sounds like magic or a miracle, but it has a human face. This is the single definitive characteristic separating the ambiguity Levinas describes from the "magic spell" Lévy-Bruhl describes, distinguishing the personal sense of a face from the impersonal sense of il y a.

The face remains "terrestrial" (TI 203), concretely in the world even when dissolving (in laughter or in tears). It is the site of a meaning that does not signify, that goes beyond the given and does not register as a fact or additional data, a meaning on which nothing gets built. And yet, a face is a source of a *personal sublimity* as opposed to the impersonal sublimity of il y a. "The face to face," Levinas insists, "cuts across every relation that one could call mystical" (TI 202). Despite the face's ambiguity, it is not an occasion for reverie or evasion. It is as though the human erupts in a face to face relation, tensioning the very core of a person to be more awake, alive, receptive—in Levinas's words, more "sober." He described this sobering-up as "a dawn of clarity in the horror of the [*il y a*]; a moment where the sun rises" (EI 51). From the neutrality of a world in which everything will be leveled in the indifferent march of history, singularities nonetheless rise. They are sources of illumination and excesses of life. The "moment when the sun rises" stands for the "Good beyond being" that Levinas borrows from Plato or Plotinus: an idea about a primary, blinding source of any subsequent illumination, a good beyond ontology, beyond any theory and instead situated in unique beings who are not single instances of an overarching Good, but particularly, differently meaningful in their own ways and in their own times. Ethics responds to deeply situational particularities and is incapable of being abstracted into a principle or general ideal. Individual faces signify as interruptions of every generality; the face signifies—which for Levinas means *speaks*—enigmatically. Faces, transcendent because unfathomable, open depths *in* the world—not outside the world or in some world that has passed away or is yet to come.

There remains, nevertheless, an element of mysticism in the way Levinas describes the face. The intense proximity of facing, like the heat of sensibility and the fluidity of "saying," is neither secure nor sustainable. Each defies comprehension and leaves behind a residual, accumulating disturbance which Levinas describes as "the overflowing of meaning by nonsense" (OB 64). James, alongside Bergson, recognized the value of non-intellectual sense, urging us to reanimate our capacity for greater intimacy and sensible contact with the world. Bergson celebrated the "sympathy" (CE 180) of a climbing vine with its trellis and called for the development of "instinct" to counterbalance the fundamental inertia of human intellect. James encouraged us to access "our earliest, most instinctive, least developed kind of consciousness" (PP 2: 32). And yet James also asked: "What are the dangers in this [mystical] element of life? And in what proportion may it need to be restrained by other elements to give the proper balance?" (VRE 476). When Levinas claims: "The face is abstract" (MS 59), or later, "We hear this way to signify—which does not consist in being unveiled nor in being veiled . . . under the third person personal pronoun *Il*" (EP 75), it is difficult to reconcile these passages with the idea that a face is the site of a personal meaning as distinct from the abstract, impersonal meaning conferred by some distant universality or some deadening neutrality. If "the face is abstract," and signifies "under the pronoun *Il*," what differentiates a face from *il y a*? What distinguishes Levinas's philosophy from a Platonism that situates the ideal beyond the real, in a perfect Form, the particular manifestations of which are simply fallen imitations?[62]

If the face is ideal, then it is just as his critics suspected, and the centerpiece of Levinas's philosophy is essentially abstract; his ethics is unrealistic. Levinas contests the duality between reality and ideality and makes a face the arena of an ambiguity that complicates both terms, insisting that the face's "abstraction is not obtained by a logical process starting from the substance of beings and going from the individual to the general. On the contrary, it goes toward those beings but does not compromise itself with them, withdraws from them, absolves itself [s'ab-sout]" (MS 59–60 / EDHH 275–76). He attempts to define a version of abstraction that does not simply move "from the individual to the general," or from the particular to the universal (a move characteristic of German Idealism and Transcendental Phenomenology). A face draws away without withdrawing into an impersonal, neutral category.

Criticizing a philosophical tradition that prioritizes the static ideal of the known for being abstract—foreign to life as it is lived—Levinas calls the face abstract insofar as it complicates life as it is known. In *Existence and Existents* he describes this in terms of getting close up, moving "from the abstract to the concrete, from the order where no instant is central to the order where the instant is *present*" (EE 75). The "order where no instant is central" is an order where instants, taken together, make up a larger fabric. This is an arrangement allowed by distance, either temporal or spatial. Backing up, one can see the whole picture just as, looking back, one can tell the whole story. The other order, "where the instant is *present*," is a discontinuous order where a single instant obscures everything else and comes entirely to the forefront, an overwhelming density marked by the absence of distance. In Levinas's terminology, this is the move from distance to proximity. Making this kind of move can't be accomplished by any mental gymnastics but requires a physical, bodily approach. In getting close, what appeared ordered at a distance disintegrates into another order—a *disorder*, where something particular and singular refuses to sink back into place.

A face "draws away"—abstracts—while remaining particular, and Levinas calls this movement a third way between relation and dissimulation. The face's abstraction resists generality in the form of a whole picture, and at the same time resists particularity in the form of a knowable particular. The face's "Illeity" (EP 75), its ambiguity, hesitates in an expressive gap between appearance and disappearance, never resolving into something definite, remaining unknowable, un-nameable, and other. It is barely a *trace*. In its resistance to being knowable generally or particularly, the face is the site of a uniquely transcendent sense, significant without signifying. It signals an empty, open interval of meaning—an abstract, yet human significance prefiguring and grounding the possibility of any definite or concrete signified. Levinas describes this in several ways, in each case dislodging dualities—subject/object, inside/outside, immanent/transcendent—between which meaning supposedly arches. The bare fact of *sens* registers obliquely as an overwhelming feeling without any subsequent revelation, stopping short of generalizing or particularizing into anything revealed.

In the abstraction of a close-up, being face to face in a way that is actually skin to skin, what we recognize later, with distance, as a particular, memorable face, is at first the abstract sense of *someone other*. There is nothing comforting in this kind of facing—no trace of recognition. Rather, one feels a sense prior to a name, before one is able to locate or distinguish, in advance of having an answer to the question "Who?" Withdrawing at the very instant of its approach, Levinas cautions that the sense of a face "is possibly nothingness" (OB 91). In many ways this sounds like the destabilizing non-sense of *il y a*. Levinas even uses the same imagery from *Macbeth* to conjure up *il y a* in *Existents and Existence* in 1947 and eighteen years later, in 1965, to conjure up the face in "Enigma and Phenomenon." In the earlier text he elaborates the "horror" of *il y a*:

> Horror is the event of being which returns in the heart of this negation, as though nothing had happened. "And that," says Macbeth, "is more strange than the crime itself." . . . Specters, ghosts, sorceresses are not only a tribute Shakespeare pays to his time . . . they allow him to move constantly toward this limit between being and nothingness where being insinuates itself even in nothingness, like bubbles of the earth ("the Earth hath bubbles"). (EE 57)

Compare this to "Enigma and Phenomenon," where Levinas writes: "The Saying, that is, the face, is the discretion of an unheard-of proposition, an insinuation, immediately reduced to nothing, breaking up like the 'bubbles of the earth,' which Banquo speaks of at the beginning of *Macbeth*" (EP 74). Both *il y a* and the face emerge from and return to hidden depths, like "bubbles of the earth." An eerie similarity conjoins the sense of *il y a* and the sense of another person—the sense of *something* and the sense of *someone*. Both are events in the dark where being and nothingness converge or where there is a refusal of a last word, a haunting after the end.

Both the face and *il y a* indicate a sensible surplus of reality—more space and time than one could ever imagine. When the sense of infinity registers negatively as the ever-recommencing, erosive tide of being leveling everything in its wake, then one might feel the horror and insufficiency Macbeth feels as he desperately tries to forestall his fate, the sense of vertigo experienced in the failure of any deed to be ultimate, any end to end all things. Despite everything: *il y a*. Yet there are multiple ways of seeing the world, different points of view.[63] Though Levinas recalls Macbeth's sense of horror in 1947, in 1965 he remembers Banquo and correctly attributes to Banquo his line in act I, scene 3: "The earth hath bubbles, as water has, / And these [the Witches] are of them. Whither are they vanished?"[64] Banquo, unlike Macbeth, is not frightened by the Witches, imploring them: "Speak then to me, who neither beg nor fear / Your favours nor your hate." Later Banquo becomes the haunting presence that torments Macbeth, the ghostly apparition who refuses to die a decisive death. Clarifying the attribution of the line in 1965, Levinas emphasizes a different, now *positive* significance to fluidity and impermanence—envisioning the surplus of infinity as an ever-opening possibility. Something beneath roils and comes to a boil; an internal depth or disorder breaks through the surface. In 1965 this is not *il y a* but the evanescent "saying" of a face. Things could go either way, and Levinasian ethics entails the sense of being held at the intersection of all and nothing. Blanchot identified this crossroads as definitive of where Levinas leaves us, giving us "a burden and a hope, the burden of hope" (WD 149, n. 8). From one vantage point the world is perforated with all-consuming holes—an infinite nothingness haunting being. From another view, these same holes are faces, lighting their own way—an infinite sense.

Faces are instances of the infinite in person, concrete events of infinity in real time. This is a critical juncture of Levinas's philosophy that causes many secular philosophers, Dominique Janicaud and Alain Badiou foremost among them, much anxiety, fueling criticisms that Levinas's phenomenology is really just theology in thin disguise. Decrying the capitalizations and hyperbolic language in Levinas's texts, Badiou flatly concludes: "There can be no ethics [in Levinas's sense] without God the ineffable."[65] Undeniably, Levinas borrows theological language to express the non-appearance of the face: "the shock of the divine," "the Absent," the "Absolutely Other." These are, perhaps, unfortunate choices in the end, since they fan the flames of a religious/secular divide threatening to overtake and stunt Levinas scholarship. Yet his word-choices are deliberately superlative without naming anything specific, be it God or anything else. They are expressions of excess, attempts to articulate the inexhaustible sense of humanity in the world.

If there is anything religious about Levinas's philosophy, it is the strictly catholic holiness of humanizing faces—a holiness descended to earth, fallen and already impure. The face, excessive, infinite and transcendent, is *at the same time:* "a banality, but one has to be surprised by it" (IRB 48). This banality is not unlike the one Hannah Arendt invoked to describe the evil of totalitarianism—another banality one has to be surprised by. Faces (and evil, Arendt argues) are much more pedestrian than one might realize or like to acknowledge. For Arendt as for Levinas, to turn one's face from the banal is to risk missing everything of real importance.

Levinas's phenomenology is a philosophy for the streets here below and not the heavens above. The question is whether contemporary phenomenologists can tolerate the ambiguity of human faces and the crush of a crowd. Can phenomenology accommodate the non-phenomenal but deeply experiential and sensibly overwhelming event of the face to face? Does it have to sacrifice the real for the surreal or the unreal, turning into theology?

Levinas suggests phenomenology can move in other directions, turning toward the depths of the world with a pragmatic openness and focus on "the human or interhuman intrigue as the fabric of ultimate intelligibility."[66] This is not phenomenology in any classical sense of the word. But can't we relinquish the impulse to classify every thought as decisively of one genre, one school, one trend or another? The only "evidence" relevant in Levinas's ethical phenomenology is a face—a trace effacing its own trace. And yet, the face is the source of a crucial ordeal, a superlative experience. Levinas insists on retaining the impulse of the phenomenological method, but also on letting phenomenology show its insufficiency, letting it fail in increasingly complicated, experimental ways. This should teach us something about the value of failure, about how to calibrate expectations and how to continue thinking in a world that is often repellent to thought. It should also dispel the temptation to look for everything in one place, or to believe that any singular method might be comprehensive enough to eradicate the necessity of additional perspectives, new approaches. Levinas, a thinker of the impossibility of self-sufficiency, is not self-sufficient. This is one reason to read him in concert with other thinkers and other traditions—to engage pluralistically with the spirit of Levinas's texts, beyond the letter.

The irreverent, radical phenomenology Levinas practices leaves unanswered who or what counts as a face, how exactly I should respond to a face, or whether the "shock" of a face and the interruption of egoistic life necessarily leads to any definitive ethical *action*. For some, this amounts to leaving out everything of real importance in any philosophy that calls itself an ethics. And yet, it is precisely the minimalism and openness of Levinas's ethics—his effort to show that theory rests on a prior *sens,* and *sens* awakens in the face to face of compounding vulnerabilities—that keeps his ethics from closing down around any *Who? When?* or *How?* that might be learned and then dispensed with. For those who cannot tolerate such ambiguity, Levinas is not without some practical advice: hold the door (*Après vous*), say hello, don't kill or crush the other. These are not rules that require memorization, but minimal practices (a single prohibition) that might allow for less driven, linear, and isolating interactions, practices that might allow vulnerability, in a variety of forms, to live.

Phenomenologists identify and analyze the features underlying everyday experience, providing reminders of the things so close to us that we continually miss them. Levinas is an awkward phenomenologist insofar as he insists that the things closest to us are not things at all, but faces—ruptures of the human in a world that is sometimes more than and sometimes less than human. Fleeting and fluid, faces are reminders of a significance that cannot be pinned down by any definition—traces evading every light. Description will be too blunt a tool for capturing the living expressivity of a face. Levinas's descriptions show the insufficiency of every methodical approach to the human, phenomenological or otherwise. The setting of Levinas's phenomenology, therefore, can feel like a mess, like the cluttered and utterly chaotic space of a city at rush hour—a place so crowded with faces that they sometimes recede in a blur of architecture, blinking streetlights, and endless traffic. Yet in the places most densely packed with life in multiple forms, one finds endless possibilities for evasion and attentiveness. Cities are certainly not the *only* sites for such evasion or attention, and ethics is not tied to a single place or time. But the most populated sites of interaction can be especially demanding. Every face is a source of exposure. Every exposure exposes differently. Moving through the streets with one's head down, one's eyes cast down, is always one possibility, but faces continue rising all around, whether one faces them or not.

THREE

EXPERIENCE

Survivors look back and see omens, messages they missed.

—JOAN DIDION, *THE YEAR OF MAGICAL THINKING*

The previous chapter centered on Levinas's fraught relationship with traditional phenomenology and his account of the face as the non-phenomenal site of "unique sense" (*sens unique*) (MS 46). Both of the preceding chapters have remained largely within the confines of Levinas's work to establish the degree to which his philosophy is rooted in the plurality of subjectivity, a focus on the human and the mere, and a radical re-thinking of *experience*. This chapter moves from the account of *sens* into the themes of Levinas's first book, *Existence and Existents (De l'existence à l'existant)*, in order to explore explicitly the relationship between Levinas's radical phenomenology and William James's radical empiricism. In *Existence and Existents,* Levinas invokes James directly, providing specific occasion for asking how and why James influenced Levinas and the degree to which their philosophies might converge. Whereas James has been present as an interlocutor in the preceding pages, now he comes decisively into focus. This chapter and the next one describe pragmatic aspects of Levinas's ethics and ethical aspects of James's pluralism. The poetic is a slightly more complicated upshot of Levinas's and James's methods of writing philosophy and reflects an internal tension considered in the last two chapters. The overall effort is to open new lines of thought leading into and out of Levinas's phenomenology—bringing together traditions and spheres of inquiry that typically hold each other at arm's length.

As we saw in the previous chapter, Levinas's "face to face" populates the Heideggerian world with "particular" and "personal" beings (TI 26). They are beings who "magnetize the very field in which the production of infinity is enacted" (TI 26), lighting the fire of sensibility and injecting the finite with infinite depth. Heidegger would undoubtedly decry this as a forgetting of Being and a misguided return to "metaphysical subjectivism."[1] Yet the encounter Levinas describes is too situational and sensible to be metaphysical and too transcendently un-experiential to be physical. Human, yet out of reach, the face complicates traditional philosophic categories and makes Levinas's philosophy particularly difficult to situate. Although Levinas criticizes the language of "experience" for being the language of totality and opts for "metaphysics" in his description of ethics, the face betrays a strange empiricism.[2] In a discussion following his 1962 lecture, "Transcendence and Height" (*Trascendance et hauteur*), Levinas explained that the face to face is "our most valuable everyday experience, one that allows us to resist a purely hierarchical world. But this is an illuminating experience, metaempirical, as Jankélévitch would say. This is not pure empiricism" (BPW 23).[3] Faces are sources of impact that redouble or sensitize sensibility itself. Levinas's new empiricism discovers in sensibility something both more meaningful and less distinct than the "strong and vivid" facts that Hume called "impressions" and credited with being the essential constituents of ideas.[4] Elsewhere Levinas admits that his prioritization of sensibility over consciousness is "congenial to empiricism, but to a very new sort of empiricism" (PN 110). He does not, however, elaborate what kind of "new" empiricism this might be.

Faces are ideal and real without either of these terms canceling the other or having the dense meaning philosophy can give them. It is a weak ideality, a thick but traversable reality. Faces express something ideal here on earth, here in the world. The mixture of ideality and reality, along with an urban sense of plurality, has roots in another tradition—one that is not at odds with phenomenology, but that too rarely is invoked with reference to Levinas.[5] It is the tradition broadly called American Pragmatism (although I am only concerned here with one particular variety of pragmatism, namely, James's *radical empiricism*).[6] Richard Bernstein defines a "pragmatic ethos" by way of five interrelated themes and concerns: (1) anti-foundationalism, (2) fallibalism, (3) de-centering the subject, (4) contingency and chance, and (5) plurality.[7] One finds versions of all of these running through Levinas's work. Underscoring his "pragmatic ethos" opens new lines of investigation and criticism which promise to be distinct from a heavily theological vein of French phenomenology, "Levinasian" readings of Levinas, or discussions pitting religious faith and mysticism against practical reason. There are many ways of reading Levinas or highlighting specific trains of his thought. Some readings make his ethics look sublime, beautiful, angelic; others make it seem disastrous, impossible, masochistic. What if it is simply messy, unpredictable, and minimal? What if it is closer to the "pluralistic empiricism" James described as "a turbid, muddled, gothic sort of affair without a sweeping outline and with little pictorial nobility" (PU 45)?

There are striking coincidences between Levinas's radical phenomenology and William James's radical empiricism. Thinking about them together provides a deflationary reading that establishes distance from what Dominique Janicaud decries as French phenomenology's "theological turn."[8] Levinas does in fact turn away from phenomena, as Janicaud fears. This need not, however, be interpreted as the destruction of phenomenology or the catastrophic transition to a Christian phenomenology of a god "whose properly phenomenological sense must fall away, for a nonbeliever, midway through the journey."[9] Demonstrating Levinas's relevance for contemporary, secular ethics requires unlinking the chain Janicaud has constructed. Janicaud situates Levinas at the head of a theological turn that shatters the promise of the phenomenological method and winds up as "Marionesque givenness."[10] Levinas's turn is not a single swerve away from the world and toward a divine, self-sustaining source, but an unending series of rotations toward an infinite variety of particular human faces. Seen in this way, his phenomenology returns more deeply to the everyday and the concrete, even as it forces one to accept that life is fundamentally fluid, plural, and resistant to concretion.

1. Captivity

Existence and Existents, published in 1947, lays the groundwork for much of Levinas's later writings yet remains free of language that has become synonymous with his ethics. In the 1940s, Levinas had not yet coined the familiar phrases, "ethics as first philosophy" and "face to face," which are now so intimately tied to his thought they have largely become cliché. This is the first reason for retrieving Levinas's older work: *Existence and Existents* provides access to new vocabulary. An overlooked and underappreciated text, it is uniquely positioned to reanimate Levinas's distinctive use of language, move his work in new directions, and recalibrate the tenor of his ethics.[11] In this early book, Levinas continues yet breaks with the phenomenology of Husserl and Heidegger, exploring a less-well demarcated area that opens somewhere between phenomenology and radical empiricism.

Levinas began writing *Existence and Existents* as a prisoner of war in a French labor camp in the years between 1940 and 1945. In the opening pages he announces his overt philosophical intention to articulate an ethical alternative to Husserl's transcendentally ideal ego and Heidegger's ontology, a project of differentiation from his former teachers that persists throughout his career. While Husserl stands somewhat in the background of Levinas's critique in *Existence and Existents,* serving as a model and a touchstone for Levinas's idiosyncratic version of phenomenology, Heidegger stands in the foreground as a more decisive point of departure—a shore not only to touch but to erode. Levinas makes this clear in his introduction, naming Heidegger first:

> If at the beginning our reflections are in large measure inspired by the philosophy of Martin Heidegger, where we find the concept of ontology and of the relationship which man sustains with Being, they are also governed by a profound need to leave the climate of that philosophy, and by the conviction that we cannot leave it for a philosophy that would be pre-Heideggerian. (EE 4)[12]

Levinas notes his debt and recognizes the importance of going *through* Heidegger to arrive at a new possibility for philosophy. Contesting the "climate" of Heideggerian philosophy, Levinas considers a meaning irreducible to Being "*in general*" (EE 2) and centered instead on the interpersonal. He bases his "other" phenomenology on the primacy of sensibility over consciousness, and the situational encounter with the face of another person.

Levinas thinks about being a prisoner of Heidegger's "climate," but his fixation on imprisonment is not a philosophic invention. The thought of confinement comes directly from experience—a real separation from the world and not, as with Descartes, an imagined or staged retreat. Serving as an interpreter in the French army beginning in 1939, Levinas was taken captive in Rennes in 1940 and transported to a labor camp in Germany, where he was grouped together with other Jews in a special work unit. Protected by his military status as a prisoner of war under the Geneva Convention, Levinas was not exported to a concentration camp. He spent five years performing manual labor. Of that time, he recalls: "It was not a period of torture. We went to work in the forest; we spent the day in the forest. Materially supported by care packages, morally by letters, like all the French prisoners" (IRB 41). Elsewhere he is less dispassionate, as he remembers: "The French uniform . . . protected us from Hitlerian violence. But the other men, called free, who had dealings with us or gave us work or orders or even a smile—and the children and women who passed and sometimes raised their eyes—stripped us of our human skin" (DF 152–53). The war and this experience of captivity colors all of Levinas's philosophy. Moreover, radical or rupturing experience dictates the themes and style of his writing, from his descriptions of horror, trauma, and insomnia in the 1940s to his asking whether we are duped by morality in the preface to *Totality and Infinity*, in 1961.

Indeed, Levinas opens *Existence and Existents* with prose that belies a self-conscious sense of how a philosophical text ought to proceed: a clean, dispassionate train of thought and argument that does not get bogged down with the details of concrete circumstances. Yet to read *Existence and Existents* is to experience the dissolution of this intellectual remove and dispassionate beginning, and to find oneself, at the end, wading in details. As they surface, Levinas begins to abandon traditional philosophic language and to forgo the typical structure of philosophic argumentation—replacing theses, proofs, and evidence with a series of compounding descriptions. One can feel in his prose the progressive and increasingly laborious effort to develop a mode of expression that says the unsayable and shows the unshowable—a quest Levinas remains concerned with for the rest of his life.

Existence and Existents takes us to a raw scene. The lines urgently cast here get tied together and neatened over the course of Levinas's later work. Yet all the critical bits appear in the first book, and in many ways it is easier to see what is at stake by surveying the rough pieces, learning from the fragments of what Wittgenstein called "primitive language games."[13] Levinas's text reads like a narration someone can only give in the midst or immediate aftermath of tragedy: a strangely lucid running account that has not had a chance for the reflection, editing, and faltering that will, later, make the story both leaner and more complicated.

2. Radical Empiricism

Formed in the crucible of captivity, *Existence and Existents* provides a critical introduction to Levinas's concerns, providing a roadmap for his later work and delivering a list of early influences that inspired his ethical thought.[14] The names and references populating *Existence and Existents* are particularly relevant insofar as they are the names Levinas recalled in isolation, without recourse to his own notes and books.[15] Some of the names that appear here reappear throughout Levinas's later writings, including (among others) Bergson, Heidegger, Husserl, Rimbaud, Valéry, Baudelaire, Shakespeare, Blanchot, Plato, Kant, and Descartes. One can begin to construct an idiosyncratic, Levinasian history of philosophy from this list, a history that deliberately and openly blurs the lines between philosophy, literature, and poetry. There are a few surprising absences, foremost Dostoyevsky, whom Levinas read in Russian as a teenager growing up in Kovno and credited with leading him to philosophy.[16] There are also some surprising additions—names that appear here and not again. Among these is William James. This name is surprising because Levinas does not claim James as a source of inspiration in any of his later interviews or reflections on philosophy. But the name is also singularly instructive in helping to understand Levinas's growing anxiety with the phenomenological methods of Husserl and Heidegger and his lifelong quest for a more radical, humane, and personal phenomenology.

There are many ways in which Levinas may have happened upon William James. In fact, it would have been surprising had he been able to avoid him. Although James died in 1910, his fame was still reverberating through Europe from 1923 to 1928, when Levinas was a young student (together with Maurice Blanchot) in Strasbourg. Many considered James's massive two-volume opus, *The Principles of Psychology,* to be a prototype of phenomenological description and a direct inspiration for Husserl's phenomenological method.[17] Husserl acknowledged the influence himself, citing James's "genius-like observations" in a footnote to the *Logical Investigations,* and in diary notes admitting that James's *Principles* "furnished me with some insights." He continued: "I saw how a daring and original man did not allow himself to be influenced by tradition and attempted to hold fast to what he saw and describe it. This influence was probably not without significance for me."[18] Several groundbreaking studies have linked aspects of James's psychology, pragmatism, and radical empiricism with Husserl's transcendental phenomenology. As one commentator notes, "Husserl himself was most generous in acknowledging his debt to James in general terms, especially in conversation with American visitors in the twenties and thirties."[19] Another possible conduit to James may have been through Jean Wahl, a lifelong friend and crucial academic mentor of Levinas's from 1947 onward (*Totality and Infinity* is dedicated to Wahl and his wife, Marcelle). Wahl was the author of texts such as *Les Philosophies Pluralistes d'Angelterre et d'Amérique* and *Vers le concret*, in which the first two chapters focus on James.[20]

Husserl or Wahl could have easily directed Levinas toward James, but the more direct connection that may have influenced the young Levinas would have been that between James and Henri Bergson, whose correspondence, open support, and encouragement of each other's work brought each of them notoriety beyond their own national borders.[21] This relationship, unlike that between James and Husserl, was a live exchange. Bergson's new philosophy imbued the university at Strasbourg with a spirit of novelty, encouraged increasingly creative and subtle accounts of life (although, as Samuel Moyn has pointed out, without any clear indication of the ethical implications of such philosophy), and formed the dominant backdrop of Levinas's earliest philosophical studies in France.[22] This influence reverberated throughout Levinas's career.[23] As he began his own investigations of time, escape, and intersubjectivity in the 1940s, Levinas returned to Bergson at critical junctures, attempting to find a way of moving beyond Husserlian or Heideggerian phenomenology and toward a more vital and—beyond Bergson—ethical philosophy.

In his 1904 paper, "A World of Pure Experience," James articulated the quest for a more living philosophy. Diagnosing the zeitgeist that informed his own thought, James wrote:

> It is not difficult to notice a curious unrest in the philosophic atmosphere of the time, a loosening of old landmarks.... The dissatisfaction with these seems due for the most part to a feeling that they are too abstract and academic. Life is confused and superabundant, and what the younger generation appears to crave is more of the temperament of life in its philosophy, even though it were at some cost of logical rigor and of formal purity. (ERE 39)

With these lines introducing the "*Weltanschauung*" James called "radical empiricism," he struck a presciently post-modern tone.[24] The feeling of "unrest" palpable in 1904 would grow exponentially and unavoidably urgent by the time Levinas began composing *Existence and Existents* in captivity in 1940, in the wake of one world war and in the midst of the second. Prior to Levinas, James questioned and hoped for an articulation of the ethical implications of Bergsonian vitalism, writing to Bergson after his second reading of *Matter and Memory:* "I think I understand the main lines of your system very well at present—though of course I can't yet trace its proper relations to the aspects of experience of which you do not treat. It needs much building out in the direction of Ethics."[25]

James, the most successful and widely known intellectual of his era in the United States, enjoyed a worldwide reputation from the 1890s through his death in 1910. The pragmatic method James inaugurated (and credited to Charles Sanders Peirce) began as a new theory of meaning and truth in American philosophy in the 1870s. Unlike rationalist or idealist philosophies (epitomized in France by Descartes and in Germany by Hegel), pragmatism emphasizes parts rather than wholes. Rather than the *absolute* or *The Truth,* pragmatists focus on the practical consequences of ideas, describing meaning in terms of dynamic, experiential effects. For James, this means that what is true today may or may not be true in the same way tomorrow. Anticipating the connection between this notion of truth and his later account of "pure experience," James explained: "Experience, as we know, has a way of *boiling over,* and making us correct our present formulas. . . . We have to live to-day with what truth we can get to-day, and be ready to-morrow to call it falsehood" (P 90). James connected the idea of revisable truths (as opposed to an eternal, immutable Truth) with his own empiricist conception of knowledge as perpetually open and *virtual:* "in transit and on its way," it is "never complete or nailed down" (ERE 67–68). Different ideas will play different roles in one's life, sometimes making a great deal of practical difference and sometimes making very little difference. Truth for a pragmatist like James is not static but perpetually in the making and context-dependent, becoming deeper and shallower over time as different ideas become more or less integrated into the fabric of one's life.

James's focus on practical consequences and a fluid conception of meaning challenged a mechanistic world-view and particularly the use (and abuse) of Darwinian natural selection for the conservative aims of Social Darwinism.[26] From James's perspective, the misapplication of Darwin's biology threatened to remove spontaneity from the world, relegating every instance of change to a blunt, biological event. James worried that this stripped the significance from *living,* since anything one did could be explained away in terms of a larger story about the future life of a species. Coincident with this worry was James's concern with an increasingly scientistic attitude in philosophy—an emphasis on experiment, predicative theory, and the accumulation of data at the expense of genuine *experience* and the cultivation of feeling.[27] The world seemed messier and less coherent than scientific theory allowed. The early pragmatists were proto-phenomenologists in their efforts to describe life in its living complexity.

At the same time, the evolutionary theories of the nineteenth century were a tremendous source of inspiration insofar as they placed new focus on the temporal nature of experience, paving the way for renewed philosophical interest in time and James's own sense of fluid, developmental, indefinite meanings. James saw the world as a deeply plural space of personal struggle, a sphere rife with novelty, uncertainty, chaos, and creative possibility. He advocated a sober optimism in the midst of so much uncertainty. Nothing is permanently stable, and yet this need not lead us toward a nihilistic rejection of all meaning. Nothing is for all time, but in the time we have to live we have the potential to make life meaningful. In 1896 James famously called this attitude a "Will to Believe," a commitment to *live* in increasingly intimate relation with a fragmentary world.[28] He named his own philosophy; one he believed was uniquely capable of attending to both intimacy and fragmentation, *radical empiricism.*[29]

What is radical about James's empiricism? In "A World of Pure Experience" he defined radical empiricism as "a mosaic philosophy . . . of plural facts" that is radical by virtue of its focus on "direct perceptual experience" (ERE 42). Admitting that this sort of empiricism is "like that of Hume and his descendents" (ERE 42), insofar as there is an emphasis on "the part, the element, the individual" (ERE 41), James insists that his empiricism differs from Hume by virtue of being "radical." Experiences, never isolated as atomized facts or things, include the sense of connectedness, or the "conjunctive relations" (ERE 44) between experiences.[30] The emphasis falls on parts, but the parts themselves are indefinitely bounded, surrounded by halos lacking definite edges. In *The Principles of Psychology,* James foreshadowed this idea in his description of the stream of thought, wherein "every definite image in the mind is steeped and dyed in the free water that flows around it. . . . in this halo or penumbra that surrounds and escorts it,—or rather that is fused into one with it and has become bone of its bone and flesh of its flesh" (PP 1: 255). In early work he used the terms "*psychic overtone, suffusion,* or *fringe*" (PP 1: 258) to describe the dimly perceived but expanding radius of every thought within a moving horizon of relations. Different aspects of thought succeed in commanding one's attention, momentarily cresting above the stream. The mistake James thinks we commonly make lies in interpreting such a swell as a singular or definitive event, as if it were the last and most significant wave.[31] Instead, emphasizing the "continuous transition" (ERE 48) of experience, James points us toward the connective tissue and compounding significance of thoughts and experiences that are never final or independent—even when they appear particularly decisive or emphatic. His radical empiricism looks to the disjointed pieces of experience. But in the attempt to lift a piece from the stream of life, James finds that each drags with it a trail of others like a fishing line gathers kelp as one reels it in from the sea. Connection and plurality are meant to save James's version of empiricism from skepticism and from despair at the futility of trying to piece things back together from a set of disjointed particulars. Connectivity is not a supersensible "third thing," but something James expresses in the *Principles of Psychology* as "a feeling of *and,* a feeling of *if,* a feeling of *but,* and a feeling of *by,* quite as readily as we say a feeling of *blue* or a feeling of *cold*" (PP 1: 245–46). The feeling of connectedness has just as much reality or truth as the weight of a stone in one's hand. James thinks traditional empiricism, reacting to rationalism, overemphasizes separation and atomic parts. Rationalism over-optimistically unites everything, but empiricism over-pessimistically dislocates everything. *Radical* empiricism aims for a hesitation between intimacy and imperfection, between total homogeneity and utter isolation, in order to be "fair to both the unity and the disconnection" (ERE 47).

Radical empiricism aspires to the real feeling of things in all their shifting weight and jumbled significance. The emphasis on plurality and experience disallows recourse to an ideal situated somewhere beyond or above the real that is the touchstone for transcendental idealism. But there is another arc within everything real, the tracing out of something thinly, vaguely, or provisionally ideal that can only be described as an ambiguous sense of plurality or endurance trailing off indefinitely. No experience is separate or final, and James concludes: "Our fields of experience have no more definite boundaries than have our fields of view. Both are fringed forever by a *more* that continuously develops, and continuously supersedes them as life progresses" (ERE 71). James's ideas of an overflowing "field" and a superseding "more" prefigure the transcendent and infinite sense of a face that Levinas describes forty-three years later.

3. Bergsonism

Although James was a larger-than-life philosophical force, Henri Bergson was the philosophical superstar in Europe in the early 1890s, expounding an earthshaking notion of temporality and plurality. As I suggested earlier, one can locate an explicit link between Levinas and James in their common interest in and influence by Bergson's work. Bergson's central ideas concerned temporality conceived as duration (*durée*) and a creative life force he called *élan vital*. Following James's conviction that mechanism could not explain all the diverse phenomena of the world, Bergson conceived *durée* and *élan vital* as alternatives to scientific conceptions of time and Darwinian natural selection.

In James, Bergson discovered an American ally in the quest for a more nuanced conception of *living* time. In a letter from 1903 Bergson wrote to James, "French students passing through Cambridge . . . must have told you that I was one of your greatest admirers, and that I have never passed up an opportunity to express the great sympathy I have for your ideas to my listeners."[32] James, seventeen years older than Bergson, made Bergson's philosophy the topic of the central lecture of *A Pluralistic Universe* and wrote of him, "Bergson alone has been radical" (PU 238) in his criticism of rationalism. James went on to praise his originality and style, at the same time writing, "I have to confess that Bergson's originality is so profuse that many of his ideas baffle me entirely. I doubt whether any one understands him all-over, so to speak" (PU 226). After reading *Creative Evolution* in 1907, James wrote Bergson an effusive letter in which he called Bergson a "magician," his work a "marvel," and concluded "I feel that at bottom we are fighting the same fight, you a commander, I in the ranks. The position we are rescuing is 'Tychism' and a really growing world" (LWJ 292). In a letter from 1908, James fondly recalled his long walks with Bergson after a recent visit to Europe. Revealing the growing friendship and intimacy between the two men, he ends his letter by confessing, "I wish that you and I and Strong and Flournoy and McDougall and Ward could live on some mountaintop for a month, together, and whenever we got tired of philosophizing, calm our minds by taking refuge in the scenery."[33] In 1911, one year after James's death, Bergson wrote the introduction ("Verité et realité") to the French translation of *Pragmatism*.

Their respective projects and concerns were by no means identical, but their mutual openness to each other's endeavors represents a crossroads of American and European philosophy, a fertile—if short-lived—forgetting of national borders.[34] Both James and Bergson insisted on the independence of their work and their mutual surprise at finding each other, rather late in their careers, so closely allied in spirit and realm of investigation. James in particular felt that the coincidence of their thought despite their physical distance from one another testified to a genuine zeitgeist, a real convergence of American pragmatism and a nascent European phenomenology yet to be fully explored.

Levinas's work is one place to look for that uncharted convergence. Second only to Heidegger, Bergson is the most cited name in *Existence and Existents*. Levinas frequently emphasized Bergson's profound influence on his early thinking and on phenomenology generally. On several occasions he protested the lack of philosophical engagement with Bergson in postwar France, describing Bergson as "a very great philosopher who remains in purgatory" (BPW 154), and insisting that "Bergson's importance to contemporary Continental thought has been somewhat obfuscated."[35] In an interview with *Autrement* in November 1988, Levinas responded to a question about his "contact" with the tradition of philosophy by acknowledging phenomenology and Heidegger, and then adding, "I have hardly emphasized the importance (which was essential for me) of the relationship—always present in the background of the teaching of those masters—to Bergson." He elaborates,

> I feel close to certain Bergsonian themes: to *durée,* in which the spiritual is no longer reduced to an event of pure "knowledge," but would be the transcendence of a relationship with someone. . . . Bergson is the source of an entire complex of interrelated contemporary philosophical ideas; it is to him, no doubt, that I owe my modest speculative initiatives.[36]

Later, in the foreword to *Proper Names,* Levinas lists his beginning interests in philosophy, describing how he "marveled, while still in school, at the prospects for renewal recently introduced by Bergson's conception of *durée.*"[37]

"The prospect for renewal" is a driving theme of Levinas's early work. In *Existence and Existents,* he invokes both *durée* and *élan vital*—a vital impulse and creative urge to begin anew that is distinct from the ruthless forward march of Darwinian natural selection and what Levinas, following Bergson, calls the "time of clocks and trains." *Durée* holds a special place for Levinas, since it provides one alternative to the Hegelian dialectic that puts every loss in the service of some future gain. Bergson stressed discontinuous time (in particular the discontinuous time of memory) and in so doing allowed for the prospect that the instants of one's life are not simply additive or determinative of the whole of life. *Durée* represents the priority of fluidity and change over permanence, opening the possibility of living time and genuine novelty.[38] Reversing the classical hierarchy of the stable over the fluid, Bergson insists that linear, measurable time derives from a more original experience of lived duration and endurance. "In a word," Bergson explains, "pure duration might well be nothing but a succession of qualitative changes, which melt into and permeate one another, without precise outlines, without any tendency to externalise themselves in relation to one another . . . it would be pure heterogeneity" (TFW 104). This sense of living time makes room for the idea of a radically new beginning and foreshadows Levinas's own insistence on the infinite opening of a living face as the embodied revelation of *heterogeneous,* discontinuous time.

In his 1903 *Introduction to Metaphysics,* Bergson relates the sense of dynamic endurance to a variety of knowledge that remains irreducible to static facts. Instead of knowledge, Bergson describes a *sympathetic acquaintance* that allows for attentiveness to the inexhaustible richness and complex interrelation of lived experience. It is difficult, if not impossible, to articulate the content of this type of knowledge, which resembles the grasp one has of a deeply familiar place—a subtle sensitivity for its shifting smells, sounds, and shades. One might describe such a place to a friend in colorful detail, with snapshots and great narrative flare; but nothing can replace the physical, sensible immersion of being there in person. Bergson argues for the importance of being engaged in a situation in such a way that one becomes intimate with its dynamic rhythms. He names such intimacy "Metaphysical intuition," differentiating it from the "analysis," which is always the abstracting aftereffect of intuitive knowledge.[39] Bergson explains,

> Metaphysical intuition . . . is an entirely different thing from the summary or synthesis of knowledge. It is as distinct from it as . . . the tension of a spring is distinct from the movements in the clock. In this sense, metaphysics has nothing in common with generalization of experience, and yet it could be defined as the whole of experience (*l'expérience intégrale*).[40]

One cannot arrive at "Metaphysical intuition" through the accumulation of facts, the "summary or synthesis" of information, just as one cannot arrive in New York through the accumulation of guidebooks and postcards. Instead, "Metaphysical intuition" prefigures analysis as an animating principle, a tension that gets thought moving in the first place.

Four years later, in *Creative Evolution,* Bergson articulates a distinction between "intellect," which always works on "the discontinuous, the immobile, and the dead" (CE 182) and "instinct," which brings organisms into contact with life in its living vitality. In human beings, Bergson diagnoses an overabundance of intellect and a dangerous diminution of instinct or intuition, suggesting that a recalibration of our means of engaging with the world "may bring the intellect to recognize that life does not quite go into the category of the many nor yet into that of the one; that neither mechanical causality nor finality can give a sufficient interpretation of the vital process" (CE 195). Echoing the Jamesian image of the stream of thought and foreshadowing Levinas's description of the fluidity of the "saying," Bergson continues, "by the sympathetic communication [intuition] establishes between us and the rest of the living, by the expansion of our consciousness which it brings about, it introduces us into life's own domain, which is reciprocal interpenetration, endlessly continued creation" (CE 195). In positing a kind of knowledge that is a pre-articulate immersion, Bergson challenges the Kantian model of a subject forever separated from the noumenal world. The Bergsonian subject could be in closer contact with things and could find, in its experiences, living sources of infinite intrigue.

Levinas saw Bergson as a champion of sensibility thanks to his suggestion of "metaphysical intuition" as a more original source of contact with the world than anything provided by "analysis" or traditional descriptions of knowledge. Though Levinas ultimately criticized Bergsonian "intuition" as a solipsistic epistemology, Bergson remained an inspirational source of a set of philosophical problems relating to time and sensible experience—driving issues of Levinas's own conception of ethical subjectivity. The depth of this influence is shown by Levinas's frequent references to Bergson in published work, and his consistent championing of Bergson as one of the five most important philosophers, along with Plato, Kant, Hegel, and Heidegger.[41] This list, and Bergson's place in it, might be surprising given Levinas's early focus on Husserl. The scope of Bergson's influence on Levinas is also surprising given the fact that Bergson retired from the Collège de France in 1920 and published little after that until 1932, when his first public foray into ethics appeared as *The Two Sources of Mortality and Religion*.[42] Bergson's years of cult-like celebrity and international renown as a dramatic teacher, wild experimentalist, and political activist took place predominantly before World War I. Later, in the years following World War II, the philosophical ingenuity attributed to Bergson was decried as "spiritualism" and "mysticism," notably the same tags applied to James and those now being affixed by some to Levinas. Nevertheless it is Bergson, and not Husserl, who Levinas credits with his initial philosophical awakening. This is significant, since Levinas missed the historical apex of Bergsonian enthusiasm (a period called *le Bergson Boom* in France) and had to rekindle Bergson's philosophy for himself.

4. Escape

In the hours of manual labor, the monotonous trips out and back from the forest, Levinas's experience of physical and mental endurance links with Bergson's conception of duration. At the same time, *élan vital* remains a profoundly hopeful thought that life is not governed by an abstract, impersonal, and predetermined end—a sealed fate. Bergson defended a profound *multiplicity* that could not be synthesized into a coherent whole. For a prisoner confined to the margins of the living, and designated by the Germans as one of those unfit for life, these thoughts were a crucial source of inspiration, motivating Levinas's early efforts to account for pluralistic meanings and living interruptions of abstract universals. Perhaps it was possible to escape the philosophical idealism and monism that put every individual in the service of a greater totality. If so, perhaps it would be possible to escape totalitarianism, or at least to escape from the labor camp to a life that would remain meaningful even though it would lack coherence and closure.

Despite the lure of these ideas, Levinas adheres to the spirit, but not the letter, of Bergson's work. This is because Bergson does not describe the multiplicity central to his thought about temporality in terms of the social, *ethical* world. Time is multiple, moving in multiple directions, but Levinas, looking for the ethical upshot of this multiplicity, discovers that he will have to articulate it himself. Unable to find an adequate account of the interhuman in Bergson, Levinas concludes that Bergson sets the stage for Heidegger's ecstatic temporality by describing time as "purely exterior to the subject, a time-object, or . . . entirely contained in the subject" (EE 96).[43] He believes Bergson is right to reorient temporality around fluidity but wrong to describe the experience of fluidity in terms of a private intuition or interior consciousness. Embracing Bergson's "creative evolution"—the idea that "to exist is to change, to change is to mature"—Levinas simultaneously contests the idea that "to mature is to go on creating oneself endlessly" or that evolution is "creation of self by self" (CE 9).[44]

Existence and Existents is a sober text that is somewhat at odds with the exuberance of a creative life force. Not surprisingly, Heidegger is the first name to appear in the book, but where one might expect to see Bergson's name, the second name cited is Baudelaire and his image of "true travelers... parting for the sake of parting" (EE 12). The line comes from "Le Voyage," the last poem in *Les Fleurs du Mal*. The entire stanza reads:

> But the true voyagers are only those who leave
> Just to be leaving; hearts light, like balloons,
> They never turn aside from their fatality
> And without knowing why they always say: "Let's go!"[45]

To part for the sake of parting, without knowing why, to always say, "Let's go!" (*Allons!*). This is the attitude Levinas describes as "an evasion without an itinerary and without an end" (EE 12). It is an attitude of joyful escape Levinas associates with Bergson's *élan vital*, a spontaneous burst of enthusiasm. Baudelaire's *vrais voyageurs* leave naively, without anxiety and without the thought of fate or death. They don't know where they are going or where they will end up. They simply set sail. Breaking with the past and the future, they embark impulsively without an attempt to reach a destination or to circle back to someplace they have been before. This is the thought of a beginning unburdened by history and indifferent to destiny. A clean slate.

But in the poem, the *vrais voyageurs* do return, and when asked what they have seen, they reply that they've seen the same things everywhere—the same stuff of life in different shapes the whole world over. They are weary of traveling. They have tried to escape, to flee or kill time, and instead of setting sail in a final, ecstatic departure, they return to say:

> O bitter is the knowledge that one draws from the voyage!
> The monotonous and tiny world, today
> Yesterday, tomorrow, always, shows us our reflections,
> An oasis of horror in a desert of boredom![46]

The return of the travelers in Baudelaire's poem parallels the collapse of Bergson's *élan vital* into solipsistic intuition. Sensitized to the profound difficulty of beginning, Levinas insists: "Beginning is unlike the freedom, simplicity and gratuitousness which these images suggest" (EE 14). Time has no exits, and every beginning is complicated by a shadow of the past and a halo of the future. There is no way of escaping reality since there is no way of escaping oneself or seeing things from the beginning: separate, distinct, and free. Levinas contends, "existence drags behind it a weight—if only itself—

which complicates the trip it takes" (EE 16). Later he stresses, "to simply say that the ego leaves itself is a contradiction, since, in quitting itself the ego carries itself along" (EE 100). The "tiny world . . . shows us our reflections." To begin from the beginning one would have to begin without taking oneself along, without the baggage of one's own ego. How then to escape? If it is impossible to shake free of oneself, how can one start over?

The promise offered by Bergson's *élan vital* winds up as naïve escapism. In the end, it does not have enough weight or velocity to be a total escape or a completely new beginning. The "explosive force" (CE 109) of *élan vital*, though powerful in its dispersive capacity, is not explosive enough. The hope fueled by this idea—a beautiful hope—is tempered with a realistic vision of what one can do given the impossibility of an entirely new beginning. It's a lovely picture of setting sail, and Levinas gives us only the promising first lines of Baudelaire's poem in *Existence and Existents,* only the departure and not the return. He leaves off at the first stanza and leaves it to his reader to discover what the *vrais voyageurs* discover. His careful dispensing of verse seems to be a way of honoring Bergson and acknowledging the force of his idea. The *vrais voyageurs'* enthusiasm is, however, a false start, and one can sense Levinas's wish that starting over was as simple as setting sail, a wish coupled with his recognition that one cannot begin that easily. Intimating the intersubjective turn that becomes the centerpiece of his philosophy, Levinas concludes: "The future, a virginal instant, is impossible in a solitary subject" (*à un sujet seul, l'avenir, un instant vierge, est impossible*) (EE 17 / EaE 40). Something else, *someone else,* will have to intervene.

5. Indolence

At this moment, William James appears in *Existence and Existents.* James, the third proper name to appear in the text, is the source of Levinas's description of "indolence" (*la paresse*). One page after citing Baudelaire's "true travelers," Levinas cites "William James's famous example" (EE 13) to describe an aversion to waking, explaining: "Indolence is neither idleness nor rest. Like fatigue, it involves an attitude with regard to action. But it is not a simple indecisiveness . . . It occurs after the intention has been formulated. As in William James's famous example, it lies between the clear duty of getting up and the putting of the foot down off the bed" (EE 13). Levinas establishes that indolence is not equal to Dasein's failure to make an ultimate choice, its inauthentic potential to "lose itself and never win itself" (BT 68). Instead, Levinas is interested in the ambiguous gap that indolence opens "between" (*entre*) the past formation of an intention and the future realization of that intention into action. In later work, Levinas will call this interminable interval the "meanwhile" (*entre-temps*), a suspended present.[47] Bergson provided the hopeful picture of a beginning undetermined by any end, but James furnishes the description of just how hard it will be to get going. Indolence entails being stuck in the moment, incapable of getting started.

Levinas turns to James for a description of the seemingly endless gap "between the clear duty of getting up and the putting of the foot down off the bed" (*le devoir clair de se lever et la pose du pied sur la descente du lit*) (EE 13 / EaE 33). The first chapter of *Existence and Existents* focuses on that gap, centering on descriptions of fatigue and work that indicate a physical, repetitive struggle. In some ways these are moods like Heidegger's anxiety, curiosity or boredom, but instead of highlighting a finding or losing of *oneself*, they show "a disquietude which his own existence awakens in man" (EE 105). They signal events in which existence feels bodily and weighty, something one must face up to or take on, as if strapping on a heavy pack. The struggle with indolence takes place in a minimal interval between waking up and getting up, without the epic span from thrownness to projection. Heidegger prioritizes the future as the most authentic possibility for Dasein's self-understanding. Indolence holds back from the future, and would be, therefore, a profoundly inauthentic mood in Heidegger's analysis, a "tempting, tranquillizing, alienation and self-entanglement" (BT 223). Yet it is a mood Levinas singles out because it exemplifies the real difficulty of getting started, a feeling of dread before the beginning. There is a space indicated by that gap, an expansion of the present where things unfold differently from a Heideggerian effort to authentically face one's own "certain and yet indefinite" (BT 356) future. It is a struggle to begin and not to end.

As one of the first names Levinas cites in *Existence and Existents,* James is particularly significant. Without recourse to a library or to his own books, the "famous example" inhabits Levinas's memory and provides a touchstone for his early philosophical thought. Though he names James only once, the phenomenological analysis of fatigue and labor Levinas adopts from James dominates the entire book. These are descriptions of what it feels like to be without will, unable to get going. The example Levinas cites comes from the second volume of *The Principles of Psychology*, in the chapter devoted to "Will." James is in the process of describing what he calls "ideo-motor action" (PP 2: 522)—a subtle, but critical, variety of action that dovetails with the mere thought of activity, something like the involuntary itch that materializes in the thought of itching.[48] Not willed, deliberate, or well-thought out, these actions arise inadvertently, without prior plan or reflection. James calls them "*quasi*-automatic" (PP 2: 523) and assigns the bulk of everyday activity to this realm, including basic activities like standing up, sitting down, walking, talking, and eating.

The privileged example of "ideo-motor action," however, James reserves for the mundane, daily routine of getting out of bed.[49] James describes this example, which captivates Levinas and organizes the first chapter of *Existence and Existents*, in elaborate detail:

> We know what it is to get out of bed on a freezing morning in a room without a fire, and how the very vital principle within us protests against the ordeal. Probably most persons have lain on certain mornings for an hour at a time unable to brace themselves to the resolve. We suffer; we say, "I *must* get up, this is ignominious," etc.; but still the warm couch feels too delicious, the cold outside too cruel, and resolution faints away and postpones itself again and again just as it seemed on the verge of bursting the resistance and passing over into a decisive act. Now how do we *ever* get up under such circumstances? If I may generalize from my own experience, we more often than not get up without any struggle or decision at all. We suddenly find that we *have* got up. A fortunate lapse of consciousness occurs; we forget both the warmth and the chill; we fall into some revery connected with the day's life, in the course of which the idea flashes across us, "Hollo! I must lie here no longer." (PP 2: 254)

For James, the daily experience of getting oneself out of bed proves that action is not always coincident with either willing or conscious engagement. Volition is not a simple relation between an internal idea and an external state of affairs. Psychic counter-currents disrupt and complicate every effort, sometimes enabling and sometimes disabling activity. This suggests that it is not easy to distinguish intentional from unintentional acts, and that action is something more complicated and nuanced than the outward (supposedly mobile) expression of an internal (supposedly immobile) idea. A level of activity subtends consciousness like a current under a canoe. The more one lies awake weighing the pros and cons of getting up, the less likely one will make the decisive leap out of bed. Instead, crossing that minimal and at the same time infinite gap between the thought of waking and the fact of waking requires a certain re-laxation of deliberation, a "fortunate lapse of consciousness" (PP 2: 524). One discovers that, despite oneself, one is out of bed. Something flares up and motivates the waking, causing one to forget both the warm bed and the cold floor. For James, the possibility of an unconscious motivational force indicates a level of activity not reducible to conceptual thought—an animating source of "quasi-automatic" action that prefigures and dismantles the traditional op-position between activity and passivity.

Not surprisingly, Levinas exploits the ethical significance of a passivity that cannot be explained as the simple opposite of action. James is primarily concerned with establishing that "consciousness is *in its very nature impul-sive*" (PP 2: 526) and that "willing" is not a super-added force that gets things moving. The emphasis in James falls on the continuously active nature of voluntary life, the significance of micro-movements in the brain, "an expres-sion of the brow, or an expulsion of breath" as much as more visible, forceful "acts of locomotion" (PP 2: 527). Action takes place at various thresholds or intensities, but action of some kind is always taking place somewhere.[50] This might lead one to conclude that James is a philosopher of action, while Levi-nas is a philosopher of inaction. But this would be a hasty oversimplification of the breadth and pervasiveness of passive activity in James and of active passivity in Levinas—both of them are attentive to the subtle and ambiguous registers of an essential, ongoing vitality.

Levinas's emphasis falls on "the restlessness of respiration" and the "trembling of substantiality" (OB 180) that are definitive of a being who is both sensibly vulnerable and capable of *patience*. Passivity becomes coinci-dent with an ethical *willingness,* a hiatus of egoistic power and judgment occasioned by the "face to face" encounter with another person. The possi-bility that one can get over one's own profound weariness, getting *past one-self* in order to wake up to a reality outpacing one's intentions, indicates an ethical potential constitutive of what it means to be a human being. Being human in Levinas's work means being able to feel motivated by something other than the *conatus essendi,* the Spinozan or Darwinian will for self-preservation and survival at all costs. Humanity demonstrates the interrup-tion of that will: caring for something, for someone, more than one cares for oneself. It takes Levinas several decades to cultivate this thought, but the seeds lie in his earliest fixation on fatigue and the experience of rising despite oneself. In particular, the phenomenology of fatigue from Levinas's first

book turns into the phenomenology of insomnia that describes ethical subjectivity throughout his later work.

From James's example of indolence, Levinas adopts the idea that there
is an animating source of activity, irreducible and prior to, conscious engagement. He also follows James's return to this most banal, non-eventful
situation in order to exhibit the drama characteristic of a much more significant event. We do get out of bed, most every day, day after day. The
repetition indicates that we are routinely inspired to activity that is (at least
initially) at odds with our own sense of comfort. For James it indicates the
reality of multiple kinds of activity and the critical importance of studying
every vague "*feeling of tendency*" (PP 1: 251) infiltrating psychic life. James
shows that not everything we feel or do is decisive or distinct. In fact, most
of what we feel and do remains murky and entangled with several simultaneous feelings and actions. But this essential ambiguity does not render action
or feeling meaningless. On the contrary, the blind spots and sheer darkness
in the human psyche are among the most significant aspects of James's psychology. Levinas takes the reality of ambiguity as an indication of meaning
that transcends the visible world and the reach of knowledge. He ultimately
locates such meaning outside the psyche in another person. The *other* becomes the flesh and blood manifestation of James's field of experience
fringed with a "penumbra that surrounds and escorts it" (PP 1: 255), edged
with a "*more* that continuously develops" (ERE 71).

6. The Sensible Flux

It is not hard to see James's appeal for Levinas as a prisoner in a labor camp.
James is a master of examples that crystallize as recognizable feelings of weight
or density; like Bergson, he valorizes sensibility. Reversing the Platonic/Car-
tesian/Kantian/Hegelian hierarchy of mind over body, James argues that the
unity of apperception Kant attributes to the *rational* subject is in fact only the
full-bodied manifestation of an underlying, passive synthesis, and he urges us
to realize that "breath is . . . the essence out of which philosophers have constructed the entity known to them as consciousness" (ERE 183).[51] There is no
"entity" uniting the subject and gathering the manifold of experience; there is
no mental cabinet for storing ideas as Locke envisioned. Instead, James suggests a bodily intimation of a pulse outside one's control. It is a *feeling* of exist-

ing along a bodily axis that sometimes feels pulled together and sometimes feels pulled apart.

The embodied, breathing subject is subject to a reality infinitely more complicated than the subject reduced to consciousness. In *A Pluralistic Universe*, James writes about the unmanageable thickness of "sensible reality," and insists that "to get from one point in it to another we have to plough or wade through the whole intolerable interval. No detail is spared us; it is as bad as the barbed-wire complications at Port Arthur, and we grow old and die in the process" (PU 247). Sometimes there is no way of getting at something just by thinking oneself there with the ease of what James calls "conceptual reality" that "skips the intermediaries as by a divine winged power" (PU 248). Concerned with the tangible heft of lived existence, James draws on Bergson's idea about the primacy of perception, which he applauds as a return to "the despised sensible flux" (PU 248). Bergson argues that sensible reality has a visceral thickness impenetrable by concepts alone, requiring a return to "that flux which Platonism, in its strange belief that only the immutable is excellent, has always spurned" (PU 252). James takes this insight as an occasion to differentiate between "theoretic knowledge," knowing *about* things, and something else he calls "living or sympathetic acquaintance" (PU 249). "Theoretic knowing" knows from a distance, but "sympathetic acquaintance" is the direct experience that rounds out "theoretic knowledge" with a fleshy density.

"Skipping the intermediaries" is one way of describing James's critique of Hegelian rationalism and Levinas's criticism of Heideggerian ontology.[52] For all its equipment and being-alongside and in-the-midst, the "world" Heidegger describes ends up feeling remarkably empty and without gravity. Even the idea of "falling" (*Verfallen*), the "*downward plunge*" (Absturz) (BT 223) which could indicate a weight, ends up feeling more like lateral drift. Heidegger explains: "'Fallenness' into the 'world' means an absorption in Being-with-one-another, in so far as the latter is guided by idle talk, curiosity, and ambiguity" (BT 220). Each of these is a way of being in the world that evades the world, a mode of what Heidegger names "groundless floating" (BT 221). The image of "groundless floating" recurs, unintentionally, via a conception of thinking that Heidegger makes explicit in his 1951 essay "Building, Dwelling, Thinking":

> When I go towards the door of the lecture hall, I am already there, and I could never go towards it at all if I were not such that I am there. I am never here only, as this encapsulated body; rather, I am there, that is, I already pervade the room, and only thus can I go through it.[53]

At first glance, this passage might seem coextensive with James's emphasis on the "fringed," expanding nature of lived experience and with Levinas's focus on the non-identical, displaced subject. And yet, Heidegger's sense of "pervading the room" instills a picture of transparent space that differs substantially from the visceral clutter and chaos of life critical to both James and Levinas. Heidegger's aim is to describe the ways in which human beings persist in and move through the world, intending—and thus being—beyond the strict limits of embodiment, in their entwining with spaces and objects. Like the bridge extends over the river between two shores, so the body Heidegger describes overreaches its sheer physicality, projecting out ahead of itself toward a future possibility, a space it has yet to inhabit or traverse. Yet this promisingly expansive description of the body carries with it a potentially troubling overstatement of the amorphous pervasiveness and influence of one's own intentionality, an overemphasis on future-oriented *projection*. The drift of conceptual thought can lightly touch down anywhere. Heidegger is already here, there, and everywhere—pervading the room and escaping through the door he has yet to reach. He doesn't need to walk, just to think. But intending to exit is not the same as actually making an exit, a distinction Beckett underlined at the end of *Endgame* as Clov hovers on the stage, "dressed for the road. Panama hat, tweed coat, raincoat over his arm, umbrella, bag. He halts there by the door, impassive and motionless, his eyes fixed on Hamm, till the end."[54] We never see him leave.

Thinking doesn't get one through the door, and Levinas and James agree that intentions by themselves, however good, are never good enough. Levinas makes this explicit, insisting:

> We are responsible beyond our intentions. It is impossible for the attention directing the act to avoid inadvertent action. We get caught up in things; things turn against us. That is to say that our consciousness, and our mastery of reality through consciousness, do not exhaust our relationship with reality, in which we are present with all the density of our being.[55]

One's own intentions may be good or bad, but intentions are entangled in a social, fluid matrix that complicates and transfigures them. There are, for this reason, no *pure* intentions. For both James and Levinas, a critique of intellectualism coincides with a criticism of disembodied forms of thinking. To be "present with all the density of our being" is to be in a relationship that is more intimate and complicated than "knowing." There is something inherently messy and specific about reality that resists and overreaches every intention, a residual resistance. "Theoretic knowledge" is a way of knowing what James admits "may indeed be enormous . . . it may dot the whole diameter of space and time with its conceptual creations; but it does not penetrate one millimeter into the solid dimension" (PU 250). "Thought," he continues, "deals solely with surfaces. It can name the thickness of reality, but cannot fathom it, and its insufficiency here is essential and permanent, not temporary" (PU 250).

Sometimes one has to wade through the whole deep, sensible swamp. Thinking won't get you through, and what you really need is something less essential and more real. Trawling through matter without recourse to any imaginable or thinkable end, caught up in the thick of things, one might experience what Levinas distinguishes as "moments of human density" (EE 7). Such moments show "the concrete forms of an existent's adherence to existence, in which their separation already begins" (EE 10). *Existence and Existents* opens with situations where action feels endless, impossible or useless, and with forms of repetitive work and labor that dismantle the *sense* of work.[56] Roughly thirty-four years later, in 1981, Levinas was asked by Philippe Nemo how thinking begins. Levinas, responding in terms that recall the setting of *Existence and Existents,* answered: "It probably begins through traumatisms or gropings to which one does not even know how to give a verbal form: a separation, a violent scene, a sudden consciousness of the monotony of time" (EI 21). His answer reflects the priority Levinas gives to the moments when a new way of thinking is called for by situations uniquely resistant to conception, by moments when things are unthinkable and one feels the insufficiency of reason or rationality. These are moments when all the thinking or intending in the world will not bring one any closer to traversing the minimal and at the same time *indefinite* interval between waking up and putting one's foot down on the floor.

There are grey areas (making up a lifetime) between being born and dying, where one finds that one's own birth was not enough of a beginning or that a loved one's death is not enough of an ending. Indolence is one example of feeling left without the effort required to begin, as if the velocity of birth, of one's thrown-ness into the world, wore off too soon and hasn't carried one far enough. Yet exhaustion, insomnia, and the effort required to rise to the new day all indicate in their sensible density ways of rising despite oneself, rising when one doesn't want to, when one is "weary of everything and everyone, and above all weary of oneself" (EE 11). A minimal rising gesture (get up, put on your coat, go out) indicates an effort and a dignity in spite of—because in the midst of—dark times. Life doesn't leave one alone. There are a thousand lives everyone lives out, endless beginnings and endings. Time, never a smooth path stretching forward and back, is "an ill-paved road" on which one is "jolted about by instants each of which is a beginning all over again" (*cahotée par les instants dont chacun est un recommencement*) (EE 13 / EaE 34). In *Otherwise than Being or Beyond Essence*, Levinas continues this train of thought, insisting: "To speak of time in terms of flowing is to speak of time in terms of time and not in terms of temporal events" (OB 34). Emphasizing "discontinuousness" (EE 13), Levinas parts ways with Bergson's sense of *durée* and James's early image of consciousness as a flowing stream "without breach, crack, or division" (PP 1: 237). This is a vision of continuity that James adjusts in later work, as he emphasizes "both the unity and the disconnection" (ERE 47) central to radical empiricism, staking himself against every absolutist philosophy in his commitment to a pluralistic, "distributive form of reality, the *each*-form" (PU 34). In Levinas, the jolting instants are faces—the eruption of personal sense from the heart of impersonal nonsense. Intersecting the feeling that nothing is possible, the world keeps moving in the pre-articulate density and ethical urgency of individual faces, but also, beyond Levinas, in texts and paintings, landscapes, streets, and noise—all of it waking a person up, calling her out of bed, outside, into life.

7. Religious Bearing

Heidegger provides the launching point for *Existence and Existents,* Baudelaire provides a picture of escape, and James tempers Baudelaire's "true travelers" with a sober description of how hard it will be to get started at all. Things become increasingly realistic, more intimate and solid as Levinas moves from Heidegger's clearing to Baudelaire's ship to James's bed. Thinking about confinement in the most confined space, Levinas questions what kind of future or hope is available given *this* reality.

Experience invades a subject. Even after one experience cedes to another—after a prisoner has been released, freedom is not as simple as walking out of a cell through an open door. James wrote about this difficulty in terms of the deep-rooted and physical basis of habit, noting that persons "grown old in prison have asked to be readmitted after being once set free" (PP 1: 121). There are experiences one can undergo that change everything, including what change means. *Existence and Existents* begins with such an experience, with a sense of maturity overly mature, too old too soon, and a parting glance back at youth and freedom left behind. Without the possibility of escape to an untainted "before," without a way of going naively forward as Baudelaire's *vrais voyageurs* hoped to do, one is left with the memory of a distant time—another life in another form, be that childhood, nature, or freedom—and the tangible reality of a *now* that has divided everything into a before and after, a now and then.

If Baudelaire's *vrais voyageurs* stand for the illusory promise of escape offered by Bergson, it is a point of departure that gives way almost immediately to weariness and the indolence that stalls effort. Levinas's digression from Bergson to James reveals his own attempt to come up with increasingly realistic descriptions of life, death, escape, and time. In particular, Levinas cannot help including a psychological account of what time feels like in particularly difficult and dense moments and how that time clings to a person for the rest of his or her life.

This is something darker. It is something that James did not fully explore until his consideration of the "sick soul" in the *Varieties of Religious Experience* in 1901–1902. Convinced that a naïve or complete "healthy-mindedness" is impossible in a precarious, shifting world, James augments his lecture on "The Religion of Healthy-Mindedness" by turning to "pivotal human experiences" (VRE 117) where "something bitter rises up; a touch of nausea, a falling dead of the delight, a whiff of melancholy, things that sound a knell" (VRE 116). It is through such experiences that even the most healthy mind finds itself left with "an irremediable sense of precariousness" (VRE 116). James describes such a mind as "a bell with a crack" (VRE 116).[57]

In the middle of his lecture James turns to the darkest episodes of the sick soul, those relating to "pathological depression" (VRE 123) and, more severely, "positive and active anguish" (VRE 124). As a case study of intense melancholy, he recounts a haunting memory of an epileptic patient in an asylum. James transcribes the description from a letter he attributes to a French acquaintance "evidently in a bad nervous condition"[58] (VRE 134)—but it could easily be his own testimony:

> A black-haired youth with greenish skin, entirely idiotic . . . used to sit all
> day on one of the benches, or rather shelves against the wall, with his knees

drawn up against his chin, and the coarse gray undershirt, which was his only garment, drawn over them covering his entire figure. He sat there like a sort of sculptured Egyptian cat or Peruvian mummy, moving nothing but his black eyes and looking absolutely non-human. This image and my fear entered into a species of combination with each other. *That shape am I,* I felt, potentially. . . . [I]t was as if something hitherto solid within my breast gave way entirely, and I became a mass of quivering fear. After this the universe was entirely changed for me altogether. (VRE 134)

The sense of things being "entirely changed for me altogether" is a radical shift. Some scenes transpire leaving everything intact. One can move through some experiences seamlessly, *this* to *that, here* to *there.* But other kinds of "pivotal human experiences" (VRE 117) remain unending and up-ending. Then it is as if, even at a distance, "sensible reality" refuses to loosen its grip and there is no movement from *this* to *that.* Such experiences provoke a change and perhaps especially maturity, but added to this is a compounding sense of being insufficient to the task of coming through such a change, of bearing certain kinds of memories or beginning again, by oneself. There is a lasting sense of what James calls "this experience of melancholia" (VRE 135) that seemed to him to have "a religious bearing" (VRE 135). The upshot of such melancholia is the realization that one requires something external and outside of one's own experience to help one through, to begin again, or simply to orient in an "entirely changed" universe. James found outside support in "scripture-like texts" he could repeat to himself: "'Come unto me, all ye that labor and are heavy-laden,'" without which he confesses, "I think I should have grown really insane" (VRE 135).

James writes about religious experience in terms of a "more" (VRE 400) with which one feels oneself connected. The "religious" dimension of the "bearing" is just an outward gesture and ambiguous contact with someone or something other. In the second lecture of *The Varieties of Religious Experience,* he differentiates between "institutional" and "personal" religion, explaining he is only concerned with the latter. He goes on to describe "personal religion" as "the feelings, acts, and experiences of individual men in their solitude so far as they apprehend themselves to stand in relation to whatever they may consider the divine" (VRE 34). A few pages later he continues: "Religion, whatever it is, is a man's total reaction upon life" (VRE 36). This is a broad and loose description of "religion," so broad that it is hardly recognizable as anything other than the basic fabric of a person's life, the things that persist meaningfully through any number of setbacks or collapses, the things that stand when everything else falls. Such things for James happened to be "scripture-like texts"—but a mantra, a photograph, a line of poetry, an object or a person could serve as a touchstone, allowing the world to balance on the tip of a single, saving point. Jean Wahl described this Jamesian sense of religion as a "pluralistic agnosticism" (*agnosticisme pluraliste*), identifying such open-minded spirituality with "the world of Peirce, the world of Whitman, [and] the world of Myers," a British psychical researcher. Wahl added that James refuses to choose between these three seemingly exclusive worldviews, instead equally embracing "pure chance, simple earthly destiny, [and] spiritual progress aided by the gods."[59]

Levinas tells a similar story of the radical experience of something transcendent in the world, but in his case the saving point of contact is called a face. Levinas describes this as an interruption of abstract space and time by the embodied space and time of another human being, an interruption "where a beyond appears in the form of the 'interhuman'" (EN 93–94). Elsewhere, Levinas contends: "Everything that cannot be reduced to the interhuman relation represents not the superior form but the forever primitive form of religion" (TI 79). In the presence of so many competing possibilities for what might constitute the "more" of someone's life, James advocated "tenderness and tolerance" (VRE 505). Rather than "tolerance," Levinas's dominant vocabulary includes responsibility, "moral summons" (TI 196), and ultimately "a traumatic hold of the other on the same" (OB 141)—indicating an intensification of the demand placed on the subject that James would likely find overly intense and too oppressive. Yet despite differences in emphasis, Levinas follows James in the essential commitment to a plurality of values and a conviction that "no philosophy of ethics is possible in the old-fashioned absolute sense of the term."[60] Facing out toward something "more" is the name for a gesture that both James and Levinas identify with religion. It is an open and vague sense of religion and not a specific dogma or set of beliefs. James insists that "whether a God exist or whether no God exist . . . we form at any rate an ethical republic here below."[61] Identifying religion with "the exceptional situation where there is no privacy" (BPW 29), Levinas elaborates a community of the interhuman, a "horizontal religion, remaining on the earth of human beings."[62] One might easily read Levinas's "Other" as a placeholder for the divine. In a sense it is. Only, insofar as divinity figures in his work, it is merely the divinity of another person—an ordinary, minimal, and secular divinity also critical to James. Both of them describe an a-religious faith based in the here and now, where the only afterlife is the life of another person who lives on after one's death, and where a holy place is a crowded street.[63]

8. Lights in the Dark

Levinas's ethics—a "turbid, muddled, gothic sort of affair" (PU 7), in the spirit of James's radical empiricism—does not coalesce into a principle one might learn and follow. If one is looking for rules, Levinas will disappoint. Describing ethics as an ongoing labor, Levinas offers no indication of what it might yield or where it might end.

Similarly, James refutes the notion of a systematic ethical theory, insisting that

> there is no such thing possible as an ethical philosophy dogmatically made up in advance. We all help to determine the content of ethical philosophy so far as we contribute to ... moral life. In other words, there can be no final truth in ethics ... until the last man has had his experience and said his say.[64]

James underscores the openness of plurality—a hopeful lack of closure that is definitive of life and allows for new perspectives, changes of heart, and innovative work. Ethics is never-ending—but thus is also perpetually possible. Sartre conceded: "If one considers living beings as finished, closed totalities, humanism is not possible in our time," adding, "we could say we are submen, beings who have not yet reached a final point, a point we may never reach, though we are moving toward it."[65] Levinas emphasizes such open potential, the plurality in oneself and others. The ethics he describes as holding the door open for another and welcoming them is the minimal, and at the same time, infinite demand to face the other every time, time after time. It is an ethics rooted in a pragmatic pluralism, an ethics of attending to experience in all its fleeting, fallible, fallen, and obscure significance.

In his 1892 public lecture for students in Cambridge, "On a Certain Blindness in Human Beings," James defended the idea of plural, indefinite meanings and articulated the ethical significance of attending to meaning in multiple forms. Noting the susceptibility to "a certain blindness" to things that are meaningful in another person's life, James explained "how soaked and shot through life is with values and meaning which we fail to realize because of our external and insensible point of view" (TT 229). Such blindness to alternative meanings limits one's ability to interact and empathize with others, but it also stunts one's capacity for wonder, curiosity, or imagination, rendering the world smaller and less vibrant.

In an earlier lecture from the same series, James uses the term *Binnenleben*, "the buried life of human beings" (TT 203), to describe an inner atmosphere or "personal tone" that colors every aspect of who a person is, sometimes for better, sometimes for worse. James argues that knowing someone in a meaningful way entails having a sense of her "unuttered" (TT 203), but pervasive, buried life. In "A Certain Blindness in Human Beings," James finds a literary example for the *Binnenleben* (the substratum of hidden meaning and inner significance) in Robert Louis Stevenson's story, "The Lantern Bearers." Stevenson describes a group of boys who have formed a secret club, in which membership consists in finding an old lantern (called a "bull's-eye"), attaching it to one's belt buckle, lighting it up, and letting it burn secretly underneath one's coat. Meeting another lantern-bearer, "there would be an anxious 'Have you got your lantern?' and a gratified 'Yes!'" (TT 236). There was little the light was good for beside this urgent, momentary exchange. Yet the lantern, the secret knowledge of its being there, gave the boys a hidden ground of joy about which Stevenson concludes,

> The essence of this bliss was to walk by yourself in the black of night, the slide shut, the top-coat buttoned, not a ray escaping, whether to conduct your footsteps or to make your glory public,—a mere pillar of darkness in the dark; and all the while, deep down in the privacy of your fool's heart, to know you had a bull's-eye at your belt, and to exult and sing over the knowledge. (TT 237)

The ground of another person's joy or sorrow is rarely, if ever, fully visible. Stevenson writes, "it may hinge at times upon a mere accessory, like the lantern. . . . In such cases the poetry runs underground. The observer (poor soul, with his documents!) is all abroad" (TT 239). In surprisingly Levinasian terms, James concludes that when—or rather, if—we succeed in glimpsing the submerged and inner life of things around us, we open ourselves to radical interruption and displacement: "Then the whole scheme of our customary values gets confounded, then our self is riven and its narrow interests fly to pieces, then a new centre and a new perspective must be found" (TT 241). The "self" splits and widens, inspired by more life. James does not identify this moment with the *subjectification* of the subject, but in Levinas the "flying to pieces" of the Ego (*le Moi*) gives rise to the self (*le soi*): "a defecting or defeat of the ego's identity" (*défection ou défaite du l'identité du Moi*) (OB 15/ AE 31). The negative claim of James's essay is: don't presume. One cannot see the bull's-eye beneath the top-coat; one never knows the whole story. As Ruth Anna Putnam puts it, one cannot know the full scope of another person's "animating ideal."[66] James's negative claim is coincident with his belief that radical empiricism attends to the imperfect intimacy of things connected in a loose, shifting way, and that one should always be skeptical of claims to total resolution or knowledge, skeptical of ultimate definitions. But there is also a positive claim: one can become an increasingly open and tolerant observer of and participant in the world. One can, with practice, be more intimate with others, seeing the glimmer of a hidden bull's-eye and finding multiple centers of gravity.

Levinas and James agree that the world can be disarmingly dark. But there are also lights in our midst. In the last pages of "Nameless," Levinas stresses: "In the accursed cites where dwelling is stripped of its architectural wonders, not only are the gods absent, but the sky itself. But in monosyllabic hunger, in the wretched poverty in which houses and objects revert to their material function and enjoyment is closed in on all sides, the face of man shines forth" (PN 149). Like a blinking light, "the face of man shines forth." Levinas's lights are faces, and he argues for their expressive, hidden depths. In the midst of life, one can awaken to and be awakened by more life, a revelation Levinas describes as the "shock (*coup*) of the Other" (GDT 145). James describes "*living* realities" (PP 2: 297) as characterized by a "single *stinging* term" (PP 2: 297). Later he adds to the sting "the zest, the tingle, the excitement of reality" (TT 234). A shock and a sting are not simply reducible to one another; Levinas clearly has the more traumatic account. But both Levinas and James express a sober hope in the unforeseeable horizons of alternate times and the infinite, if chaotic, plurality of new perspectives. Nothing is closed and settled—not the meaning of ethics or religion, not the subjectivity of the subject or the nature of experience. Taking one by surprise, life swells in the interruptive flash of innumerable lights, glimmering like a lambent sea of sometimes dimly and sometimes brightly burning bull's-eyes.

FOUR

EMOTION

Since feeling is first
who pays any attention
to the syntax of things
will never wholly kiss you;
wholly to be a fool
while Spring is in the world
my blood approves
and kisses are a better fate
than wisdom
lady i swear by all flowers.

—E. E. CUMMINGS

In 1868, at the age of twenty-five, James sailed to Germany in hopes of immersing himself in a foreign language, studying physiology, and recovering from a variety of ailments that would continue to plague him through the following year. In the midst of his ongoing depression in Berlin, James wrote a remarkable letter to his friend Thomas Ward, who was suffering his own "inward deadness and listlessness" (LWJ 1: 127) across the sea in New York. Extolling the powers of positive thought, James encouraged his friend (as well as himself):

> Remember when old December's darkness is everywhere about you, that the world is really in every minutest point as full of life as in the most joyous morn-

ing you ever lived through; that the sun is whanging down, and the waves are dancing, and the gulls skimming down at the mouth of the Amazon, for instance, as freshly as in the first morning of creation; and the hour is just as fit as any hour that ever was for a new gospel of cheer to be preached. I am sure that one can, by merely thinking of these matters of fact, limit the power of one's evil moods over one's way of looking at the Kosmos. (LWJ 1: 128)

Knowing there was no way of eradicating "one's evil moods" altogether, James held out the possibility that one might temper them through an attention to concrete instances of good in the world. He expressed a belief in the rehabilitating power of setting one's mind on the tasks at hand, and forgetting about the ultimate end or final aim of one's life. In essence, his advice to Ward was to remember specific instances of beauty and goodness. Later in the same letter, James entreated Ward to give up the notion of a paramount struggle—it will only cause anxiety—and instead to focus on the details of living ("these matters of fact"). The details included, foremost, the "*real* relations with [one's] brothers": relations, James acknowledged, that are always "personal, finite, conditional, [and] mixed" (LWJ 1: 131). Such relations will not be the source of any ultimate conclusions, but they are as real as anything one will ever have in one's life. "However mean a man may be," James urged, we have "no revelation but through man" (LWJ 1: 131).

Not until 1896, twenty-eight years later, did James formalize his outlook into a principle he called "The Will to Believe." Articulating the vital role of "passional tendencies and volitions" (WWJ 722) in every aspect of deliberative life, James underscored the importance of not only recognizing, but *cultivating,* one's own emotional attachments so as to better let them impact and reconfigure "pure insight and logic" (WWJ 723). James argued that without emotional resonance, no fact, however strong, ever registers as a "living option" (WWJ 718). His advice to Ward was to seize the day and let himself be moved, however insignificant the day and its mundane duties might seem at the time. His advice years later remained largely the same: attend to life's fleeting and idiosyncratic sources of affection and emotion. In the moments when things become inexplicably momentous, these sources will play a disproportionately large role in how one makes any decision or takes any next step. Just as he described holding fast to a single line of scripture in the *Varieties of Religious Experience,* in "The Will to Believe" James emphasizes the attachments and feelings that emerge as critical touchstones of sense when everything seems to be falling apart.

The claims James makes for the scope and role of the "passional," position him outside of any tradition that sees "reason" or "intellect" as self-sufficient mechanisms of thought or paradigmatic accomplishments of the human. As James sees it, the waters of intellect are inevitably stirred by emotion. The emotional depth of a current of thought is not indicative of a weakness or defect but of a vast potential.[1] As we will see in this chapter, Levinas follows James in arguing for the centrality of emotion and feeling in any account of what it means to be human, and moreover, in an account of what it means to be ethical. Neither James nor Levinas view reason as the pinnacle of a human possibility, or epistemology as the summit of philosophy. Instead, they strive to articulate a more nuanced, ambiguous account of what it means to feel alive to and engaged with a fragmented world that continuously expands beyond one's grasp. The last chapter left off with the sober hope that Levinas and James find in plurality and lack of closure; this chapter picks up with the *emotional* depth definitive of a subject who, without recourse to a foundation, finds herself and loses herself repeatedly, drowning in and cresting on feelings.

1. Pragmatic Phenomenology

Before turning to emotion, it is worth considering the strange blend of optimism and skepticism that results from defending the "passional," the plural, and the mere. One can hear the dissonance of this mixture in James's letter to Ward cited above—his ironically self-titled "new gospel of cheer," which entails a belief in the power of positive thinking and attention to the everyday and involves a simultaneous recognition of the transience and fallibility of all things. In the pluralistic universe James defends against monism, happiness is possible; but no instance of happiness guarantees future happiness, since no experience is ever static or determinate. The "cheer" he envisions is, therefore, always provisional and tied to a particular time and place.

James worried about deterministic accounts that negated the potential of individual action and precluded the possibility of free will. Yet he retained a realistic vision of the limited scope of any action, declaring that blanket optimism or pessimism in the face of complex realities is "equally daft."[2] Levinas, suspicious of any mythologizing of the human will, nonetheless shares James's anxiety about determinism, about "being in a world without novel possibilities, without a future of hope, a world where everything is regulated in advance" (EI 28). Levinas resists situating hope beyond the world, refusing to provide an "optimistic philosophy for the end of history."[3] Finding hope in the embodied futures of other lives, he admits hope's fragility and the degree to which "there are precisely no assurances."[4] In a 1984 interview with Salomon Malka, Malka used the term "optimistic morality" to describe Levinas's postwar philosophy, to which Levinas protested: "Why optimistic? I will tell you, optimism and pessimism are not the ultimate categories of evaluation. Is the idea that the human takes on meaning in the relation of man to the other man optimistic or pessimistic?" (IRB 98). Levinas leaves the answer to this question deliberately open. Given the even mixture of hope and risk Levinas and James recognize in the world (and in light of their aversion to a stark either/or between optimism and pessimism), they could be read as pragmatic pessimists or realistic optimists. Either way, they sketch a precarious, non-naïve hope that will look bleakly hopeless to staunch "idealists" and overly ideal to staunch "realists."

Levinas, in particular, is often criticized for being naïvely hopeful about the ethical force of a face and overly idealistic, to the point of being unrealistic, in his expectations of human responsibility. If one reads him this way, one is struck by the mystical character of the face to face and a sense of the impossibility of being responsible for *everyone*. All of the responsibility will seem too heavy and too impractical. One might then decide that Levinas is irrelevant to moral philosophy and is primarily of religious or literary interest. Or else one could decide—as Hilary Putnam suggests—that Levinas is an example of a Cavellian "moral perfectionist" (as opposed to a "moral legislator"), and therefore strategically relevant insofar as impossible demands are essential to moral *striving*.[5] In this view, Levinas gives us something to aim for, even if it is nothing we can ever achieve.

The idea of Levinas as a "moral perfectionist" is appealing for at least two reasons. First, it is a way of justifying Levinas's own insistence that ethics precedes politics: the ideal we have to strive for is separate from the rules and principles that govern how we actually get things done. And second, it lets Levinas remain relevant in the realm of moral philosophy and even puts him in the good company of Kant. As alluring as this reading seems, this characterization of Levinas underestimates the complexity of his thought. It is a way of agreeing with those who criticize him for being abstract and impractical (a nod to the "legislators"), while at the same time insisting that we need ideals to orient our practices. Taking this middle-of-the-road position (yes, it's too hard to do, but we should try to do it anyway) is supposed to be a defense of Levinas. But it seems like "defending" something by taking its teeth. Like the poets outside the city walls in the *Republic,* we admit that Levinas is inspiring, and perhaps even wise—but essentially useless in the day-to-day.

Putnam's moral perfectionist reading ends up highlighting the mystical and/or religious dimension of Levinas's work at the expense of its ordinariness and realistic spirit—two aspects that the comparison with James help bring into sharper focus. The idea of a "moral perfectionist"—Cavell's idea of "an absolute responsibility of the self to the self . . . to make itself intelligible"—seems too much in the service of a "true but unattainable self," too much in the service of an authentic, forever future, overly ideal self.[6] One can find a less puffed-up variety of ethical minimalism at work in Levinas and James, which has nothing to do with perfection but still has something to do with being good.

Levinas's few examples of ethical action are not abstract ideals, but much more ordinary and practically demanding. He describes an infinite responsibility—but concretely he is talking about the *"Après vous, Monsieur!"* (OB 117; IRB 47, 106, 191) before an open door, about the "miracle . . . in the fact that I say *bonjour!"* (IRB 59), and the "goodness [that] appears in certain isolated acts" (IRB 81). The real difficulty is that one's failure to hold the door, or a tendency to do so selectively, allows for a progressive insensibility to other lives. James identifies this as the risk of a compounding "blindness to the feelings of creatures and people different from ourselves" (TT 229). Both Levinas and James focus on the complexity of the ordinary interval and the difficulty of day-to-day ethics (decency, manners, respect). Ethical responsibility is hard, not because it takes a saint to remember to hold the door, but because it is relentless and limited only by the number of faces one encounters in one's day or in one's life. It is hard because we are all prone to slipping in small or big ways all the time: when we are tired, in a hurry, distracted, or just unaware. It doesn't make anyone a demon not to hold the door. The frequency and ease with which we forget such a gesture indicates that it is surprisingly easy to forget others and much more difficult to get over oneself.

Like Levinas, James questions the very possibility of erecting an ethical *theory,* and instead attends to individual and discreet acts of human goodness as they manifest themselves in the world: "this unidealized heroic life around me" (TT 275). It is not that we are bereft of ideals, but James insists on the ever-open reconfiguration of what goodness means and what a good life includes. In his 1891 address to the Yale Philosophical Club, "The Moral Philosopher and the Moral Life," James argued for the open-ended and ongoing project of ethics, concluding, "there can be no final truth in ethics any more than in physics, until the last man has had his experience and had his say" (WWJ 611). In similar terms, Levinas wrote: "It is not the last judgment that is decisive, but the judgments of all the instants in time, when the living are judged" (TI 23). This view entails a recognition of the conflicting demands and values competing among different lives. James's and Levinas's insistence that ethics remains incomplete and that individuals incrementally contribute to the endeavor to realize a more ethical world opens them to the criticism that their philosophies are subjectivistic, that ethics is reduced to a chaotic play of unregulated whims. James answers this critique by accepting the label of "subjectivism" insofar as it means a *humanist* conviction that "all present beliefs [are] subject to revision in light of future experience" (ERE 251). James does not fully articulate or dwell on the weighty responsibility inherent in living up to the demand of every face in the way that Levinas does, but he does insist on the urgency of contextual, lived exposure that grounds any good with "personal support" (WWJ 618).

In the 1930s, Husserl suggested that James had pointed the way toward phenomenology by foreshadowing intentional analysis through his invocations of "fringed" experience, the "specious present," and "pure experience."[7] Levinas, as Derrida noted, forced phenomenology toward an "empiricism" radicalized by "an audacity, a profundity, and a resoluteness never before attained" (VM 151). Yet James does not give us a phenomenological pragmatism, and Levinas does not give us a pragmatic phenomenology; each contributes several elements of a perspective that has yet to be articulated. Together they open a terrain of problems and possibilities we can only explore if we keep both figures in mind and willfully ignore the tendency to delineate and separate American and Continental thought.

Despite similarities, there is of course no one-to-one correspondence between Levinas and James, or between phenomenology and pragmatism. It may seem that Levinas's focus on ethical interruption is at odds with James's classic metaphors of the ever-flowing "stream" of thought and the "flux" of pure experience, metaphors suggesting continuity rather than rupture.[8] Levinas provides a more troubling and visceral account of traumatic encounters; yet Levinasian interruption itself entails an incessant, an ever-new breach. The modern picture Levinas sketches is more jolting than flowing, but both Levinas and James are thinkers who contest closure in order to appeal to a living sense that transcends any static known. James defends the priority of "pure experience" as an ambiguous, undifferentiated "that" which only later, by an act of reflection, becomes categorized into a distinctive, discernible "what." Levinas insists on the priority of another's face—an "original epiphany," "a first language"—interrupting the ego with a unique injection of sense.[9]

Perhaps the most glaring contrast between the two philosophers is Levinas's suspicion of "experience."[10] The face refuses to terminate in an experience or appear as a phenomenon. Levinas's philosophy, therefore, contests the "experience" that is crucial to pragmatism and the phenomenality that is crucial to phenomenology. Surprisingly, in critiquing both, Levinas shows how close they are and how much James's radical empiricism looks like a radical phenomenology. Philosophy has room for phenomenology in a new key—for an attention to the unique sense and expressivity of a face combined with James's effort to see things connected without any separate third thing or connective tissue: "without bedding, as if the pieces clung together by their edges, the transitions between them forming their cement" (ERE 86). This is a different kind of unity than either pragmatism or phenomenology can account for by themselves. It is a unity by virtue of plurality, a loose hanging-together of things that move and change and don't make up any coherent, larger fabric, except momentarily, or in flashes, without permanent texture.

2. The Feeling of Reality

The human subject James and Levinas describe is, herself, an instance of fluid plurality. Populated from the inside out, she embodies multiple possibilities. This means that subjectivity is not reducible to any single framework or decisive feature, and particularly not to intellect or reason. Insistent on "the ambiguity of subjectivity" (OB 165), both James and Levinas emphasize the subject's sensibility and her emotional depth, aspects James calls "the darker, blinder strata of character" (VRE 395).

Emotion has been both a source of suspicion and a source of grounding in the history of philosophy—often within the same body of work. The complexity of emotion's definition, role, and range has been, and continues to be, particularly complicated as it relates to ethics.[11] Broadly, the worry is that emotion is too personal, fleeting, and subjective to be meaningful in the serious and objectively impartial business of ethics. A classic example of this bias can be found in book X of the *Republic,* where Socrates identifies the emotions with the weakest, most irrational part of the soul. A person swayed by his emotions is prone to erratic, unreasonable behavior. Socrates warns that art, and particularly tragic poetry, incites and strengthens the emotions, thus rendering a person increasingly unreasonable. The risk of emotional instability (especially for the impressionable young guardians) is Socrates' basis for banning art from the city.

From the ancient coupling of reason with rationality and emotion with irrationality evolves a history of attempts to purify the human psyche of every irrational impulse threatening to stunt its rational growth or render it brutishly animal. Philosophy has a history of treating human beings as the progressive triumph of reason over the passions, the mind over the body. There are, however, critical moments of resistance to this hierarchy.[12] Despite the historical march toward the ideals of the Enlightenment, one could read an alternative history of philosophy in the countless stutters and breaks with every attempt to describe the human in terms of reason alone. Even in Plato, the education Diotima describes in *Symposium* begins with the erotic love of beautiful bodies, and it is *eros* that drives the philosopher onward toward wisdom. Aristotle pays special attention to the emotions (particularly to fear, anger, and pity) in book II of the *Rhetoric,* describing emotions in uniquely powerful and pragmatic terms as "things which so change men as to affect their judgments."[13] Of course, this transformation could be for the better or for the worse. But Aristotle identifies and celebrates the potential inherent in becoming better practiced with a wide range of emotions, linking emotional flexibility and the willingness to experiment with pleasures and pains to a more expansive, nuanced capacity for judgment and wisdom. In the *Poetics* he underscores this point, arguing for the importance of tragedy in moral education insofar as it helps one practice with overwhelming emotion in the safe environment of the theater. For Aristotle, moral education entails learning how to feel the right emotion at the right time.

Aristotle provides a strong basis for the contemporary thought—for instance, that of Martha Nussbaum—that "practical reasoning unaccompanied by emotion is not sufficient for practical wisdom; that emotions are not only not more unreliable than intellectual calculation, but frequently are more reliable, and less deceptively seductive."[14] Nussbaum argues for the robust role of emotion in moral reasoning, though she is careful to differentiate her view from any foundationalist assertion that would describe emotions as "self-certifying sources of ethical truth."[15] The idea of a *pure* judgment, devoid of any emotional tenor, has been largely relegated to a myth (and a caricature) of Cartesian rationalism—a vision of disembodied reason "personified" in its own terrifying inhumanity by the figure of H.A.L. in Kubrick's *2001: A Space Odyssey.* If Plato worried about the risks of regression toward unreliable, emotional, animal instinct, then modern anxiety runs largely in another direction: fear of becoming machine, mechanized, and increasingly alienated from one another and from the living world.[16] It was, in part, this anxiety (fueled by conservative applications of Darwinism) that led Bergson in 1911 to propose an ambiguous admixture of intellect and intuition, matter and vitality, as definitive of humanity. "A different evolution," Bergson argued, "might have led to a humanity either more intellectual still or more intuitive." He then lamented: "In the humanity of which we are a part, intuition is, in fact, almost completely sacrificed to intellect" (CE 291).

Bergson believed that philosophy (and also art and poetry) could fuel the creative potential of human beings, nourishing a long-dormant and depleted "intuition," and leading toward increasingly intimate, living forms of engagement. The ideas Bergson articulated in *Creative Evolution* directly inspired Levinas and arose in immediate conversation with James's publications.[17] Bergson, however, inherits and relies upon a complicated history of theories of perception and emotion. Hume famously questioned the emphasis on reason and argued that moral distinctions are founded on sentiment: "Reason is, and ought only to be the slave of the passions, and can never pretend to any other office than to serve and obey them."[18] Adam Smith's sympathy, Rousseau's pity, Kant's respect, Nietzsche's joy, Kierkegaard's faith, and Heidegger's moods could all be seen as important ruptures in the description of a human being as primarily *thinking* and only secondarily *feeling.* Yet a persistent shadow of irrationality or inauthenticity haunts many accounts of the emotional depth of subjectivity and the role of emotion in ethical sensibility. James and Levinas are distinctive in their attempts to give emotional engagement a central place in what it means to be human without simply reversing an old hierarchy (reason over emotion) or instating a new one (emotion over reason). Neither of them singles out an emotion as *the* definitive ethical emotion requiring careful cultivation in isolation from, and perhaps at the expense of, other emotions. Instead, they describe being affected in various ways as a critical component of what it means to be a person who can take things personally. In Levinas's language, this is what it means to be uniquely subjected or to be the kind of being who can be both open and vulnerable—that is, ethical.

The previous chapter ended with an example from the middle of James's "A Certain Blindness in Human Beings." That is a good place to return to, for James's conception of feeling.[19] James begins that essay with the following assertion:

> Our judgments concerning the worth of things, big or little, depend on the *feeling* the things arouse in us. Where we judge a thing to be precious in consequence of the *idea* we frame of it, this is only because the idea is itself associated already with a feeling. If we were radically feelingless, and if ideas were the only things our mind could entertain, we should lose all our likes and dislikes at a stroke, and be unable to point to any one situation or experience in life more valuable or significant than any other. (TT 229)

James insists on the role of feeling in the experience of value and significance. Another way of putting this would be to say that, for James, there are no facts independent of values. This might lead one to conclude that James reduces everything to mere personal preference; yet James is not arguing that facts are whatever one feels them to be. Instead, he insists that every fact is intimately tied into a matrix of experiences, feelings, and beliefs—and these are necessarily personal, idiosyncratic, and fallible.[20] Our inability to discern or appreciate the feelings of others with respect to their own, unique sources of value and significance defines the "blindness" James worries about. We have a tendency to assign value solely to the things that inspire feeling in us: the things that inspire the strongest feelings are the things one values the most. These feelings are not irrelevant, subjective attitudes or arbitrary, irrational forces; they are the ground of attachments that shape and amplify a life.[21] James's essential claim is: where there is no feeling, there is no life. The problem is, where there is feeling—and particularly where there is strong feeling—there is a particular life that is distinct from, and potentially at odds with, other lives. Feeling is therefore both necessary for being *alive* to life and a stumbling block to being alive to more than *one's own* life. Without feeling we would be blind to everything, but feeling itself blinds us to some things.

This perpetual risk of becoming blind leads James to advocate the cultivation and education of feeling, so that it can become increasingly expansive and receptive to multiple stimuli. In the lectures comprising his "Talks to Teachers," he stresses the importance of travel, reading literature and poetry, working with one's hands, and walking outside (at *long* stretches) in the city and the country. These are only a few of the examples he uses to suggest an education rich with experiences outside of any classroom and outside of one's comfort zone. It is not a dry, academic education in a particular subject or derived from any series of lectures or set of books. In fact, James argues that an over-abundance of formal education can deaden one's capacity for expansive feeling, and particularly for unbridled, instinctual joy.[22] It is not, therefore, more schooling James advocates, but more *life,* more experience. This is similar to the education Rousseau envisioned in *Émile,* an education that requires precisely a lifetime and does not culminate in any saleable skill or formal degree.[23] Yet this education is the basis for every practical activity insofar as it is an education in becoming a more tolerant, open, and increasingly *feeling* person.

In this context, the goal of education is not to specify *what* or *how* to feel, as if subjecting a person to a series of experiments to see if she exhibits the appropriate emotional response. Instead, James envisions instilling a more abstract openness to feeling in general, feelings of all kinds. The gist of his commitment to ever-more feeling and emotional engagement is that in the instances in which we *feel* one way or another more intensely, we also believe things to be ever more *real* and thereby more urgent or alive.[24] The psychology of belief is something James was increasingly concerned with, culminating in his investigation of the most disparate and deeply seated beliefs in the *Varieties of Religious Experience.* There he criticizes science for trying (in vain) to purge the subjective elements from experience, concluding that "the recesses of feeling, the darker, blinder strata of character, are the only places in the world in which we catch real fact in the making.... Compared with this world of living individualized feelings, the world of generalized objects which the intellect contemplates is without solidity or life" (VRE 395). James's point is that feeling animates thought and suffuses ideas with color. The propensity to believe is tied to the propensity to *feel,* and both determine one's perception of reality.[25] Widening the scope of one's emotions thus deepens one's sense of reality.

Becoming more practiced in one's capacity to feel entails subjecting oneself to some discomfort. James describes such practice in terms of relinquishing the ballasts of equilibrium that keep us anchored in a steady state, immune to extreme sorrow and intense joy. These ballasts might be the comfortable confines of one's routine, one's home or city, one's customs or religion. The problem with any routine is that it becomes so physically and psychologically ingrained that it no longer requires active engagement or thought. The ability to execute unthinkingly certain kinds of routines, to tango for example, is one indication of mastering an activity. It is only when one stops thinking about the individual steps that one begins to dance. The same is true for a variety of other complex activities that require ongoing practice: swimming, skiing, or playing a musical instrument for example, and in the earliest stages of life, walking and talking. In *The Principles of Psychology,* James describes this transition from intense focus and stuttering effort toward increasingly fluid activity in terms of the physical basis of habit. An action becomes habitual when "mere sensation is a sufficient guide, and the upper regions of the brain and mind are set comparatively free" (PP 1: 115–16). Habit is a critical part of progression and acclimation, but it is also the source of stubborn anchorage in patterns that diminish one's capacity for creativity and blind one to alternative possibilities for action. James uses the imagery of riverbeds to describe the neural pathways deeply carved in the brain by the repetitive currents of habit. (In this, as well as in the "stream of thought," James seems to be drawing on memories of the rivers he navigated in Brazil with Louis Agassiz, in 1865.)[26] Well-worn paths allow an action to flow easily from start to finish, but well-worn paths also dictate and encourage the predictability of habitual action. Echoing Aristotle's picture of the soul as pliant and impressionable, James notes that the mind's essential "plasticity" (PP 1: 105) allows for the formation of habit, *and,* with considerable attention and effort, for the transformation or de-trenching of habits already formed. The notion of "plasticity" dovetails with James's commitment to a notion of experience as formative without being (necessarily) determinative. This is one of the central insights of his *Principles of Psychology:* the mind, never fully solidified, can change.[27] The point is that even *after* one becomes a proficient dancer, swimmer, skier, or musician, improvement will depend on the degree to which one can continue to challenge oneself and reengage the feeling of being a novice, actively refusing to let practice become *merely* habitual. James ends his chapter on "Habit" with the following advice:

> *Keep the faculty of effort alive in you by a little gratuitous exercise every day.* That is, be systematically ascetic or heroic in little unnecessary points, do every day or two something for no other reason than that you would rather

not do it, so that when the hour of dire need draws nigh, it may find you not unnerved and untrained to stand the test. (PP 1: 126)

There is an echo of Stoicism in these lines—a demand for giving up a life of pleasure and seeking out the harder paths for the sake of challenging and shoring oneself up—not surprising coming from a New England son of a religious thinker steeped in the Emersonian tradition of self-reliance. James is a tireless advocate of the idea that living requires effort and that effort has moral significance. But he is decisively un-Stoic in his emphasis on feeling and emotion as critical components of every effort and in his definition of emotion itself as intensely physical.[28] "A purely disembodied emotion," James concludes, "is a nonentity" (PP 2: 452). James's conception of emotion entails bodily entanglement, an idea often misconstrued by James's critics as the *identification* of emotion with specific physiological expressions or brain states, resulting in charges of emotional behaviorism or materialism. In the chapter on emotion in the *Principles,* James provides some ammunition for such a critique, but also goes to great lengths to anticipate and answer his critics. He describes both strong and weak "organic reverberations" (PP 2: 449) as indicative of varying intensities of emotion, portraying the body as a "sounding-board, which every change of consciousness, however slight, may make reverberate" (PP 2: 450). James continues: "Our whole cubic capacity is sensibly alive; and each morsel of it contributes its pulsations of feeling, dim or sharp, pleasant, painful, or dubious . . ." (PP 2: 451). In the case of less subtle emotions, James argues that bodily manifestations can be extreme: tears, flush, trembling hands. Yet he is careful not to reduce any emotion—however strong or weak, apparent or invisible—to a determinate physiological trait or set of traits, instead insisting on the inherent complexity and ambiguity of emotional life. This is one reason James ardently disputes attempts to classify the emotions.[29] No emotion exists singly or separately as an entity (either mental or physical). No description of emotion can have "absolute truth" (PP 2: 448). James offers an experiential, fluid description of emotion in which feeling, infinitely fringed, seeps through a porous body that remains enigmatically susceptible and precariously sensitive—at the mercy of its world.

Stoicism teaches a doctrine of desensitization, calling for the reining-in of the emotions so one might lead a more reasonable, measured life. As Pierre Hadot explains, *prosoche* (tension) is "the fundamental Stoic spiritual attitude. It is a continuous vigilance and presence of mind . . . a constant tension of the spirit."[30] In response to all this tension, the Epicureans pleaded for a little relaxation and a healthy dose of pleasure. James falls somewhere between these extremes. Sheer effort, strength, and will are not enough to ensure one retains a sense of openness to life. Rather than stoically standing firm in the face of every obstacle, James insists on practice in relaxation and the passivity of letting oneself crumble and be crushed, letting oneself rejoice and be elevated.[31] The sense that emotional engagement is fundamental to ethical attentiveness, to an expanding field of values and significance, goes together with James's conviction that emotion must be *exercised* rather than exorcised, for only in expanding the heart and honing a whole-bodied capacity for feeling does one stand any chance of expanding one's mind.

3. Hypostasis

Levinas's account of ethical subjectivity as insomnia, a constant vigilance and radical tension of the psyche, sounds cryptically Stoic. Levinas is often accused of giving a masochistic account of subjectivity with too little room for relaxation and a dangerous lack of self-interested well-being or happiness.[32] He would certainly contest James's assertion that, in addition to heightened sensitivity to and intimacy with other lives, "moral holidays" are also sometimes in order (P 41–42). Nonetheless, both Levinas and James share the sense that being a subject entails feeling uncomfortable most, if not all, of the time. The discomfort may be as subtle as feeling ill at ease or slightly anxious in a new social setting or as overt as feeling consumed with grief, jealousy, love, or exhaustion. Levinas, like James, describes feeling as a definitive component of what it means to be alive and to be human. Also like James, Levinas acknowledges that one can feel more or less alive at different times, on different days. The tension of subjectivity Levinas describes is not, however, the result of purging emotion and tightening one's grip on oneself. It is, instead, the tension produced in finding oneself gripped by a world outside of one's control. In a world populated with faces, each one demands attention. The fact that one does, routinely, pass faces by or overlook them does not negate the potential for becoming increasingly open and tolerant, increasingly able to be affected by or exposed to multiple realities. To be a human subject in Levinas's account is to be able to *feel* more exposed and more alive, without any sense of whether this will feel better or worse. Opening up to more feeling is not a masochistic flagellation of the self, but a relaxation of the self's egoistic and insulating defenses.

In the effort to relax defenses, James provides some concrete, practical advice: get out more, read more, meet more people, and subject yourself to more challenges. He also advocates finding something—anything—to believe in and care about, and even suggests taking up yoga and meditation as ways to practice becoming more receptive and emotionally flexible.[33] None of these are ethical prescriptions; they do not form a set of rules one might follow to ensure moral behavior. In large part, James draws examples from his personal experience and merely describes the things he has found make life feel more significant.

Levinas offers even less in the way of prescriptions. Like James, he is not interested in establishing a moral code or universal set of ethical maxims. Instead, he describes multiple ways in which something *humane* shows up in the human ("the appearance in being of these 'ethical peculiarities'" [EI 87]), the ways humanity shows its face. The kind of attention required to let oneself be impacted by multiple faces is not something that can be memorized or learned, but Levinas is not without *some* practical advice for keeping oneself open and responsive to an infinitely demanding world. His very few examples of ethical action include holding the door open for someone and saying *bonjour.* He concludes *Otherwise Than Being or Beyond Essence* by emphasizing "simple politeness [and] the pure polish of manners" (*pure politesse et de pure polissure des moeurs*) (OB 185 / AE 283). Such emphases reveal Levinas's ethical minimalism. It is a commitment to incremental, ongoing interaction, and practice in letting another go ahead of oneself.

Returning to *Existence and Existents,* we see that Levinas is not naïve about the real difficulty of such seemingly simple gestures, particularly in times of isolation, exhaustion, and despair. In the struggle of indolence that Levinas borrows from James, he discovers a span of weighty infinity packed into the moment between waking up and getting out of bed. According to the clock on the nightstand, it may only be a few minutes, but according to the feeling of dread and impossible effort, those minutes last a lifetime. In the opening chapter of *Existence and Existents,* Levinas shows that the time of labor, fatigue, and work bear down on a subject physically and mentally, rendering temporality a deeply sensible, physical duration. The trajectory of *Existence and Existents* moves from a deadening, eternal present experienced as insomnia, indolence, and *il y a* toward the jolting interruption of a new beginning and future time provided by another person. Levinas succinctly described his text in terms of two phases: "The first half of the book turns around the subject, and toward the end, the other appears" (IRB 46).

The driving issue of Levinas's text is the possibility of a transition from the impersonal to the personal: *from* Existence (in general) *to* the Existent (in particular). (Sadly, the momentum is lost in the English translation of the French title, *De l'existence à l'existant.*) The movement is, concretely, from the confines of an anonymous prison that refuses to differentiate between inmates, identifying each one by a number rather than a name, to a personal realm wherein one is granted both a name and a face. In the more technical terms Levinas uses in *Existence and Existents,* this transition is synonymous with the temporal event of an "instant" as it stands out against the ambiguity of *il y a.* An instant expresses an "articulation" (EE 2) that interrupts "the eternal, which is simple and foreign to events" (EE 2). The temporal dimension of an instant is a break in the even flow of *il y a,* a shock of difference in the usual feel and pace of time. The instant stands alone, momentarily gathering everything together in its singular emphasis, giving Levinas a metaphor for the positioning of a personal being in impersonal Being, a suspension of anonymity he ultimately calls "hypostasis" (*l'hypostase*). It is a positioning that Levinas describes spatially in terms of a "here" and temporally in terms of a "now."[34]

Tracing the interpenetration of an "instant" and *il y a,* Levinas chronicles the arising of a person out of anonymity. But how will something as ephemeral as an "instant" stand up at all, let alone on the elusive ground of *il y a*? The differentiation will not be easy to show, since both the "instant" and *il y a* are resistant to disclosure. The instant in its momentary flash resists from one direction, while *il y a* in its interminability resists from another, as if the one is too finite (a blinding flash) and the other is too infinite (an indefinite field). Both of them lack the borders that mark something as substantially present or absent.

"Hypostasis" derives from the Greek, *hupostasis.* Etymologically it breaks down into *hupo* (under) and *stasis* (standing): that which is "standing under," in the way that a pillar stands beneath and supports a roof, for instance. In this connection with the ground, hypostasis expresses "substance" (in the Latin sense of *substantia,* from *substo:* "to stand firm, hold out")—a solid point that anchors something at its base. Hypostasis thus entails a sense of vertical support that is crucial to Levinas's account of the ethical relation's asymmetry. The face to face is not a horizontal configuration of standing eye to eye. In the face to face, the other is always higher. The ethical subject emerges in a critically supporting role, as called upon to be there for someone else. In hypostasis, a subject rises out of the anonymity of *il y a*, not to rise above the faceless crowd and assert her singularity and independence, but to rise *to* the height of a face standing above her, calling her up and out of herself.

As an event in which a subject finds an occasion for standing up, hypostasis is Levinas's early attempt to express what he later calls *substitution:* the theme Levinas identifies as "the centerpiece" (*la pièce centrale*) (OB xli / AE 10) of *Otherwise Than Being or Beyond Essence.* The basis for standing is not a stationary, stable point on which the subject might balance or rise indefinitely. Instead, the subject is pulled from the slippery ground of *il y a* by the magnetic force of a face, which particularizes the ego and renders it momentarily unique and irreplaceable. Levinas calls this the "subjectification" (OB 17) of a self that emerges not by force of will, intention, or as a free choice. Substitution describes the way in which an *ego* that is essentially for-itself, reverts into a *self* arising for-another.[35]

This reversal defines the instant when the ego becomes meaningfully personal, becoming *someone* in particular. Standing up, abstract existence assumes a place and finds a name. In conversation with Philippe Nemo, Levinas explained his notion of hypostasis as "the passage from *being* to *something,* from the state of a verb to the state of a thing" (EI 51). In *Existence and Existents,* he describes hypostasis as "the apparition of a private domain, of a noun [or a name]" (*l'apparition d'un domaine privé, d'un nom*) (EE 83 / EaE 141). Levinas envisions the tension between the fluidity of *il y a* and the solidity of hypostasis in grammatical terms as a difference between verbs and nouns. *Il y a* represents the interminable, verbal aspect of *existence.* Hypostasis represents the nominal, nameable footholds of specificity interrupting being as *existents* raise their heads from the sea of *il y a.*

Hypostasis is a precursor of substitution, but the noun/verb distinction between hypostasis and *il y a* in *Existence and Existents* prefigures Levinas's later differentiation between the "said" and the "saying." A web of interrelated terms runs through Levinas's early and late work. At a basic level, he remains consistently concerned with privileging the terms that indicate rupture, interruption, or movement—anything that challenges closure and totality. These are the terms of infinity that Levinas thinks have been overlooked and undervalued in the history of philosophy. A beginning list of such *infinite* terms include: *il y a,* "saying," "verbs," and "emotion." All of these signify inarticulate, destabilizing aspects of existence that inject life

with a living sense. A corresponding list of *totalizing* terms signifying closure and anchorage include "hypostasis," "said," "nouns," and "identity."

Levinas privileges infinity over totality, openness over closure. Verbs,
therefore, (and ultimately *il y a*) have a certain priority insofar as they resist
objectification and express the *movement* that is definitive of expression
itself (as well as the *motion* of emotion). Levinas ultimately credits verbs with
"producing language, that is, in bringing forth the seeds of poetry which
overwhelm 'existents' in their position and positivity" (*à produire le langage,
c'est-à-dire à apporter les germes de la poésie qui bouleverse les "existants"
dans leur position et dans leur positivité meme*") (EE 82 / EaE 140).[36] This is
a striking passage. It recalls Bergson's differentiation between "instinct,"
which "proceeds organically" and is "molded on the very form of life" (CE
182), and "intellect," which "dislikes what is fluid and solidifies everything
it touches" (CE 52). The organic forces which Levinas calls "the seeds of
poetry" are the seeds of *il y a* at work in language, provoking a defection
toward more open, expansive forms of meaning and toward a sense that
registers emotionally. No noun or name, however definitive, can withstand
the power Levinas associates with verbs, emotion, *il y a,* and poetry. Each of
these represents a force—in language, in life, in time, and in art—that
threatens and ultimately topples every instance of hypostasis.

No meaning is entirely secure just as no self is entirely identical or pulled
together. This is an insight shared by James, one that is reflected in his broad
commitment to pluralism, his notion of the mind as "a theatre of simultaneous
possibilities" (PP 1: 288) and of the self as "a fluctuating material" (PP 1: 291).[37]
Individuation recurs incessantly in a world where different selves are called
forth for different times and different places. Following James, Levinas emphasizes the deeply pluralistic and fallible aspects of the self. "The Mind," he
insists, "is a multiplicity of individuals" (OB 126)—an image that calls to mind
Goya's 1824 drawing of an infinite cascade of bodies pouring out from the ear
of a giant head. Bodies within bodies, minds within minds. James concludes
his chapter on "The Consciousness of Self" with a variety of case studies
grouped under the heading "The Mutations of the Self," chronicling minor
"mutations" such as a routine forgetfulness and more substantial disruptions
including insanity, multiple personalities, epilepsy, and trance states. Yet this
description of the self as multiple, as a precarious sieve for an identity that is
never permanent or secure, is also the description of a self that is able to reconfigure, rebound, and relax. This is the other side of both James's and Levi-

nas's imagery. The subject, not an ego helplessly pinned to itself, is threaded through and tied to others. Plurality gives the subject unique chances for being otherwise, for emerging in a new way and for not having any single experience or identity become definitive for the whole of one's life. Levinas's imagery for the dephasing of subjectivity is hyperbolic and traumatic; but the subject can survive or return from trauma to find that trauma is not permanently present or all-consuming. This seems to be Levinas's other agenda in both *Existence and Existents* and *Otherwise than Being or Beyond Essence:* to sketch the way forward from trauma via new faces, to combat what Jean Améry called "loss of trust," and to remain open to the openness of the world.[38]

4. Emotion

Through hypostasis, what is initially undifferentiated from impersonal Being comes forward as a unique, substantial being with a name. Taking a stand, a person refuses to be counted as simply one among many. Hypostasis is meant to solve the problem of the many and the one—the move *from existence to the existent*—by providing an account of solidity and substantiality in the midst of the eroding fluidity of existence and *il y a.*

There is, however, a strangely impersonal upshot to hypostasis that results in the "return" of *il y a* (EE 84). In the move toward particularity, another generality shows up. Levinas writes: "The hypostasis, in participating in [*il y a*], finds itself again to be a solitude, in the definitiveness of the bond with which the ego is chained to its self" (*L'hypostase, en participant à l'il y a, se retrouve comme solitude, come le definitive de l'enchaînement d'un moi à son soi*) (EE 84 / EaE 142–43). Although Levinas was looking for a drama that prefigures any opposition between ego and the world, hypostasis ends up describing the "solitude" of an ego that has closed in on itself. The *here* of hypostasis leads to the *there* of *il y a* as soon as a person's identity becomes fixed or knowable, and this slippage between the personal and the impersonal shows the way "*here* and *there* come to be inverted into one another."[39] What first looked like awakening turns almost immediately into a rigid self-confidence and fixation on one's own ground. This is the description of the way a subject settles down—a settling down that is simultaneously a closing down. In Levinas this is literally the way that a subject comes home, moving into an enclosed space where she can retire. The move toward substantiality and identity occasions the risk of "stupefication, a petrification or a laziness."[40] In stepping onto a base or behind the closed door of one's home one also steps out of "the vivacity of life."[41] It is as if a person risks becoming her name, becoming a static idol or type. Then everything personal about the person is reduced to her name, as if she could take one stand for all time, as if a name could be so definitive that it eclipses the person behind it.

What happens in the move from the impersonal to the personal? Something solidifies. Someone stands up from among the crowd. She is particular and unique—differentiated. But *who* is she? She has a name and a history. In all the ways we can begin to describe and know a person, to recognize her, there is simultaneously the risk of letting this description *stand for* her, as if to know her once is to know her always. Hypostasis can tend toward stasis—toward the immobile and fixed idea or image. What was once impossible to pin down stands still, and in this standing loses that ability to move that is crucial for the difference between a painted image and reality, a statue and a living body, or "a mask and a face."[42] Socrates describes such a difference to Timaeus as the feeling of someone who, "on beholding beautiful animals either created by the painter's art, or, better still, alive but at rest, is seized with a desire to see them in motion or engaged in some struggle or conflict to which their forms are best suited."[43] To be immobile, "alive but at rest," also serves as the description of having a fixed sense of identity that keeps one from becoming anything else. Levinas frequently invokes Macbeth as an example of the "underlying tragic element of the ego" (*le tragique foncier du moi*) which keeps the subject "riveted to its own being" (*rivé à son être*) (EE 84 / EaE 143). But this is equally, or perhaps more so, King Lear's fixation on his sense of being king, a rigid sense of identity and ownership—of "mineness" (*Jemeinigkeit*) with regard to his land, his children, and their love—that blinds him to any other way of being.

What begins as hypostasis turns into something else, as if there is a detour or a sudden swerve in the road. You think you have taken a stand. Perhaps it feels like your strongest position, and you dig in your heels. But the digging-in can turn just as suddenly into your trench, your grave. There is an interval between here and there where nothing is finished, where there is an openness and flexibility. In that interval anything could happen. Hypostasis tends toward stasis as soon as the interval is closed—as soon as you get all the way there.

But one never gets all the way there, and the interval never closes completely. Against the "petrification" at work in hypostasis, there is another current at work eroding the subject's base. *Il y a* is one way of describing this erosion of a subject's *here,* but Levinas also talks about this erosion in terms of "emotion." In either case it is an issue of being moved off one's base, set back into motion, or brought back to life.

Just as hypostasis names the standing—the sediment in the midst that settles down—*emotion* undoes that standing. "Emotion," Levinas explains, " . . . prevents the subject from gathering itself up, reacting, being someone" (*elle l'empêche de se ramasser, de réagir, d'être quelqu'un*) (EE 68 / EaE 121). Overwhelming a subject, emotion literally moves her off her stable base. In opposition to finding a position, emotion signals "the destruction of the subject, the disintegration of the hypostasis" (EE 68). *Existence and Existents* oscillates between these two possibilities: solid and fluid, standing up and breaking down. Levinas thinks from multiple sides of experience, following James in conceiving experience itself as essentially plural and plastic, "a quasi-chaos" with "vastly more discontinuity in the sum total of experiences than we commonly suppose" (ERE 65). On one side there is the stability of gathering oneself up and pulling oneself together. On another side there is the instability of being overwhelmed or shaken. In standing the subject finds a place, a *here,* and becomes a subject. Emotion disengages a subject from her place so that "what is positive in the subject sinks away into a nowhere" (*ce qu'il y a de positif dans le sujet s'abîme dans le nulle-part*) (EE 68 / EaE 121). Hypostasis gives a subject a *here;* emotion gives her vertiginous *il y a.* Between these cascading possibilities subjectivity flares up, falters, flashes, burns out, and flares again.

Emotion subjects a subject to *il y a.* Moved from his pedestal—from being reasonable, knowledgeable, and pulled together—the subject loses his *here* and, though overwhelmed, nonetheless finds "a way of holding on while losing [his] base" (EE 68). There are ways of falling into and out of subjectivity—ways of finding and losing oneself. To describe the "I" as an "instant," as Levinas does, is to describe subjectivity as flickering and ephemeral. It's a momentary positioning, like raising one's head above the water. A subject is never all the way up or down, pulled together or falling apart. One has to get from *here* to *there* and from *there* to *here* not once, but an infinite number of times and in an infinite number of ways. No single resolution is entirely resolved; no single emotion is completely overwhelming. At the height of the most stable stance, something moves; in the heart of the most obliterating emotion, something hangs on.

5. Solitude and Obsession

The *motion* of emotion is critical to Levinas's description of the rupture of hypostasis by *il y a*—the return of ambiguous, inarticulate, and depersonalizing sense. Emotionally subjected, one finds oneself "over a void" (*au-dessus d'un vide*) faced with "the absence of place, the [*il y a*]" (*l'absence de lieu, l'il y a*) (EE 68 / EaE 121). Hypostasis and emotion describe a subject's oscillation between standing up and falling apart. But the oscillation itself, the movement from *here* to *there*, relies on a motivating force outside the subject. Emotion puts a person in touch with *il y a*, while hypostasis puts her in touch with "I am"—yet neither puts her in touch with another person. Although hypostasis was supposed to lead to a personal being, it leads instead to a *private* being through an "event by which existence in general, anonymous and inexorable, opens to leave room for a private domain, an inwardness" (EE 104). The anonymous opens onto the private, as if there were a door in existence that leads to an intimate room of one's own.

Levinas associates the "private domain" (*un domaine privé*) with a distinctive possibility of consciousness that allows one respite from *il y a* and an exit out of "existence in general." One can hole up with oneself in the interiority of a daydream, fabricating in thought a world less threatening than the one experienced in fact. This capacity for inner escape is of critical importance; it is among the psyche's mechanisms of equilibrium and rehabilitation.[44] In a poignant passage of his 1966 essay, "Nameless," Levinas underscores this fact, insisting on the necessity of teaching "new generations the strength necessary to be strong in isolation, and all that a fragile consciousness is called upon to contain in such times" (PN 121). Twenty-five years earlier, in the midst of his own captivity, he described consciousness as a room with a threshold across which one could emerge in waking or retreat in sleeping—opting into or out of being-there.

A subject can find expansive space in the inner recesses of consciousness. This can be a crucial access to movement and a source of strength, especially in instances when one is denied the physical space to roam. The problem is that the escape inward via consciousness, while it may connect one more deeply with oneself, still leaves one essentially alone. Levinas associates the privacy, interiority, and closure of consciousness with "solitude." Asked by François Poirié about whether he conceives of solitude as "something sad," Levinas replied:

I do not have any sympathy for solitude. There is something good, something relatively good in solitude. It is perhaps better than the dispersion in
the anonymity of insignificant relations but, in principle, solitude is a lack.
My whole effort consists in thinking sociality not as a dispersion but as an
exit from the solitude one takes sometimes for sovereignty, in which man is
"master of himself as he is of the universe." (IRB 57)

Admitting that there is "something relatively good in solitude," Levinas simultaneously warns against valorizing it as a sign of self-sufficiency or heroic individualism. The sanctuary of one's inner life may prove crucial in
desperate times. And yet, the escape Levinas conceives in *Existence and
Existents* is not an inward retreat, but a concrete, outward liberation into the
world of other people.

Solitude is one solution to the anonymity of *il y a* and the fear of being
emotionally overwhelmed. One can try to safeguard oneself by hiding, closing the door and refusing to come out. Faced with the risks of exteriority, a
subject can become radically interior. Yet in spite of its strategically positive
potential, in Levinas's work, solitude ultimately hangs together with knowledge, vision, light, theory, and consciousness—all instances of being driven
by the ego toward closure.[45] All of these terms express an intentionality
projecting from the locus of a private domain and coloring everything it
meets with an initial "my." Levinas criticizes phenomenology for being unable to dispel the filter of "mineness," stressing: "For phenomenologists . . . a
meaning cannot be separated from the access leading to it. *The access is part
of the meaning itself.* The scaffolding is never taken down; the ladder is never
pulled up" (MS 44).[46] The metaphor of a scaffold is helpful in understanding
Levinas's project. Levinas criticizes traditional phenomenological accounts
for treating meaning as an endless building project overseen by an individual ego who is always in control and always onsite. Insofar as phenomenology remains tied to intentionality, Levinas thinks it is held captive to a
predetermined register of meaning that is always weighted by the anchor of
an ego that cannot get past itself. This is the "blindness" James was worried
about in his "Talks to Teachers," a blindness to meanings that are not meaningful *for me.*

Pulling up the "ladder" would entail finding a non-intentional meaning—a type of meaning that originates outside the ego and separates the
subject "from the access leading to [meaning]" (MS 44). The "private domain" (EE 104) of consciousness is like an echo chamber. Levinas tries to

throw away the ladder of consciousness in order to make room for ambiguous, indeterminate forms of meaning.[47] These instances of *sens* will not be sturdy like a building. They will not be able to be stabilized by the scaffolding of a transcendental subject like the endless renovation project Levinas finds in Husserlian phenomenology. Instead, *sens* remains disorganized, an impact of bare meaning or the meaningfulness of meaning. Levinas situates the de-formed meaning he names *sens* at the level of sensibility and makes the locus of sensibility the face: the face is a site where meaning issues abstractly and withdraws as soon as it becomes a point of focus. Yet without becoming a theme or a fact, without appearing, *sens,* uniquely, provides a personalizing, humanizing undercurrent and an animating spark.

Consciousness, ego, knowledge, light, theory: all of these terms signify the solitude of a subject who finds refuge in a "private" interiority that Levinas associates with a coincidence of the "Same." The problem with a phenomenology limited to the interiority of consciousness is that the only relationship it can have with anything exterior is based in a fundamental narcissism. What is ethical in the face to face is an immediacy of impact that undercuts the scaffold of the self—or maybe shows the self to be a rough building project of scaffolding and ladders fiercely but barely held together. "Face" is Levinas's name for the sensible impact that doesn't organize into *something* significant. Or as soon as this impact organizes it trembles and falls along with the scaffold, even as it is already being erected again in an endless cycle of standing (hypostasis and the event of being a subject) and falling (emotion and the event of being subjected).

The subject is subjected to something beyond her grasp.[48] This is why, against the closure and composure of knowledge, Levinas emphasizes the emotional/physical exposure and extreme non-indifference of "obsession." In chapter 3, part 6 of *Otherwise Than Being or Beyond Essence,* Levinas defines obsession as "a shuddering of the human quite different from cognition" (*par rapport au connaître, un frémissment de l'humain tout autre*) (OB 87 / AE 138). He takes the word "shuddering" from Plato's *Phaedrus,* from the description of the soul painfully struck and viscerally altered by the beauty of its beloved. The soul, pricked all over, begins to grow wings. Obsession, a physical intensification of the subject's emotional potential (as insomnia is the intensification of her waking potential), overwhelms the thinking subject and renders her radically prone. The heat and abandon characterizing obsession render it dramatically distinct from the cool remove of knowledge, the lukewarm proximity of *sympathy* or the sterility of *care*. Levinas is careful in his choice of words here. Obsession is not just another name for an innate impulse or natural instinct at the root of moral sensibility. It is not the "pity" that Rousseau identifies in his *Discourse on the Origin of Inequality* as the distinctly human "repugnance" at seeing a fellow creature suffer.[49] Unlike Rousseau, Levinas does not make any distinction between a state of nature and a civilized state. Obsession, therefore, is not a first step on the way to a more reasonable or genuinely ethical engagement. Indicating an inability to maintain any reasonable distance, obsession describes the way something takes up all of one's emotional and physical time and space, the way something (someone) matters when there is no longer any scaffolding to hold onto or hide behind.[50]

6. Imperfect Intimacy

The interior room of the "private domain," which was supposed to provide a safe haven from the anonymity of *il y a*, ends up feeling a lot like "existence in general"—as if, in the end, there is no difference between solitude and anonymity. Or else, there are different types of anonymity and solitude—the one like the loneliness of living in a city surrounded by other people, the other like the loneliness of living in the middle of nowhere surrounded by no one. In both cases (inside or outside, private or public, all alone or all together), these are stark alternatives that preclude a more ambiguous register and possibility for being together—a level of intimacy where one is partially hidden away from the world without therefore being left entirely alone.

In his 1983 article, "Nonintentional Consciousness," Levinas invokes the "intimacy (*l'intimité*) of the nonintentional in prereflexive consciousness" as an alternative to "the *envelopment* of the particular in a concept, the *implication* of the presupposed in a notion, [and] the *potentiality* of the possible in a horizon" (EN 129). Intimacy here stands apart from "envelopment," "implication," and "potentiality." A substratum of consciousness, older than intentionality, opens the subject to being entwined with things in a deeper, more obscure and personal way than what is allowed by the "scrutinizing, thematizing, objectifying, and indiscreet eye of reflection" (LR 128). Levinas insists that this other possibility for consciousness is not "some childhood of the mind to be outgrown" (LR 129). Elsewhere, describing Jean Wahl's critique of intellectualism, Levinas writes about Wahl's "intimate itinerary" leading to "this immediate consciousness of feeling," which in no way evokes "the life of childhood, the lost paradise to which instinctive life clings."[51] Feeling, emotion, and obsession are not stages surmounted on the way toward increasingly mature minds. Instead, they are thresholds to an insurmountable intimacy, a "delightful 'lapse' of the ontological order" (TI 150), that allows one to be ambiguously outside and inside at once, or alone together with someone. "The warmth of intimacy" (la chaleur de l'intimité) softens the soul, drawing the subject out of solitude and positioning her face to face.

These are incremental steps toward sociality, and the face to face remains, from one perspective, a "private domain." Not for the world to see, it is between just two. Since the face to face remains deeply situational and between two, there is no way of generalizing the situation or abstracting a rule one could follow that could apply to every face. Seeing this as private in a negative way defines the perspective from which some moral philosophers criticize Levinas, arguing that he is fixated on a situation that is so intensely private and ephemeral that it has no concrete moral significance or practical upshot.

The intimacy Levinas describes is, however, somewhere in between the privacy of solitude, of being alone in one's room, and the public domain he associates with politics, justice, and le tier (the third). Intimacy defines a more ambiguous form of privacy: private insofar as it is personal or close but not private insofar as it is essentially plural and insecure, destined to interruption by yet another face. Levinas is interested in the vagueness of an intimacy between strangers, an intimacy distinct from the erotic intimacy of lovers or the familiar intimacy of friends. This intimacy complicates the privacy of a solitary ego but also every subsequent level of privacy a subject tries to install: the privacy of one's family, one's circle of friends, one's neighborhood, state, or nation.

Just as there seems to be a level of meaning below the surface that phenomenology misses in its focus on intentionality and phenomena, there seems to be a level of intimacy below the surface of both solitude and anonymity. It is like a lining of sociability, a two-in-one that shows through subjectivity as a "dephasing, a difference at the heart of interiority."[52] Aristotle calls this two-in-one friendship and makes it the basis for the best political arrangements.[53] With Levinas it is a less definable, less friendly intimacy that cannot become the basis for anything concrete—not an ethical theory or a social contract that could ground a definite political configuration. It is a minimal, shifting relationship—a "dephasing" that happens repeatedly. Even in Aristotle, friendships require this constant care and friends who become distant physically or emotionally are not friends in the same way anymore. It is not clear that the Aristotelian idea about friendship means anything besides an ongoing obligation to keep in touch. Similarly, the face to face is not the description of a single transformative event after which a subject is made eternally, finally ethical. These are more minimal and fragile experiences of being impacted and being together. There will not be any way of being face to face once and for all—or next time, like the last time. There won't be any rule or principle to follow or deduce.

Husserl's early phenomenology, at least, unfurling in the extreme interiority of the transcendental subject, precludes intimacy and ends up being essentially solitary.[54] Heidegger's alternatives between a *found* authentic self and a *lost* inauthentic "they"-self also disallow intimacy, despite his emphases on *care* and being-in-the-world. There is a sense of all or nothing in Heidegger—ways of being either solitary or anonymous. Levinas tries to complicate these alternatives by showing that life is not an either/or between being lost or being found, shirking or choosing, being confused or resolved, standing up or falling down. There is no simple identity, not even with oneself. Never pulled entirely together, the Levinasian subject exists in perpetual motion.

Insofar as intimacy defines the relationship between singulars who remain particular and refuse to sink back or generalize, intimacy is at odds with laws and justice, and thus at odds with the state. Intimacy in fact corrodes the ordered state that sees individuals in the service of a whole. This is just another way of saying that intimacy complicates things, making it difficult to remain impartial or disinterested. Such "complications" arose, for example, as the result of the 1914 "Christmas Truce"—a spontaneous suspension of war in which soldiers, previously anonymous to each other, emerged from their trenches, exchanged cigarettes, stories, and photographs, sang carols, played soccer, and found it much more difficult to slaughter one another in the following days.

7. The Present Hour

Those who are anxious to acquire an ethical *theory* have no time for the narrow register of activity which Levinas and James reserve for ethics: an order of overwhelming, emotional entanglement requiring single, repetitive steps. If one reads either of them looking for rules, one will be frustrated and disappointed. The plurality James describes will seem overly chaotic and his appeals to feeling naïvely romantic; the responsibility Levinas describes will seem onerous and impractical, the face to face too ephemeral and mystical.[55] From a bird's eye, impersonal vantage point there emerge history, laws, and justice—perspectives through which things become comparable, reconcilable, and orderable. Levinas acknowledges the importance of such perspectives and knows that every face to face succumbs to an interruption by yet a third, a fourth, a fifth face. This is a political reality; and it is here that Levinas situates *morality*, as distinct from ethics. It is a distinction he explains in these terms: "The ethical fact owes nothing to values, it is values that owe everything to the ethical fact" (GCM 147). Elsewhere he underscores the fragility of the face to face, admitting that "the origin of the meaningful in the face of the other, confronted with the actual plurality of human beings, calls for justice and knowledge; the exercise of justice demands courts of law and political institutions, and even, paradoxically, a certain violence that is implied in all justice."[56] Morality and justice signify the rules and compromises that make sense of multiple faces at once, assigning "values" to incomparable "facts." Ethics stands for the disorganized, bodily, emotional impact that prefigures any value and complicates every rule.

There are ways of getting a foothold for an overview, but there is also the dense feeling of the *here and now*. The overview will come later—looking back, thinking back, retelling, reflecting. In the meantime, an impact devoid of organization elicits a sensibility prefiguring consciousness. It is a wakefulness more awake than knowing, a feeling for being impacted that only later allows one the distance for focus and deliberation. Initially it is just an overwhelming feeling.

Moving outside of Levinas and James, one can connect their thought with another account that prioritizes a dense entanglement and *feeling* in relation to ethics. Proximity, vigilance, insomnia, and intimacy all entail an *immediacy* that Cora Diamond reserves for moral feeling. She describes the feeling of immediacy in terms of an impersonal and yet urgent sense of being on the side of life—and being bound together by an anonymous sense of being on the same side.[57] She writes about such a feeling in terms of a unique impersonality (one she wants to distinguish from utilitarian or consequentialist impersonality). It is a unique type of abstraction (a poignant obscurity, like that of a close-up) that complicates one's ability to conceptualize.[58] This part of Diamond's moral theory is interesting in relation to Levinas and James, because, for each of them, there is an emphasis on the abstract, ambiguous sense of being impacted by life and an attempt to differentiate *enlivening* abstraction from other forms of deadening abstraction.

Many of Diamond's examples of such a sense of moral urgency come from Dickens. In "How Many Legs?" she quotes a scene from *Our Mutual Friend* in which Rogue Riderhood, a generally despised character, fished out of the river nearly dead, has been brought to the local pub, where everyone unites around him to see if he might be revived. The passage concludes with these lines:

> See! A token of life! An indubitable token of life! The spark may smoulder and go out, or it many grow and expand, but see! The four rough fellows, seeing, shed tears. Neither Riderhood in this world, nor Riderhood in the other, could draw tears from them, but a striving human soul between the two can do it easily.[59]

Neither Riderhood *here* nor Riderhood *there* could awaken the sense of urgency and desperate hope for life, but the struggle—this interval *between* being here "in this world" and being there "in the other"—has an overwhelming emotional effect and lets "rough fellows" be touched by what Diamond calls "the characteristic temporal shape of human life."[60] These "rough fellows" snap into action. They are moved by the crisis and a sense of "more life" than just their *own lives*. It is a sudden sense that Riderhood, no less than themselves, had a history and lived-through experiences that led him to this moment. There can be an awakening to a depth in one's own or another person's life, as there was for Scrooge—the memory of one's own childhood and the many lives that everyone lives out—the possibilities opened and closed within every life, of the roads not taken, the near misses, and the all-at-once sense of how it has all led *here*.[61] In a crisis, but also in moments of great joy or love, one's own life story can collapse into a dense sense of being *here* that resists reflection or formulation. It's just a feeling, but it's a feeling of being suddenly intensely alive to life.

In Diamond's account moral feeling is not a rational feeling, not the cold stare of reason that knows how to judge and get distance. Rationality is not the centerpiece of Diamond's description of what it means to be human. Instead, she focuses on a physically overwhelming sense of being in the heat of the moment that is paradigmatically emotional. Merleau-Ponty described such a feeling this way:

> Suddenly there breaks forth the evidence that yonder also, minute by minute, life is being lived: somewhere behind those eyes, behind those gestures

or rather before them, or again, above them, coming from I don't know what double ground of space, another private world shows though the fabric of my own, and for a moment I live it.[62]

Practicing and honing emotional responsiveness (particularly through reading literature) is central to what Diamond calls "the development of moral sensibility."[63] In her account, reading is one way of learning how to let oneself be impacted and of opening oneself to the idiosyncrasies of other lives. In recent work, she describes this in terms of exposing oneself to "difficult realities," and suggests the realities of poetry and (drawing on J. M. Coetzee) animal life as particularly challenging and important instances of potential exposure.[64]

For Diamond, developing moral sensibility includes widening the role of the imagination (and narrowing the role of argument) in moral philosophy. In her work, imagination is tied to a capacity for being emotionally impacted.[65] James, who enthusiastically celebrated "the personal poetry, the enchanted atmosphere, that rainbow work of fancy that clothes what is naked and seems to ennoble what is base" (TT 240), would likely embrace Diamond's train of thought. Levinas (who prioritizes "beings of flesh and blood" [OB 74]) would not adopt Diamond's emphasis on imaginative engagement, but her insistence on emotional receptivity resonates with his argument for the precedence of sensibility before consciousness and, more specifically, for the "proximity" of being face to face. These are all ways of expressing the priority and gravity of the personal. They are variations on the theme of how important it is to resist systematizing responsivity, to resist clarifying generalizations, which preclude what James calls "a more profound and primitive level . . . of pure sensorial perception" (TT 257) and Levinas calls the "obscurity of feeling" (EE 105). Such obscurity has its own role. It will never lead in the direction of a system or set of rules. It remains abstract. Yet it is similar to something Emerson described when he wrote:

> Let us be poised, and wise, and our own, today. Let us treat the men and women well; treat them as if they were real; perhaps they are. Men live in their fancy, like drunkards whose hands are too soft and tremulous for successful labor. It is a tempest of fancies, and the only ballast I know is a respect to the present hour.[66]

Despite many differences between Emerson, James, Levinas, and Diamond, there is for each of them an ambiguous sense of feeling attuned to the present moment—an insomniac refusal to opt out or turn away and a "respect to the present hour"—at the basis of respect and responsibility specifically, but more broadly, at the root of feeling alive. We feel that we are on the same side, despite difference, in large part by getting past the need to feel the same, by withholding judgment and being moved. This sentiment is central to Levinas's sense of the *here and now* and to James's sense of "the teeming and dramatic richness of the concrete world."[67] The ethical attention each of them associates with vigilance to the particular and the mere entails suspending knowledge in order not to see past "the present hour" to some other horizon. Such a deferral of overarching concepts and readymade categories leaves one devoid of footholds and open to destabilizing impact, yet the same deferral allows one to imagine with urgency and to live intimately.

8. Transitional Depths

Levinas's radical empiricism offers a clue to a new phenomenology, the thread of which has yet to be fully taken up. Recognizing the importance of his lived experience and the relentless effort to describe everything about life that is most elusive and resistant to description, one sees that Levinas has yet to be situated in a single philosophical tradition and that new roads have yet to open from these lines of thought. The work is unfinished. Holding Levinas next to James, one can recognize that he is writing about something minimal and pragmatic. This claim might be at odds with characterizations of Levinas that emphasize metaphysics, "the good beyond being," infinity, and "ethics as first philosophy," all of which seem grand and otherworldly. All of these ideas are, without doubt, central to Levinas's philosophy, but they are meaningless without their contextualization in the much less dramatic, much more ordinary aspects of his thinking: his focus on fatigue, the body, a face, emotion, and holding the door for another to pass through.

Levinas is, in the end, a philosopher who tried to think about the everyday intervals between one person and another—the dimension of the interpersonal—without transforming it or deadening it by scrutiny. Describing the import of Vassily Grossman's *Life and Fate* for his conception of ethics and the interpersonal, Levinas explained: "In the decay of human relations, in that sociological misery, goodness persists. In the relation of one person to another person, goodness is possible. . . . Every attempt to organize the human fails. The only thing that remains vigorous is the goodness of everyday life." A few pages later he describes this as a "mad goodness, the most human thing there is in man."[68] James also argued for letting the world impact us in ways that are disarming and potentially at odds with everything we think we know to be true, urging us in "A World of Pure Experience" to "take it just as we feel it, and not to confuse ourselves with abstract talk *about* it" (ERE 48). There is in both Levinas and James a reverence for the ordinary, average ways that people pass, meet, turn, ignore, and embrace each other. They couple their focus on the mundane with a nearly obsessive attention to the vicissitudes of how it feels to live in a peopled world, the highs and lows of never being left alone. James described the world as "chaotic" and insisted that "there is room in it for the hybrid or ambiguous group of our affectional experiences, of our emotions and appreciative perceptions" (ERE 141). The world has room for all kinds of facts; some are more emotionally significant than others. In Levinas's language, faces are all around. They are the most common stuff of experience and the most pervasive features of human space, all of them turning and passing each other all the time. Yet every face is also a world unto itself, and the face to face is the collision of infinitely deep and infinitely distant worlds. There are worlds within worlds and times within time. Making these worlds vivid requires a pragmatic phenomenology, one that is plural, messy, specific, fallible, emotional, and personal—that is, a philosophy that *feels* humane and alive. Provoking such feeling requires a philosophy that is not only reasonably convincing, but also emotionally engaging and artfully said. Achieving these goals means very different things for James and Levinas, the one a master of the succinct and the clear, the other a master of the baroque and the opaque. Yet for both, a *style* of philosophizing is a crucial component of the content of their philosophy, both in how it delivers its message and what it has to say. This brings us to the edge of art and the aesthetic dimension of ethics.

—

Every life is deep without being eternal—infinitely deep in its own time and its own way. The infinite within the particular is a way of describing the infinite without the eternal. This is a new version of metaphysics where the metaphysical is not above or beyond life in another life or a world beyond the world but is an unfathomable depth within particular lives. There are no hyper-heavenly universals, just a thin and weak universality of differing and unknowable depths. And this depth deepens in us every time a face surfaces. We surface to each other without showing all the movement across the depth, and yet the very fact that we surface speaks of a depth. Occasionally we glimpse a depth through breaks—the sound of your voice belies your expression or your expression belies your voice.

We need a little a bit of every sense to be able to hear the "unique sense" (MS 36) of a face. In the end it is only a unique sensibility that meets the "unique sense"—a synaesthesia or crossing-between the bounds of every sense toward a more open, heightened sensitivity. Being open to what things have to teach and to say includes being open to a variety of faces surrounding us and even to the "elemental" Levinas describes as "the surface of the sea and of the field, the edge of the wind" (TI 131). In spite of his criticisms of theory and light, Levinas gives us a phenomenology of the world we inhabit, and particularly of the faces of people we encounter abstractly, without ever meeting. It is a sense of openness to being impacted by the flash of a face in a crowd—a particular kind of impact by something in motion and entirely out of reach. Yet Levinas, in his attentiveness to the human, may have underplayed other dimensions of humanity, namely the faces of things, animals, landscapes, rubble, and art. This is a juncture where James can supplement Levinas. Particularly through his attention to literature and poetry, James gives us a sense of the ambiguous meaningfulness of life—the sense of this living manifold that can strike us like a face in many ways, can make us better readers of the faces of things, and can help us learn to be more awake and alive.

Levinas also relies heavily on literary and poetic examples, but reluctantly, without the enthusiastic abandon one finds throughout James. Levinas's texts are, as a result, fraught with a more acute tension between form and content. Put differently, there is a voice in Levinas against Levinas. One voice, the "said" of his texts, tells us "ethics is first philosophy." It is a sober, philosophical voice. What this voice says, however, and what Levinas shows are somewhat different. His other voice, the "saying" of his texts, deflates the first voice in a variety of ways, speaking poetically, visually, emotionally. This voice employs a set of deceptively simple and specific words and images, like flashcards of things we know viscerally and by name: *insomnia, face, emotion*. On the one hand, Levinas insists on the non-phenomenality of the face and the priority of language that never appears but lights its own way. Seeing is forever tied to power in his account, and from the moment I see your face, it is as if we have lost all the ethical ambiguity of being unrecognizable, untouchable, and in the dark—we have crossed unwittingly "from the lived to the known" (TI 130). At the same time he tells us that the face "can come from a bare arm sculpted by Rodin,"[69] that "the face is not exclusively a human face,"[70] and that the face is also the nape of the neck of the person in front of you. The face speaks, even when it is a face without recourse to an audible voice—even when it is an arm chiseled out of stone. This shows that "speaking" is not simply audible or primarily verbal: there is something to see and hear at same time, or more broadly, something to feel.

Anticipating Levinas, Heidegger thought about a commingling of sight and sound and wrote, "the hard thing consists not only in the difficulty of forming the work of language, but in the difficulty of going over from the saying work of the still covetous vision of things, from the work of the eyes, to the work of the heart."[71] Envisioning the depth of an immanent domain, he insists: "The widest orbit of beings becomes present in the heart's inner space."[72] Heidegger characterizes the "work of the eyes" as covetous—as grasping. But what is "the work of the heart"? A mysterious phrase, it points to an ambiguous intermingling of senses or a fully embodied, whole-hearted capacity for feeling.

The priority of the audible over the visual defines one point (among several) of coincidence between Levinas and Heidegger—as much as Levinas would like to suggest otherwise. Both of them prioritize the ear over the eye, emphasizing language, poetry and the audible word. Levinas rarely comments on Heidegger's late writings on poetry, art, and technology, although one can hear these essays echoing through Levinas's work in the 1960s and later. Already in *Totality and Infinity*, Levinas describes ethics as "an optics" that is a "vision without image, bereft of the synoptic and totalizing objectifying virtues of vision, a relation to intentionality of a wholly different type" (TI 23). Ethics "is an optics" that empties the visual of its usual relationship with appearances. Sight stops short of insight. This different type of intentionality breaks with the framing horizons of subject and object. It is a type of vision that doesn't lead in the direction of an image—that doesn't fix an object in any frame. Yet if ethics is this non-visual vision—a vision without an image—then why does Levinas simultaneously use and reject the language of optics, resorting to so many images, so much description? As we saw in Chapter 1, the tension around the visual is particularly acute in Levinas's description of the ethical subject as an insomniac—as one who can't close her eyes. The description of such a subject requires an extraordinary artistry. Levinas's texts thereby intensify the ancient and acute tension between ethics and art.

And this leads us to the next story.

FIVE

POETRY

We may climb into the thin and cold realm of pure geometry and lifeless science, or sink into that of sensation. Between these extremes is the equator of life, of thought, of spirit, of poetry—a narrow belt.

—R. W. EMERSON, "EXPERIENCE"

1. Style and Vision

Reading Levinas in light of James's radical empiricism brings the personal and pragmatic aspects of Levinas's ethics into focus, and helps to underscore the ethical implications of James's pluralism. Reading them together also has a therapeutic effect: James provides a welcome dose of conversational clarity alongside Levinas's demanding prose; seeing their very different approaches to writing widens one's expectations about what a philosophy text is, sounds like, or can include.[1] They have distinct voices, come from different continents and different generations, but both experiment with the borders of philosophical writing. As a result, both have been criticized for their unconventional styles and suspected of being un-philosophical and overly artful. Levinas is criticized for the abstractness and density of his texts; one commentator calls his writing "infuriatingly sloppy," citing this as the reason Levinas "is largely ignored in the Analytic tradition."[2] James is criticized, rather, for being folksy and flashy—but also un-rigorous; or as one critic concludes, James is "inconsistent and illogical at heart."[3]

Despite their dramatically different styles and authorial voices, Levinas and James have incessant recourse to artistic examples. They also share the conviction that description plays a crucial role in philosophy and has its own performative value. Instead of linear argumentation, both employ an arsenal of literary devices, unapologetically contaminating discursive prose with metaphors, imagery, and poetry. James argued for the importance of expansive, inclusive prose in any effort to write about ethics, insisting that "ethical treatises . . . can never be *final*, except in their abstractest and vaguest features; and they must more and more abandon the old-fashioned, clear-cut, and would-be 'scientific' form."[4] This seemed crucial to James if ethical texts were to have any persuasive power and genuine connection with the emotional tenor of life. In the effort to make ethics personally relevant to his readers, James includes countless stories in his texts, descriptions of things he has seen or experienced that have changed his mind about one thing or another and have led him to a new belief.[5] "On a Certain Blindness in Human Beings," the exemplar of this strategy, is comprised of a series of stories and images drawn from personal experience, alongside excerpts from Stevenson (as discussed), Whitman, Wordsworth, Tolstoy, Emerson, and Royce. Stories and images make James's vision vivid. They lend his philosophy a dramatic, exploratory quality—as if one were getting to know him in a variety of settings as he sorts his way through each new question. The degree of personal intervention and autobiographical narration in James's philosophy can be disarming and disorienting, but it is also one of the joys of reading him. He addresses his reader as a friend and fellow traveler.

In his series of "Hibbert Lectures," delivered at Manchester College and published as *A Pluralistic Universe* in 1909, James attacked various forms of absolute idealism for being rigid and abstract. In the process, he articulated a central tenent of his philosophical outlook: that every philosophy is only a "summary sketch" (PU 8) and that every philosopher's conclusions are "at bottom, accidents more or less of personal vision which had far better be avowed as such; for one man's vision may be much more valuable than another's, and our visions are usually not only our most interesting but our most respectable contributions to the world in which we play our part" (PU 10). The idea that "vision" is always partial and personal is crucial to James's radical empiricism, which refuses the finality of any concept or experience.

Advocating the open admission of how one has arrived at one's "tempera-
mental vision" (P 12), James urges philosophers to write from personal experience and to show the tracks to their thought. At the same time, he advocates a method of reading that will allow one to "catch the centre of [the
author's] vision" (PU 87), encouraging a sensitivity to the atmosphere of the
work and to the over- and undertones of an author's language. This more
expansive, creative, and experimental notion of writing and reading goes
together with James's emphases on the "passional" dimension of thought,
and his critique of logic being seen as the only (or best) paradigm for philosophical reflection. Philosophy, James concludes, "is more a matter of pas-
sionate vision than of logic" (PU 176). Following his own advice, James gives
us texts rife with anecdotes and imagery that blur the lines between philosophy and literature and that grip his readers with their intimate detail.[6]

With Levinas, there is a decidedly different tenor. He does not employ
autobiographical narration in his writing, and his texts do not induce
friendly intimacy with their author. He experiments with more disruptive
forms of writing, culminating in the distinctively complex and interruptive
prose of *Otherwise Than Being or Beyond Essence*. James issued the challenge
for more open, living, and experimental forms of writing about ethics in
1891, and Levinas takes up this challenge in 1971, making the style and
method of delivering his ethical message as important, if not more so, than
the content of that message. Levinas is the more radical experimentalist in
his writing technique, akin to Joyce or Faulkner in his attempts to capture
in prose the nonlinear movement of consciousness and a multiplicity of
perspectives. *Ulysses* and *The Sound and the Fury* are essentially stories, but
they unfold with a syntax and rhythm that demand an experimental way of
reading. Although Levinas does not describe or explain his writing method,
he provides a telling description of Derrida's prose that could easily serve as
an analysis of his own: "At the outset, everything is in its place; after a few
pages or paragraphs of formidable calling into question, nothing is left inhabitable for thought, this is, all philosophical significance aside, a purely
literary effect, a new *frisson*, Derrida's poetry."[7] The effect of this kind of
prose is cumulative. It seems to be progressing in one direction, but it unravels as it goes, much like Penelope weaving by day and undoing her work
each night. It is nearly impossible to provide excerpted examples of this effect in either Derrida or Levinas (particularly in translation); extracting
single passages or sentences is like pulling a few words from a poem, or try-

ing to explain a Pollock by focusing on an isolated drip. The effect of Levinas's own philosophical poetry is holistic, requiring a holistic method of reading—a way of *absorbing* the text.

The degree to which Levinas's texts are poetic intensifies over the course of his life. His early texts rely on examples and images he draws from poetry—particularly from Baudelaire, Rimbaud, and Valéry—but in later texts his prose becomes increasingly imagistic and poetic in its own right. Levinas is helped in this direction by modernism's tolerance for experimental methods of writing, and particularly by the example of his lifelong friend, Maurice Blanchot, whose literary texts hover ambiguously between philosophy and literature. One can find a similar intensification of imagery and personal intervention in James's late writings, notably in the *Varieties of Religious Experience* (1902) and *A Pluralistic Universe* (1909), but James (despite anxiety about his own style) never questioned the philosophical legitimacy of *visual* language. Unlike Levinas, he did not condemn the totalizing pretensions of vision as inherently unethical. The tension between what James says and *how* he says it is, therefore, less acute than in Levinas—for whom the very possibility of writing about ethics becomes a central problem. Given the greater complexity of the problem of style in Levinas, the present chapter follows the development of his poetic prose, proceeding chronologically from his early writing on art in *Existence and Existents* and his 1948 article for *Le Temps Modernes,* "Reality and Its Shadow," and ending with his 1975 writings on Blanchot. The trajectory shows a growing interest in ambiguity and experimental methods of writing that exploit the poetic possibilities of language. Ethics and aesthetics become increasingly entwined as Levinas devises a "language that no full meaning guides,"[8] looking for a way of writing a text that engages in ethical "saying" without resolving into anything final or "said."

2. Saying the Unsayable

There is no easy relationship between Levinas's prose and his theory, in part because he refuses to have a theory in the way philosophers generally expect one.[9] This is one reason many descriptions of Levinas's project end up seeming discordant with the feeling one can have while reading him. Efforts to restate him drag one into interminable contradictions and miss everything important or moving about his work. All of the clichés ring hollow, and the repetition of the "face to face" starts to look like a caricature—as if the whole world were peopled with riveted, horrified faces unable to move or turn away. Quickly, as Levinas himself noted, "the caricature turns into something tragic" (RS 134). Description is a slippery slope. Instead of ethics in the desert, ethics after desertion, the flaring up of life, and the hot density of a peopled world, there is a tendency to envision Levinas's ethics in an ice age—everyone fixated to the point of being frozen in the last circle of Dante's hell. Once this picture takes hold it is especially hard to dislodge.

Levinas's effort to unseat the primacy of light, knowledge, phenomena, theory, and vision, are often read as a polemic against art; indeed, he is frequently interpreted as being openly hostile to art.[10] As this interpretation goes, art is the decadent, playful, and seductive distraction from the serious business of ethics. Art is not ethical. However, as soon as one has collected all of the quotations to support the idea that Levinas's ethics is allergic to art, one is faced with two difficulties: (1) a writing style that relies heavily on figurative language and imagery, and (2) Levinas's reliance on works of art—literature, poetry, sculpture, music, painting, and film—in the course of writing his ethics. Worried about orienting in the dark, Levinas prioritizes sound over sight, insisting that the face, though invisible, *speaks.* Insofar as aesthetics is preoccupied with vision and light, and particularly with the shining light of beauty, Levinas is suspicious. And yet his work is both artful and suffused with art. In a footnote to "Violence and Metaphysics," Derrida goes farther than this and calls *Totality and Infinity* a "work of art and not a treatise."[11]

Levinas's writing is fraught with an internal tension. His prose relies on elements his ethics seem to preclude, hinging on aesthetic examples and a style of writing that proceeds by compounding and competing descriptions. Above all, perhaps, it is the "face to face" that ends up being such a vivid image in (and of) Levinas's philosophy, an image that draws its force in large part from the intuitive sense that there is something ethically relevant about looking another person in the eye. Of course, Levinas denies the idea that we can ever fully see another person's face, which is always expressively moving and withdrawing out of reach. Challenging the philosophical dominance of light, Levinas describes the face as uniquely resistant to disclosure, reverberating beyond every horizon. Ethics takes place in the dark.

Still, images retain a certain priority, even for Levinas. This means that focusing on his emphases on sound, rhythm, and language will not exhaust the aesthetic dimension of his work. It also means that Levinas's own hierarchies (sound over sight, word over image) are much more complicated than any simple reversal of terms. His prose forces his readers to experience the dissolution of meaning that accompanies the fixation on any single point or term, and it does so by dismantling itself: contesting definition, enacting the indefinite openness of sense, and exploiting the metaphorical and poetic dimensions of language. His writing shows that meaning is not reducible to an additive, cumulative event, and it illustrates his claim that ethics is not reducible to a golden rule. This is something James also stressed, claiming that "in a question of significance . . . conclusions can never be precise" (TT 296). Ethics requires an ongoing vigilance and attention to the specificity of particular faces. Reading Levinas's prose forces one to hold one's attention to particularity and acclimate to the absence of ultimate definitions. His texts are training grounds for hearing residual meanings and for reading in the absence of a definitive plot.

Levinas's discomfort with the aesthetic is less a way of excluding it than a way of highlighting its powerful hold. In his captivity from 1940 to 1945, Levinas found a way of writing a text, *Existence and Existents,* that is riddled with art and imagery. To write about an image and to paint or draw an image are not the same thing, and Levinas does give priority to language. But at the limits of what one can say, an image can emerge and express things differently. A face is not a picture—but a picture, like the flash of a face, has something to say about humanity, and sometimes has a way of carrying us through dark times. Beyond more talking, additional description, or theory, an image can pick up where everything else has left off. At the very least, an image or a picture can mark an interruption. It can stay put after we have left off or begun again. For all these reasons, Levinas's writing is not simply centered on the serious ethics of response and responsibility. It is also enmeshed in the serious aesthetics of trying to show something unsayable.

3. The Transcendence of Sound

Two hierarchies stand out in Levinas's writing about ethics. The first is the priority of sound over sight, and the second is the priority of prose over poetry. These are stumbling blocks in any discussion of aesthetics in relation to Levinas, because they seem to exile all visual imagery and poetic language from the realm of ethics. Painting, sculpture, video, theater, dance, performance, poetry—they fall by the wayside. We are left with a hesitant possibility for music (if it is purely audible) and perhaps certain forms of literature (if it could be aurally recited and not require looking at a page). These are unreasonable and unsustainable limitations, ones which Levinas neither condones nor suggests. Still, it is useful to begin with the most conservative, literal reading of his ethical hierarchies to show how they contain the seeds of their own destruction.

Levinas reserves hearing as the privileged sense that can attend to a face, insisting on a hierarchy between the ears and the eyes insofar as the ears seem capable of receiving and following a sound without contaminating the reception. In section 6, "Expression and Image," of the "Conclusions" to *Totality and Infinity*, Levinas makes his polemic against images and vision explicit and offers a justification for his privileging of sound and hearing. He writes: "Images . . . are always immanent to my thought, as though they came from me" (TI 297). Images align with the immanence that is fundamentally at odds with exteriority and transcendence. Incapable of speech, images stand mutely at a crossroads between vision and a totalizing idea, manifesting themselves entirely and exhausted at first glance. The eyes grasp things and hold them in their powerful gaze, but the ears hear without grasping, touched by an invisible vibration.[12] Moreover, the ears, unlike the eyes, have no lids—no way of closing off or turning away. Listening, therefore, stands for the pure passivity, radical vulnerability, and openness of a unique sensibility that Levinas reserves for the moving *sens* of a face.

If the ethical is going to be contaminated by the aesthetic, it will happen through the *musical* quality of art that preys on the very sense Levinas tries so hard to reserve for ethics, enticing the ear away from its responsibility to hear the call of a face. Levinas claims that all art is, to some degree, musical. In his early work he uses "music" and "poetry" interchangeably to describe the essentially rhythmic quality of all art, whether the color composing a painting, the notes composing a song, or the syllables composing a poem. He then differentiates between art's rhythmic quality and the a-rhythmic interruption of ethical speech, explaining in *Totality and Infinity*: "Poetic activity . . . is opposed to language that at each instant dispels the charm of rhythm . . . Discourse is rupture and commencement, breaking of rhythm which enraptures and transports the interlocutors—prose [*La discours est rupture et commencement, rupture du rythme qui ravit et enlève les interlocuteurs—prose*]» (TI 203 / TeI 222). These are Levinas's alternatives to Heidegger's elevation of poetry—

prose and not poetry, *interruption* and not rhythm. Like Heidegger, Levinas prioritizes the audible over the visual, but unlike Heidegger, the sounds Levinas has in mind are not the mystical verses of any poem or song but a cacophony of questioning voices that refuse to harmonize.[13]

In this respect, Levinas follows the most aesthetically conservative moment in Plato, the exile of the artists from the city in book X of the *Republic.* Like Plato, he dismisses painters as mere imitators of imitations and singles out poets as the real threat, since what they produce can sound so much like the "discourse" that it is not. Painters are obviously working in the realm of the visible; they are easy to identify and keep outside the city walls. Poets, however, hover in an ambiguous space between the visual and the audible, using a rhythmic, visual language that can lull or charm its audience into the blind obedience Levinas associates with a naïve, complacent participation. This kind of participation lies at the root of either delirious enthusiasm or dangerously irresponsible silence.

And so prose, not poetry, takes precedence as ethical language, while the ethical and the aesthetic remain on opposite sides of a divide between the sober and the mad, the responsible and the irresponsible, rhythm and interruption. This is complicated, as I have suggested, since Levinas more often than not has recourse to imagery, and specifically to poetry, in the midst of his ethical descriptions. One encounters a similar tension throughout Plato, who bans poets in the *Republic* while insisting elsewhere that they are divinely inspired. Even in the *Republic,* the censorship of art comes in the midst of a philosophical *drama*—a vividly enacted story structured as a dialogue and rife with myth. So too with Levinas—and one must therefore read him for both literal and poetic sense, accepting that these may be distinct and perhaps irreconcilable, but equally important and meaningful.[14] The hierarchies Levinas puts in place in ethics bear an internal tension. Speech and sight, poetry and prose, the audible and the visual: these are not easy to separate or distinguish. The infiltration of the ethical by the poetic is particularly striking in *Existence and Existents,* where a chapter devoted to art occupies the central position, providing a bridge between the analyses of solitude and fatigue in the first sections and the rupture of plurality and hope in the last sections. Furthermore, as Jill Robbins and others have noted, Levinas's imagery and his own prose rely heavily on a mode of discourse that is more aptly characterized as poetic than prosaic.[15] If we take either Plato or Levinas literally, we will have to ban their works along with the work of other artists.

4. Opacity

The tension between ethics and aesthetics intensifies over the course of Levinas's work. Although Levinas never devoted a separate book to art or aesthetics, in the 1940s he wrote several articles focused on art. Among these, "Reality and Its Shadow" (*Le Réalité et son ombre*), is significant for its sustained discussion of the value of art and for foreshadowing many of the ethical concerns that emerge twenty years later in *Totality and Infinity*. This early essay reflects Levinas's insistence that a living person is infinitely more meaningful than any work of art. But it also reflects a bind he finds himself in as he begins to realize the importance of art for conveying his own ethical message. Even in this early work, where Levinas is concerned with questioning the significance of art, he never dismisses art as *unethical* but leaves its value intentionally ambiguous and open.

In "Reality and Its Shadow," Levinas critiques the "contemporary dogma of knowledge through art" (RS 132), arguing that art deals not with discernable truths, but with "obscurity" (RS 131). He criticizes the "phenomenology of images [that] insists on their transparency," continuing: "The intention of one who contemplates an image is said to go directly through the image, as through a window, into the world it represents" (RS 134). These remarks illustrate Levinas's accusation that intentionality remains indifferent to the tangible resistance of things, the density of lived, bodily experience. A suspicion of facile clarity runs through Levinas's work as a whole. Accordingly, Levinas criticizes theories of art that privilege transparency and wonders instead about "a certain opacity of the image" (RS 135).

The turn to opacity follows Levinas's general concern with rescuing the neglected, secondary, or underprivileged terms of traditional philosophic hierarchies and showing that the favored terms draw their life from something that has been forgotten. Rather than totality he thinks about infinity— he thinks not light but darkness; not knowledge but sensibility; not ontology but ethics; not Being but beings. The list could go on.

In the field of art, Levinas's alternative terms read like an anti-aesthetics. He forgoes beauty, light, and truth in favor of wretchedness, opacity, and inauthenticity. He invokes shadow, materiality, unreality, and erosion. These terms reflect Levinas's concern with moving away from purity in any form to the cluttered, embodied world we actually inhabit—moving back to meaningful particulars. In his 1976 lecture, "Philosophy and Awakening," he voices a need to "change levels," insisting that "we must return from the world to life" (EN 83). In *Totality and Infinity* he describes this as a "possible *reversal* of the lived into the known, which feeds philosophical idealism" (TI 130, my emphasis). The same thought is articulated, in *Otherwise Than Being or Beyond Essence*, as a confounding of the dichotomy between the transcendental and the empirical: a "*fall upward, into the human*" (tombe vers le haut, *en l'humain*) (OB 184 / AE 281). The movement Levinas envisions goes from abstract thought *about,* back to lived immersion *with*. This is the same idea James expressed when he described the sterility of absolute idealism, urging us to "seek reality in more promising directions . . . among the details of the finite and the immediately given" (PU 129) and to return "to the turbid, restless, lower world" (PU 218). Such directionality might seem at odds with Levinas's well-known emphasis on transcendence, but his is a new version of transcendence that moves *toward* sensible life—a descent into an opaque, infinite depth.

"Reality and Its Shadow," written for Sartre and Merleau-Ponty's journal, *Les Temps Modernes,* in 1948—a year after the publication of *Existence and Existence*—redeploys examples from the middle chapter of that book, but now Levinas's pressing agenda is to question two prevalent ideas in aesthetics: (1) the idea that art is *useful* as a source of truth or knowledge, and (2) the idea that an artist is *engaged* in an ethical or political act by producing a work of art. The first idea is something Heidegger expressed in his descriptions of works of art as illuminating sources of truth and beauty.[16] In questioning the elevation of works of art as avatars of truth, Levinas contested the postwar valuation of the aesthetic as a new frontier for meaning and truth and decried the romantic cult of the artist as a creative genius. His challenges served as reminders to a public embracing new forms of art that the politicization of images was a critical part of the Nazi mobilization in Europe. Powerful symbols and carefully selected visual propaganda helped fuel the passion for war early on and at the same time helped to *immobilize* a public stunned into submission by the spectacle.

The second idea, the conception of art as ethically and politically engaged, relates to Sartre.[17] "Engaged art" (*littérature engagée*) and the idea of the artist as "committed" to something greater than the work itself were ideas Sartre described and defended in a variety of texts in the early 1940s. Insisting that prose (unlike poetry) can be committed to ensuring moral responsibility, Sartre argued that the prose writer plays a critical ethical/ political role. To fulfill this role, the prose writer has a responsibility to choose topics and themes that force her reader to confront moral questions or to experience an existential crisis that provokes a change in how one thinks about and acts in the world. The epitome of this "committed" prose was Sartre's own philosophical novel, *Nausea,* published in 1938.[18]

Levinas disputes Sartre's distinction between committed prose and un-committed poetry, despite his own hierarchy of prose over poetry in ethical discourse. In the realm of art, Levinas refuses to grant one form of expression the upper hand or to qualify it as uniquely valuable or distinctively ethical. The gist of his claim is that there are no *ethical* works of art. This is because the term "ethical" only relates to the living expressivity of a face as a source of meaning that refuses to remain still or silent. Works of art—whether they are the most abstract, modernist poems or the most literal, narrative novels— remain essentially bound in their place and fixed on the page. "Every image," Levinas contends, "is in the last analysis plastic, and . . . every artwork is in the end a statue" (RS 137). Later he intensifies the point by adding that "time, apparently introduced into images by the non-plastic arts such as music, literature, theatre and cinema, does not shatter the fixity of images" (RS 139). Art stands still in the unending interval Levinas names the "meanwhile" (*l'entre-temps*) (RS 139), whether it is a statue or a play unfolding on a stage. This stasis, however, renders art not *un*-ethical but *a*-ethical: art is outside the alternative between the ethical and the un-ethical. The practical upshot of this claim is that responsibility as it relates to a face is of a different order than the responsibility to make or view a painting, to write or read a book, or to compose or listen to a piece of music. Works of art and faces make qualitatively different kinds of demands, and the shirking of the demand in each case has radically different consequences.

5. Rodin

In viewing works of art as opaque, Levinas distances himself from Heidegger's description of Van Gogh's painting that "speaks" and opens the peasant woman's world. If a work of art spills light in Heidegger's account, Levinas counters with the spill of shade. Deliberately underplaying Heidegger's sense of "earth" (the dark matter and materiality of the work), Levinas focuses instead on his account of "world" to challenge the notion that the work of art is a clearing where the truth of Being takes its place.

In *Existence and Existents* Levinas turns to Rodin to illustrate the "exoticism" (EE 46) of artistic objects—the way in which they appear as unrecognizable, foreign, separate, severed from the world's normal proportions and pulled from its horizons. Rodin makes the wrenching-away of the artwork from the world visible in his "undifferentiated blocks from which . . . statues emerge" (EE 49). What is visible in these statues is neither the emerging figure nor the raw form, but the very pulling-apart of the one from the other that obscures both.[19] Levinas continues: "Reality is posited in them in its exotic nakedness as a worldless reality" (*Le réalité s'y pose dans sa nudité exotique de réalité sans monde*) (EE 49 / EaE 88).

Unique among Levinas's examples, Rodin appears in both the middle chapter of *Existence and Existents,* and in "Reality and Its Shadow."[20] This recurrence might be attributed to the temporal proximity of these works, published in 1947 and 1948 respectively. But forty years later, in a 1988 interview with the journal *Autrement,* Levinas responded to a question about the face with the following explanation: "The word face must not be understood in a narrow way. This possibility of the human of signifying in its uniqueness . . . can come from a bare arm sculpted by Rodin" (EN 231–32). He followed this with a reference to Vassily Grossman's descriptions from *Life and Fate* of a line of people waiting for word of their imprisoned friends and relatives in Moscow, "each reading on the nape of the person in front of him the feelings and hopes of his misery" (EN 232). Grossman's image is tied to Levinas's description of Rodin, to the experience of sensing "feelings and hopes" without having to see a person's face, or without recourse to a literal face. In his 1984 essay, "Peace and Proximity," Levinas invokes the same image from Grossman and quotes at length: "Persons approaching the counter had a particular way of craning their neck and their back, their raised shoulders with shoulder blades tensed like springs, which seemed to cry, sob, and scream."[21]

Rodin, who was obsessed with expression reverberating through the bodies of his figures, and not only in their faces, helps make sense of Levinas's preoccupation with issues that diverge from traditional aesthetic categories of beauty, form, and truth. Of one of his best known figures, *The Thinker,* Rodin explained: "What makes my Thinker think is that he thinks not only with his brain, with his knitted brow, his distended nostrils and compressed lips, but with every muscle of his arms, back, and legs, with his clenched fist and gripping toes."[22] Many of Rodin's statues were fragmented bodies: legs, torsos, arms, and hands. In his book devoted to Rodin, Rainer Maria Rilke marveled at the heaps of body parts littering Rodin's studio, noting in particular the hands:

> Independent little hands, which are alive without belonging to any single body. There are hands that rise up, irritable and angry. . . . There are hands that walk, hands that sleep and hands that wake; criminal hands weighted with the past, and hands that are tired and want nothing more, hands that lie down in a corner like sick animals who know no one can help them.[23]

How can fragments be expressive? The experience of expression devoid of totality, the expression of ruins, lies at the root of Levinas's fascination with Rodin.[24] Over the course of his life Rodin worked with increasingly fragmented pieces, as if experimenting to determine the minimum needed to indicate an emotion, to transfigure clay, steel, and stone into flesh, to signify a human body. In the process he created works that demonstrate a mysterious inversion: the minimal can be the maximal, the least articulate can be the most expressive.

6. Modernism

Levinas finds in Rodin's figures an example of "a situation where totality breaks up" (*une situation où la totalité se brise*) (TI 24 / TeT 9). The terms he uses to describe Rodin's achievement are striking and important, because they are the same ones he uses to define ethics in *Totality and Infinity*. In *Existence and Existents* the rupture of totality is an effect he also attributes to "cinema close ups" (*les gros plans*) (EE 49 / EaE 88), and "modern painting and poetry, which attempt . . . to remove from represented objects their servile function as expressions" (EE 49). In each of these, Levinas finds the significance of the obscure and a register of meaning that does not rely on any horizon: "a meaningful content somehow prior to form" (EN 232). In a close-up, a camera generally zooms in on a face, as Rodin narrowed in on a hand. At a certain point the features of the face dissolve, yet it looms with a density and poignancy it never had at a distance.[25]

Overflowing their frame, close-ups produce an uncomfortable intimacy: "dense, opaque, dark, blind, bare, contact" (PN 114). Holding one in the presence of something evocative but illegible, they engender a sensation of *il y a*, which is not the feeling of something definite, but the haunting sense of the indefinite. Levinas differentiates the troubling disorientation of *il y a* from what he calls the "happy beauty" (RS 141) of classical art that allows one to admire ideal forms from a distance. Levinas continues his critique of classical beauty through *Totality and Infinity*, where he identifies "the beautiful" (*le beau*) with "indifference, cold splendor, and silence" (*indifférence, froide splendeur et silence*) (TI 193 / TeT 210). In modern art generally, and "modern painting" (EE 50) in particular, Levinas finds a new effect, explaining: "From a space without horizons, things break away and are cast toward us like chunks that have weight in themselves" (EE 51). The feeling Levinas attributes to modern art is fraught with discomfort. Unable to see past or through a surface, unable to find any opening, Levinas discovers a suffocating density: all earth and no world. The work of art, no longer a window, is a wall. The material itself blocks up the view.

Modern art breaks with classical art by refusing to use material to express anything recognizable. It gives up representation. In painting, to relinquish representation is to abandon or break up figures, horizon lines, and perspective. In poetry it means giving up meter, form, and narrative, closing off every access to an overview that might reassemble the "naked elements, simple and absolute" (EE 51), into a seamless whole. The matter is impenetrable. Modern art, unlike classical art, does not make anything appear except this blunt materiality that refuses to organize and only registers experientially as the abstract but overwhelming sensation of something opaque, anonymous, and unknowable. Nothing stares forth. But of course nothing is ever simply nothing, and Levinas's description of the materiality of modern art in *Existence and Existents* leads immediately to the indeterminate murmuring of *il y a*.

It is helpful to recall some specific examples from the 1940s, when Levinas was writing *Existence and Existents* and "Reality and Its Shadow." Gerald L. Bruns, in his essay, "The Concepts of Art and Poetry in Emmanuel Levinas's Writings," begins this way, helping to contextualize Levinas's fixation on the materiality of modern art by reading him against the background of what he calls Mallarmé's "radical thesis of literary modernism, namely that a poetic work is made of language but not of any of the things that we use language to produce."[26] Bruns also notes the explosion of controversy surrounding the social significance of art in Paris, and in particular, Sartre's series of essays in 1947—in which he situated the poet "outside of language" as opposed to the prose writer who uses words to actively grasp the world. We might fill out this picture with a few additional names. André Gide won the Nobel Prize in literature in 1947 (deferring to Paul Valéry in his acceptance speech); T. S. Eliot won the next year, followed by William Faulkner in 1949. This was the period that saw the rise of Abstract Expressionism— Gorky's free-form organic shapes, the exodus of European artists to America during and after World War II, and the shift that put New York at the center of an art world dominated by Rothko's color fields, de Kooning's ribbons, and Pollock's drip paintings. Following the war, Modernism reflected a struggle to make *anything* and a feeling that nothing could be made in the same way again. There had to be a new model for expression, and part of that model emerged from a revolt against classical ideals of beauty.

For many artists and critics, though not for Levinas, the revolt against beauty entailed a valorization of the sublime. Thus, in the same year that Levinas was writing "Reality and Its Shadow," decrying the "hypertrophy of art" and warning against art's "inhumanity" (RS 131), Barnett Newman was writing "The Sublime is Now" in America, proclaiming the superlative value of the artist's inner life and differentiating the expressive painting happening in the new world from what he criticized as the "beautiful" tradition of European art.[27] Modernism dealt with destabilizing formlessness, and it is not surprising that Newman, among others, saw a connection between the effects of Modernist art and the effects of Kant's sublime—that overpowering, disorienting counterpart to the beautiful that inspires "*astonishment* amounting almost to terror . . . that takes hold of one gazing upon . . . mountains ascending to heaven, deep ravines and torrents raging."[28] Newman described his own work in terms of overwhelming natural phenomena, insisting that the viewer stand up against them so that she would feel as though she were standing under a waterfall, awash in a field of color.[29]

Levinas does not invoke the sublime.[30] His refusal of that word marks an important divergence from the terms of Modernism and the trajectory of Newman's work, for instance, which developed into monumental, smooth fields of color. It was not surmounting beauty, purifying the arts to their essential elements, or achieving ideality that concerned Levinas. In 1948 he was writing about art but was thinking about ruins, fragments, and rubble, thinking about a unique resistance of the human figure to full disclosure on the one hand, and to total disappearance on the other. Just as the face remained the grounding center of his ethics, an abstract figuration remained the touchstone for his reflections on art. One breath after mentioning modern painting and its abstract materiality, he returns to Rodin's figures "arising from a shattered world" (*surgissant d'un monde cassé*) (EE 49 / EaE 88).

7. Carried Away

During the modernist fervor of the 1940s and 1950s, Levinas was a skeptical observer. He remained particularly skeptical of the hierarchy of the sublime over the beautiful and the coincident prioritization of the artist's psychology or inner life. Levinas dwells on the disorienting power of art. He stalls at the rupture of imagination and understanding, without the reconciliation provided by the Kantian dawn of reason—the sublime turn of mind. And between the alternatives of the classical cult of the beautiful and the modern cult of the sublime, Levinas articulates a third way. Navigating between sublimity and beauty involves two steps: first, refusing to mythologize the artist as a creative genius in order to treat him "as a man at work" (RS 142); and second, refusing to treat artworks as sources of empowerment, in order to underscore the value of disempowerment and the un-reasonable or a-reasonable effects of art.

Rather than leading in the direction of the sublime, toward the enlightened space of reason, Levinas argues that art opens an obscure realm, one he compares to "dreams and magic" (RS 132). James, endorsing such a mysterious space, describes the art in everyday experience. Quoting Emerson, he invokes "snow puddles, twilight, a clouded sky"—which grasp the soul and allow "its life-currents [to be] absorbed by what is given," making one "glad to the brink of fear" (TT 257). Although both Levinas and James advocate the ethical importance of a letting oneself be impacted by something outside of one's control, Levinas is far more cautious than James in his evaluation of art's effects and the potentially dangerous evasion allowed by dreams and magic. Images take hold of us. It is no longer a question of a subject intentionally confronting or grasping an object but a situation in which a subject is held, possessed, haunted, or infected by an image that won't let her go. The subject being riveted to a work of art is an instance of something Levinas calls "a fundamental passivity" (RS 132) and a "strange reversal of power into participation" (RS 133) that he associates with "rhythm" (RS 132).

The "reversal" signifies a curtailed freedom in the face of something that carries one away.

The experience of being carried away by art's rhythm, by a suspension wherein "the whole world . . . can touch us musically, can become an image" (RS 134), marks the convergence of two possibilities: the two sides to Levinas's description of art's obscure event. The first is the experience of stunningly beautiful silence and the corresponding danger that art can be an escape—a way of looking *away* from life. This was an escapism James also warned against, citing "the most worthless sentimentalists and dreamers, drunkards, shirks and verse-makers, who never show a grain of effort, courage or endurance" (TT 293). Elsewhere he condemns "the habit of excessive novel-reading and theatre-going," which can blunt one's ability to translate intentions into action: "the weeping of a Russian lady over the fictitious personages in the play, while her coachman is freezing to death on his seat outside" (PP 1: 125). In Levinas, the "reversal of power into participation" can indicate an uncritical involvement and a radically unethical failure to sober up or take responsibility. Of this possibility, Levinas cautions: "There is something wicked and egoist and cowardly in artistic enjoyment. There are times when one can be ashamed of it, as of feasting during a plague" (RS 142). This warning remembers and rekindles the "old quarrel between philosophy and poetry" familiar since Plato's *Republic*.[31] Levinas, like Socrates, worries particularly about art as idolatry, and the possibility of taking respite in an image, allowing a turn away from life. For Levinas this means art is susceptible to being used in the service of a bad transcendence: "in the midst of being, the possibility of detaching oneself from being" (EE 50). Blinded by beauty, one might worship an object and exchange life for the frantic grip of an idol.

As an antidote to idolatry, Levinas insists on the necessity of the critic, "the one who still has something to say when everything has been said" (RS 130), and of criticism, "the word of a living being speaking to a living being."[32] The critic brings the work back into dialogue, breaking the spell and silence of the picture, providing a wake-up call. The humanizing, dialogic gesture shows the critic's refusal to participate in the image's mysticism or indulge the artist's genius. Unseating the work from its pedestal, the critic sees art as a product of human labor and "treats the artist as a man at work" (RS 142). In between the work of art and the spectator, the critic intervenes to reestablish the interhuman, restoring the ethical dimension by reconnecting the image with a peopled world. This grounding activity and demystification let the work of art be worked on and let the viewer "enter into relation with someone, in spite of or over and above the peace and harmony derived from the successful creation of beauty."[33] The critic reasserts the power of the human over the inhuman, wielding prose over poetry, refusing to let the work of art render her speechless, refusing to participate blindly or silently.

Artworks can become idols, but they can also function another way. Levinas tells two stories. The first—the dominant one—is about art's insignificance compared with the living significance of a person. Art is the dead letter, the still life. This is the story Robert Eaglestone emphasizes, arguing that art is, for Levinas, "only a dangerous and wicked distraction or swindle."[34] But the second story is about the significance of that insignificance, about the way in which the seemingly marginal refuses to be *simply* inconsequential and, instead, compounds and condenses. In the first story, art fails to measure up to life; but in the second story that failure fails to *be* a failure, and ends up expressing something dense and real. The first story underscores the need for criticism and the addition of an expressive human face into the silent and inhuman world of art. The second story is about the faceless, neutral expression of *il y a:* "a mute, absolutely indeterminate menace" (EE 54).

Il y a returns via certain forms of art. Yet to say "art" as if we were concerned with particular, recognizable aesthetic objects would be overly precise. In the end it is an issue of borderless, shifting spaces of meaning—one personal and one impersonal—and their strange proximity. Art can say *il y a* by provoking experiences of formlessness that register as anonymously, terribly meaningful. The characterization of art as *il y a* is not the description of a class of objects but the description of an experience where, in the absence of a face, something else grips you or looks back.

In addition to the dangers of participation and getting carried away, Levinas considers the positive value of art's overwhelming power: "We have to understand the value of this disengagement, and first of all its meaning. Is to disengage oneself from the world always to go *beyond,* toward the region of Platonic ideas and toward the eternal which towers above the world? Can one not speak of disengagement on the hither side?" (RS 131). Different varieties of transcendence operate with distinct directionalities. One transcendence leads in the direction of a beyond. Another transcendence arises "behind every experience of transcendence, which tries to surround, circumscribe or circumvent, fasten or bind, transcendence."[35] A second transcendence transcends the first one in another direction, just as a new face rises to make a unique demand. Levinas borrows the word "transdescendence" from Jean Wahl to describe this possibility for art and images—"the disengagement on the hither side" (RS 131)—that bears no trace of aesthetic distance or disinterest but feels more like being held close to something that has pinned you and won't let you go.[36] This is a feeling similar to the obsessive proximity or the radical insomnia considered in the previous chapters. Art can inspire disengagement, but it can also be the source of intense engagement, the stimulus for emotion that has nothing to do with acquiring additional information or knowledge but that has everything to do with feeling urgently present and alive.

8. The Face of Words

There is a deepening series of qualifications as one follows Levinas's discussion of art across his career. At the beginning it looks like a series of binary oppositions between ethics and aesthetics, light and dark, sight and sound, critique and silence. Quickly the oppositions break apart into increasingly subtle pieces that in turn engender new pieces. It becomes a tangle of possibilities, all of them overlapping and looking more and more undifferentiated without any definitive either/or.

What is clear from Levinas's writing in the 1940s is that, despite an attempt to differentiate between classical and modern art, identifying a particular subset of ethical objects or works of art is never the issue. There are not ethical/unethical paintings or ethical/unethical poems—there are just paintings, just poems. They are neutral. Yet sometimes they reflect a human face and help us connect to each other and to the world. They can say something we can't say ourselves. They can provide experiences of density—a minimal sense of significance—a sense of things rising or falling out of their place, impinging like close-ups and opening up new dimensions of space and time. Works of art, whatever they are, might be these ambiguous, minimally bordered spaces where we can be touched or moved by the reality of things long after the world has "shattered" (EE 49). Art can help us move among shattered pieces.

Not until writing about Blanchot from the 1950s to the 1970s did Levinas find another way of voicing the neutrality of *il y a* as it relates not only to art, but to different possibilities of language. If we stop with *Existence and Existents* and "Reality and Its Shadow," we leave off with an account of art where, despite an effort to keep an opening for certain forms of modern art, the emphasis falls on the risks art poses to ethical wakefulness and engagement. *Existence and Existents* and "Reality and Its Shadow" fixate on the materiality and "sad value" (RS 141) of modern art. Levinas's later writings on Blanchot have a new emphasis on language that reflects Levinas's own efforts to differentiate the "saying" from the "said" in *Otherwise than Being or Beyond Essence* and to find an *ethical* method of writing about ethics that subsists in the "saying." The simultaneously closed and open nature of language becomes a critical component of Levinas's late work as he becomes increasingly concerned with writing a text that refuses to reconcile into a theory—a system of ethics that might be codified and systematized. Levinas's ethics reorganizes with every interruption of a face. If there is any way of writing ethically about ethics, it will have to be one that resists a final interpretation or reiteration that might take the place of the ongoing engagement with particular faces. The text must remain open. Ensuring this openness involves exploiting the aesthetic dimension of language as an interruptive countercurrent to propositional meaning. Levinas finds a model of this method in Blanchot's work.[38] Tracking Levinas's writing *about* art from the 1940s onward, one can read a subtle but progressive shift in what he has to say and in how he goes about saying it.

The last section of Levinas's 1975 anthology, *Proper Names,* includes a collection of essays and one interview grouped together under the heading "On Maurice Blanchot." Blanchot and Levinas first met when they were students together in Strasbourg in 1923. They quickly became close friends, and would remain so, despite political and intellectual differences, over the course of their lives.[39] They wrote as if in conversation with one another, often invoking similar themes and pursing similar rhythms of expression. Describing his first encounters with Blanchot to François Poirié, Levinas recalled their mutual interest in philosophy and literature, noting that Blanchot introduced him to Proust and Valéry (two figures who appear repeatedly throughout Levinas's writing). He went on to describe Blanchot himself as "the very epitome of French excellence; not so much on account of his ideas, but on account of a certain possibility of saying things which is very difficult to imitate, appearing like a force from on high" (IRB 30).

In his 1956 article, "The Poet's Vision," Levinas reviews Blanchot's 1955 text *The Space of Literature* (*L'Espace littéraire*), describing it as "situated beyond all critique and all exegesis" (PN 127). Concretely, *The Space of Literature* explores aspects of Mallarmé, Kafka, Rilke, and Hölderlin, but far more than this, it ventures a radical set of questions about the essence of art, literature, and death. Stressing the degree to which Blanchot's work refuses to consolidate into literature, literary criticism, or philosophy (partaking in all three), Levinas explains: "Blanchot's research brings to the philosopher a 'category' and a new 'way of knowing' that I would like to clarify, independently of the philosophy of art proper" (PN 133). Blanchot, employing a style of writing irreducible to any single genre, expresses an artistic possibility that has epistemological implications outside the realm of art. It is something Levinas, in another context, calls "a new approach to the meaningful."[40] Both Levinas and Blanchot attempt to describe a form of meaning that breaks with the lighted horizons of Being and registers instead as an inarticulable, unstable rustling. From the perspective of utility, it is a form of meaning that is meaningless. "The work [of art]," Blanchot writes, "can have no proof, just as it can have no use."[41] Levinas calls such ambiguous meaning *sens* and reserves it for the expression of a face, while Blanchot reserves this distinctive variety of meaning for "the space of literature."

Blanchot's descriptive terms for the "space of literature" include the "Night" and the "Neuter" (*le neutre*). Both of these terms express an essential darkness and ambiguity. In another text, *The Step Not Beyond* (*Le pas au-delà*), Blanchot explains that "the Neuter derives, in the most simple way, from a negation of two terms; *neuter* neither one nor the other."[42] Emphasizing the ambiguity of the word and its scintillation between multiple senses, Blanchot continues: "The Neuter: paradoxical name: it barely speaks, mute word, simple, yet always veiling itself, always displacing itself out of its meaning."[43] Elsewhere, Blanchot describes the "Neuter" as "un-knowledge" and "the un-manifest" (WD 63). The "Neuter" literally neutralizes meaning by refusing to settle into a category or a name, refusing to terminate into what Levinas calls "the said." Blanchot sees this refusal to be still as emblematic of the indistinct, dark "space" of literature, and more generally of works of art. Blanchot's "Night" and "Neuter" clearly resemble Levinas's use of *il y a* and illeity (*illéité*)—his expression for the enigma of a non-signifying, doubly elusive trace.[44] Both sets of terms indicate an impersonal neutrality that is resistant to phenomenological description. On the other side of this impersonal neutrality Levinas offers the face as the non-phenomenological dawn of a uniquely personalizing expression. Yet as I said at the close of the last chapter, the face sometimes shows itself otherwise: as with Rodin's chiseled arm, as with the nape of a neck. Levinas tells us that "there is a subtle ambiguity of . . . the mask and the face," "the face must not be understood in a narrow way," and that "the face can assume meaning on what is the 'opposite' of the face!"[45] What then is the relationship between Levinas's face and Blanchot's literary space? Both of them describe non-places, a "null-site" (*le non-lieu*) (OB 10 / AE 24) without definite edges or borders.[46]

Blanchot complicates any stark differentiation between art and ethics, between *il y a* and a face. Returning to "The Poet's Vision," Levinas credits Blanchot with the definition of writing "as a quasi-mad structure within the general economy of being" (PN 132), and he describes Blanchot's prose as "a discontinuous and contradictory language of scintillation" (PN 147). It is a form of writing that resembles the dense, material opacity of modern art which Levinas detailed in *Existence and Existents*. The "quasi-mad structure" of writing refuses language any window-like clarity, signifying a reversal of intentionality: rather than the author wielding power over language, "the words look at the writer" (PN 132). Contesting the lucidity of language, Blanchot deals with its maddening opacity and, in the process, rekindles "the obscurity of the elemental" (PN 133).

Levinas, following Blanchot, names opaque language "poetic language" (PN 132).[47] In "Literature and the Right to Death," Blanchot identifies poetic language with one "slope" of literature, a slope upon which meaning defects from words. Describing the "stifling density of an accumulation of syllables that has lost all meaning,"[48] he insists on the *positive* failure of language to signify, invoking the materiality of a word condensing like a "a concrete ball, a solid mass of existence." He continues: "Language, abandoning the sense, the meaning which was all it wanted to be, tries to become senseless. Everything physical takes precedence: rhythm, weight, mass, shape, and then the paper on which one writes, the trail of ink, the book."[49] It is not that poetic language is distinct from ordinary language—as if there were a stockpile of decisively poetic words. Instead, poetry unleashes a materiality, opacity, and disturbance at the heart of language, a restlessness or anarchy disrupting the closure of every "saying" into a definite "said." In an earlier essay, Blanchot expressed the destabilizing nature of poetry in terms that would have been particularly resonant for Levinas, writing: "Poetry is an encounter, in language, of what is strange, an encounter that preserves it and keeps it in the absolute distance of separation."[50] Picking up Blanchot's description, Levinas describes poetic language in explicitly ethical terms as "the mode of revelation of what remains *other*, despite its revelation" (PN 130). He goes on: "It is not telepathic; the outside is not distant. It is what appears—but in a singular fashion—when all the real has been denied: realization of that unreality" (PN 131). The poem, like a close-up, eclipses every horizon and takes up the whole screen of language. The poem resists explanation, but more significantly, in appearing in such a way that it resists theory, it leads away from totalizing knowledge and opens a possibility for a meaning that registers outside the alternatives between fact and fiction, the true and the false, the philosophic and the aesthetic.

In his 1966 article, "The Servant and her Master," Levinas turns from Blanchot's critical/philosophical works to his more "properly" (PN 143) literary texts. Focusing on the poetic dimension of Blanchot's language and grammar, Levinas explains: "Poetry can be said to transform words, the tokens of the whole, the moments of totality, into unfettered signs, breaching the walls of immanence, disrupting order."[51] The poem pierces "the moments of totality," wielding singular, anarchic words. It is as if a poem disengages words from the house of language, allowing them to rise to the surface through the poem and stand out as uniquely meaningful in a way they do not or cannot when they are heard prosaically—overheard or underheard in the stream of language. A poem releases words in a way that lets them resound, not because the words are extraordinary or haven't been used before. We've heard them all before, only now, in a poem, it is like hearing them for the first time. Subjecting words in a way that manifests their "unique sense" (MS 46), poetry releases them from their servitude to a language in which they are only meant to signify in context and as part of a whole. In a footnote, Levinas offers a definition of poetry as an interruption of language, explaining: "Poetry, to me, means the rupture of the immanence to which language is condemned, imprisoning itself" (PN 185). There is a clear proximity between Levinas's notion of poetry and his concept of "saying" as the interruptive, fluid, and expressive dimension of language. His definition of poetry also recalls the language of anarchy and resistance from *Totality and Infinity,* echoing his description of the ethical break with totality signaled by the infinite *sens* of a face. Elsewhere Levinas describes poetry as "the first of the languages" (PN 41), and (in explicitly ethical terms) as "response preceding the question" (PN 41). Poetry, like a face, perforates "the moments of totality" and offers, in language, a way to another side of language. A poem is a place where words show their faces.

Poems are anarchic protestors of sense and meaning. They are the figures of resistance to the closure of what Levinas, in *Otherwise Than Being or Beyond Essence,* calls the "said." The poem disengages words from the house of language, challenging "the apparently unquestionable claim of a certain language to be the privileged conveyer of the meaningful—to be its beginning, its middle and its end" (PN 142). Levinas asks: "Does the meaningful depend upon a certain order of propositions built upon a certain grammar in order for it to constitute a logical discourse? Or does meaning make language explode, and then mean among these broken bits . . . ?" (PN 142). There is a form of language that conveys meaninglessly if meaning requires the whole story or the complete narrative. Another dimension of language conveys, against the grain of progressive prose, a sense of meaning undoing itself. Levinas describes the effect of this aspect of language as "a new feeling: a new 'experience,' or, more precisely, a new prickling sensation of the skin, brushed against by things" (PN 143). Similar to the effects of certain kinds of modern art, the sense of being "brushed against by things" is intimately tied to sensibility, as if poetic language works on the body more than the mind.

Language's internal restlessness can awaken suddenly in the dark space of a poem. Levinas credits Blanchot with showing that poetry is a sensible interruption of everything language tries to contain or convey. Language, not the dawn of light and truth, is shot through with expressive, dark space.[52] There are different degrees of darkness, different shades of meaning. Poetic language, uniquely, shows the meaningfulness of those degrees. Levinas notes the similarity between Heidegger and Blanchot in their fixation on poetry, but he credits Blanchot with articulating poetry's "exclusive vocation" (PN 134): "to call us obstinately back to error, to turn us toward that space where everything we propose, everything we have acquired, everything we are, all that is disclosed on earth, returns to insignificance" (PN 135). Poetry does not provide a building site for meaning. It remains defiantly fluid, allowing for the defection of meaning in multiple directions. Poetry thereby places us face to face with ambiguous pluralities, inviting us to "untie, erode, relax, [and] obliterate" (PN 145) meaning as we know it.[53]

9. Nomadic Sense

In the last section of "The Poet's Vision" Levinas writes: "The literary space into which Blanchot . . . leads us has nothing in common with the Heideggerian world that art renders inhabitable. Art, according to Blanchot, far from elucidating the world, exposes the desolate, lightless substratum underlying it, and restores to our sojourn its exotic essence" (PN 137). The description of Blanchot's "literary space" recalls Levinas's descriptions of Rodin and "exoticism" from *Existence and Existents*. Now, however, the idea of the "exotic" is intimately tied to an ethical alternative to a Heideggerian sense of ownership (*Jemeinigkeit*) and enrootedness. Blanchot's "literary space" becomes an alternative to the inscribed space of settlement, Pascal's "place in the sun"—"the beginning and the image of the usurpation of all the earth."[54]

Blanchot's identification of poetry with the "slope" (*pente*) of literature on which language maintains its ambiguity and relinquishes its hold on definitive meaning is at odds with Heidegger's description of poetry as a shining place of truth.[55] Heidegger defines poetry as the origin of language, but Blanchot sees poetry as an interruption of meaningful language that restores to words their essential vagueness and openness: "this sickness [that] is also the words' health."[56] This is the swerve Levinas follows in Blanchot, a swerve that keeps poetry on the side of an inessential, inarticulable, formless meaning. Levinas separates Blanchot from Heidegger, and he does it along the seam between a Heideggerian conception of poetry's unique "disclosure of being" (PN 136) and Blanchot's conception of poetry disclosing "in an uncovering that is not truth, a darkness" (PN 136). The darkness a poem uncovers does not give the things in themselves or give things over to their presence. The poem makes present a darkness without giving anything: saying *il y a* without *es gibt*.

Poetry, useless in the service of the truth, is helplessly *inauthentic*. Levinas describes Blanchot's thought as a way of "calling us back to error" that is not "a nihilistic or diabolical substitution of falsehood for truth" (PN 135). The call to "error" is a call to attend to the fleeting poignancy of things that have no ultimate or final significance. This idea resonates with a core principle of James's radical empiricism, his insistence that "life is in the transitions as much as in the terms connected; often, indeed, it seems to be there more emphatically, as if our spurts and sallies forward were the real firing-line of the battle, were like the thin line of flame advancing across the dry autumnal field which the farmer proceeds to burn" (ERE 87). Rather than lighting up beings in their truth, poetry helps us operate within a darkened realm of meaning, helping us descend from the daylight to the night as if from the blinding light outside Plato's cave back into the depth and the shadows. We return to nuance and ambiguity, to the unresolved meaning of *il y a* that traverses like a countercurrent, eroding every fixed meaning.

Levinas compares Heidegger's conception of poetry to a founding while characterizing Blanchot's as erosive and displacing, thus describing this difference as one between settlement and "nomadism" (PN 136). Invoking a nomad, Levinas critiques the afterimage imprinted by a Heideggerian world dominated by hammers, jugs, temples, and bridges—the equipment and stuff of settlement. Heidegger describes the poem as a clearing, an open space (*Raum*) like the land "cleared or freed for settlement and lodging."[57] One needs tools to clear the land and a hammer to build there, but one needs art to see the space as inhabitable—to see the blueprint or "rift design" (*Aufriss*) of a house one might call one's own. Levinas critiques Heidegger at the level of his imagery and responds with alternative images. Not a bridge, but a door; not a house, but a makeshift shelter; not the woods, but a desert. It is imagery that tries to counter Heidegger's sense of entitlement to a space determined by the thrownness of fate and guaranteed by the projection of destiny. Just as emotion is not a primitive mentality to be overcome on the way to reason, nomadism is not a stage that is surpassed on the way to settlement. It is not "the distracted not-tarrying [that] becomes *never-dwelling-anywhere*" (BT 398). Nothing is settled, and yet there is meaning without settlement—without the light reflecting off the marble, without a house, without building or dwelling. Levinas credits Blanchot with the insight that poetry provides a dislocated, moving space for meaning whose only truth is "the authenticity of exile" (PN 136). It is a truth that has no homeland, owns nothing, and keeps moving—a nomadic truth without a house, unable to settle in one place for all time.[58] This is precisely the plural, fallible, and radically empirical kind of truth Levinas seeks to enact in *Otherwise Than Being or Beyond Essence*, employing a poetic form of writing that refuses any last word.

Language, poetry, and art can move us. Language's poetic possibilities work against fixed meaning and propositional truth, working against the forces of sedentary existence. We need a little bit of anarchy against the conservatism of getting old in language and growing deaf to the world. We need to be moved sensibly, without knowing what has touched us. Poetry and art are not sensible in the sense of good, common sense—but they are not nonsense. Blanchot's poetic language stands for a more sensory, difficult, anarchic, and nomadic possibility—and perhaps Levinas is wrong to characterize it as "a more mature thought" (PN 135). Perhaps it is more like a resistance to "old age," the youthful possibility of *movement* that Emerson expressed:

Nothing is secure but life, transition, the energizing spirit. No love can be bound by oath or covenant to secure itself against a higher love. No truth so sublime but it may be trivial tomorrow in the light of new thoughts. People wish to be settled; only in so far as they are unsettled is there any hope for them.[59]

10. Tremulous Hope

In a 1971 conversation with André Dalmas, Levinas explained: "I think Maurice Blanchot's thought can be interpreted in two directions at the same time." The first direction is toward a "loss of meaning . . . as if one were at the extreme pinnacle of nihilism" (PN 154). Meaning becomes meaningless and all that is left is the horrific sense of an impersonal and threatening "nothing." Nihilism names the sense of *il y a* in its erosive instability. But the other direction is toward the rupture of totality that is signaled by the unraveling of meaning. Describing this other direction, Levinas insists:

> An uninterrupted noise . . . does not let the world sleep, and troubles the order in which being and non-being are ordered in a dialectic. This Neuter is not a someone, nor even a something. It is but an *excluded middle* that, properly speaking, *is* not even. Yet there is in it more transcendence than any world-behind-the-worlds ever gave a glimpse of. (PN 155)

This is the sense of *il y a* as a minimal resistance. Its uninterrupted "nothing" says "not yet." Interpreting Blanchot's work "in two directions at the same time" allows Levinas to specify the simultaneous threat and value of Blanchot's "Neuter." From one direction Blanchot's writing can feel like the destruction of everything stable—a dead end. From the other direction the same instability feels like the enlivening source of a movement toward "more transcendence"—opening up a whole new terrain within language: an invisible, "excluded middle." The invitation to interpret Blanchot in two directions offers a clue for interpreting Levinas, whose work also drifts between neutrality and ambiguity, between a threatening and a saving *il y a*.

We are not alone in the world—not alone with one face or alone with faces only. Even when one is called and riveted by the obligation of the inter-subjective, radically subjected and forgetful of everything one knows or owns, even then, the intimacy of the face to face is insecure. The world is cluttered. Occasionally, from out of the clutter, something stands out. Writing about Blanchot, Levinas describes "the strangeness of things heavy with their insignificance: a glass of water, a bed, a table, an armchair, each of them exiled and abstract" (PN 143). Things that look "exiled or abstract" have come loose from their place in the background. They have lost their world. This may feel like a terrifying abstraction and loss of context, but it might also feel like the intimate poignancy of a close-up. Sometimes the merest thing suddenly occupies a room, taking on a monumental density. Then it becomes a space of sense that can spill over the world of objects, making heavy with significance the most abandoned, unpopulated or deserted place.

We sometimes lean into this space. Perhaps it is the space of a poem or a painting, a piece of music or a scene from a film. Perhaps it is just a line or an image that comes back out of nowhere when things have become unimaginably hard. One can read Levinas leaning into such a space at the beginning of *Existence and Existents,* bearing memorized lines of poetry from Baudelaire, Rimbaud, and Valéry with him into captivity to scatter in the pages of his first book. This was also the space of poetry that James discovered, repeating a single line of scripture ("come unto me all ye that labor and are heavy-laden" [VRE 135]) in the midst of his breakdown, returning incessantly to Whitman and Tolstoy—and to Browning's "A Grammarian's Funeral" (LWJ 1: 129). Sometimes the least tangible things carry one the farthest.

Art can be dangerously disorienting, but its ability to disorient is its special power. We can be brought back to life, brought back from the margins of life. The fact that art remains suspended in an ambiguous time, that its meaning can't be exhausted by any truth, lets it remain in play after the fall of truth. After the end, ambiguously and without any allegiances, art can stay in play. It can "arise from a shattered world" (EE 49). Its persistence is the minimal, ambiguous promise found in something that stays the same despite everything. It is one reason we go back to see the same painting year after year and that, sometimes, it might look tragically, indifferently the same. It is one reason we turn back in hard times to the names, words, and images that have stood with us—and without us—through time. We can get carried away, and "in our relationship with the world we are able to withdraw from the world" (EE 45). But recalling a poem, revisiting a painting, or replaying a song can also be a way of letting oneself be turned when one can't turn by oneself any more. It can be a way of feeling *il y a—there is*—a miraculous, hard reappearance that can in time help one appear again and bear appearances again. Art's material reality can restore a weight and can be grounding, since it is the product of blunt human work and one way in which humanity surfaces. Works of art might be, as Blanchot wrote, *useless* for the practical demands of the day. "Literature," he admitted, "is unquestionably illegitimate, there is an underlying deceitfulness about it. But certain people have discovered something beyond this: literature is not only illegitimate, it is also null, and as long as this nullity is isolated in a state of purity it may constitute an extraordinary force, a marvelous force."[60] This was the force that Georges Bataille envisioned, describing art as a "positive squandering of energy" through which "excess of energy shines."[61]

Art says *il y a*. This means that Levinas's philosophy shares an artistic ambition to show the unpresentable and say the unnamable. Images crowd into his texts. "Imagine nothingness," he tells us—and immediately pictures rush in. Something remains and returns. It is not clear what it is or how it returns. We are brought back to the shrinking margins between life and death, a breath and noise, the ability to stand up or raise one's hand—some minimal bodily gesture and resistance that keeps one on the side of life. This was the minimal, essential differentiation Emily Dickinson discovered when she wrote:

> It was not Death, for I stood up,
> And all the Dead, lie down.[62]

Standing up, lying down, getting up again. Hypostasis, emotion, hypostasis. *Il y a*, face, *il y a*. The triumph of life, but without taking a triumphant shape— the triumph of life in its minimal but essential differentiation, like the triumph of waking or standing. Stripped of all the things that indicate a whole, full life, and even without the basic things Levinas enumerated after returning from the labor camp in 1945—without "meals and rest, smiles, personal effects, decency and the right to turn one's key to one's own room, pictures, friends, countrysides and sick leave" (PN 121)—life persists. This perseverance, life welling up and returning or just carrying on, is what Levinas calls *il y a*. *Il y a* indifferently threatens everything personal and particular, and at the same time offers a minimal, ambiguous hope that nothing is final or finished.

What kind of hope is this? Minimal, marginal, uncertain; it is a non-idealistic hope James expressed in terms of radical empiricism's commitment to ongoing elaboration and plurality: an "order being gradually won and always in the making," requiring genuine effort—"sustaining, persevering, striving, paying with effort as we go, hanging on . . . " (ERE 183).[63] This is a "decidedly tremulous and conditional optimism" (P 12–13), a non-naïve hope Levinas described in the closing pages of *Existents and Existence* in terms of a future, though non-compensating, time. There he reminds us that "it is not enough that tears be wiped away or death avenged" (EE 93); "It is not enough to conceive of hope to unleash a future" (*Il ne suffit pas de concevoir un espoir, pour déclencher un avenir*) (EE 91 / EaE 153). Hope entails more time than that available to any solitary subject. It demands an embodied dimension of "fresh air" (EE 93) and a radically new beginning. For both James and Levinas, real hope is possible only in a social world, where, outlived by other lives, one encounters futures irreducible to the parameters of one's own horizons. In the midst of delivering their visions of living, interpersonal hope, both Levinas and James give us richly imagistic philosophies, reminding us that images are not merely decorative, dispensable appendages to serious prose. Complicating the closure of the "said," images propel a text beyond its letter and let it scintillate in vivid complexity long after the turn of the last page. In this sense, the aesthetic components and the distinctive *styles* of Levinas's and James's ethics ensure the transcendence of their works, the irresolvable murmur of *il y a* that is, also, the hope of art.

Maybe what is hopeful is just the endurance of something, however small, when it seems from every reasonable indication or expectation that the curtain has closed, or should close, on the last scene. "A turn of the Kaleidoscope," James writes, "when one is utterly maimed for action" (LWJ 2: 297). Life whittled away finds another way of living that bears a trace of a full life, as a deserted place bears traces of an inhabited time, echoes of shouts and street life. Not only death infects and haunts the living. Life is infectious and leaves its mark— its happy beauty, sad beauty, and glimmer of hope. What is so devastating— and so hopeful—is to see someone make something out of nothing, the extravagant, unreasonable, gesture of artists, of *poiēsis* and poetry. It is Levinas's gesture as he tries to make philosophy feel alive and significant after the loss of life and meaning, in the wake of "world wars (and local ones), National Socialism, Stalinism (and even de-Stalinization), the camps, the gas chambers, nuclear weapons, terrorism, and unemployment."[64] Life persists, a ceremony in the midst of ruins—weeding the gardens in Hamburg after the bombing . . . the blooming yellow flowers growing rampant in the rubble that no one of a generation could bear to see.[65]

SIX

PAINTING

I should have been a pair of ragged claws
Scuttling across the floors of silent seas.

—T. S. ELIOT, "THE LOVE SONG OF J. ALFRED PRUFROCK"

1. Making Progress

It is always hard to disengage from an author's language and find the right distance for reflection. This is particularly difficult with Levinas, whose texts feel like nets. In rendering language opaque and meaning unsettled, he gives us arguments that operate more like poems than proofs, requiring a method of reading that moves slowly enough to feel the sense accumulating in the wake behind every sentence. His ethics resists description, and this is critical if it is to resist becoming a theory one might memorize and unreflectively put into action—an axiom, a rule. There is no rule for ethical response and responsibility, since the ethical opens anew with every face. The aesthetic dimension of Levinas's prose ensures the openness of his ethics. That is, poetry keeps his words alive.

An unintentional upshot of Levinas's ethical prose and the patience required for reading him is that he gives us an alternative set of aesthetic values, exchanging transparency, beauty, symbolism, and truth for opacity, wretchedness, allegory, and error. We have, as a result, the first indications for a Levi-nasian aesthetics. This is not to suggest we can apply these terms in a theoretical framework to interpret or explain works of art. Instead we can, with these new values, begin identifying overlooked or undervalued works in a history of art in which beauty and truth have historically reigned supreme. If we relinquish the traditional quest, new values come into focus, new works become significant, and an alternative history of art emerges that does not depend on the successive overcoming of old models or the progressive purification of existing ones. Levinas gestures toward this hidden history in his examples and interpretations of various works of art, but it was never his goal or focus. We can thus move beyond Levinas in order to put him to work in ways he could not have envisioned himself.

One of the central, radically empirical aspects of Levinas's philosophy is his refusal to define ethics in terms of an absolute ideal or ultimate end. Levinas warned against conceiving the human subject "at the service of the system" or "effacing itself before the true" (*s'effaçant devant le vrai*) (OB 132 / AE 208). James, strikingly postmodern in his suspicion of systemization and his commitment to pluralism, was particularly critical of a Hegelian dialectic that put everything in the service of "*the* truth, one, indivisible, eternal, objective, and necessary" (PU 100). James feared that such a notion of truth makes "a spherical system with no loose ends hanging out for foreignness to get a hold upon" (PU 103). In ethics, a rigid notion of "*the* truth" commits one to a concept of moral progress in which every action leads to an ultimate goal. James acknowledged the consolation and security of the Hegelian picture, in which everything works out in the end. But he, well before Levinas, saw the danger in leveling everything to a moment of the absolute and in focusing on the future at the expense of attention to the present.[1]

In art, as in ethics, fixed ideas about what constitutes progress predetermine the horizons one is able to see and the history one is willing to tell. James and Levinas contest the archetype of a single, grand narrative. Turning to the details, messy and specific, they encourage a more minimal and pragmatic approach to ethics and a more creative and open-minded approach to philosophy, to writing, and to art. Without a guiding image or a fixed set of values, they leave things open and undone. In the process, they demonstrate a concept of incremental, indeterminate progress that is not modeled on a linear, one-way ascent. Instead, the trajectory they defend looks like a spiraling revolution, circling out without any end in sight.

The relationship I have been tracing between James and Levinas is crucial for showing the pragmatic minimalism of Levinas's ethics and the ethical importance of James's radical empiricism. But it is also important for showing the convergence of American and French theory at a time when philosophy was much less polarized and divided than it is today. Phenomenology and pragmatism grew up in atmospheres of radical ingenuity and experimentalism. James and Bergson exemplify the spirit of collaborative effort and mutual enthusiasm which allowed American and French thought to flourish beyond both continents. Rekindling that spirit and looking for the moments when, knowingly or not, highly original thinkers think together is one way of reminding ourselves of the narrow trenches philosophical specialists occupy today and encouraging ourselves to look beyond the edges of our own disciplines and schools.

In that spirit, this chapter focuses on a concrete example of a break in systematic development, moving beyond Levinas and James to consider a convergence of French and American theory in another vein. In the same years that Levinas was in France insisting on the sense of the personal and the ethical value of ambiguity, Philip Guston was in America, breaking with Abstract Expressionism to produce paintings of ordinary objects, figures, and junk—his imagery hovering between reality and cartoons. Levinas and Guston are both famously difficult to categorize in their respective fields and have only recently come into focus as critical, if deeply unresolved, catalysts for contemporary ethics and painting, respectively. Both meditated on the human and searched for a means of articulation that refused any simple reconciliation into abstraction or figuration. Both refused the alternative between the beautiful and the sublime to work in a more ambiguous, less ideal, more humane margin, giving aesthetic and ethical (and ultimately, political) relevance to the ordinary, the mere, the neglected, and the ruined. Guston's pictures provide a visual analog to Levinas's and James's radical move towards particularity, helping us to read their prose with an eye for the material and visual consequences of their language. With the possibility of a Levinasian aesthetics in mind, Guston's late paintings emerge as distinctly relevant and important for considering an alternative history of art and for illustrating, in pictures, transcendence *toward* the human and the ethical minimalism that Levinas and James put into words.

2. Proper Names

Levinas never mentioned Philip Guston. I don't know if he knew about him, liked him, or hated him, but in 1970 Guston, like Levinas, was thinking about ruins, "sad beauty," minimal hope, and a return to human faces. There is a similarity between their styles—an extraordinary ordinariness that feels raw and rough and, at the same time, artful. The style reflects grief and hope at once, the same mixture of optimism tempered with melancholia characteristic of James's radical empiricism and Levinas's radical phenomenology. Levinas and Guston seem driven by a sober realization of what it feels like to be hyper-sensitized to life in their own time. Their light shines, like Diogenes' lantern, on rubble: Levinas's describes *il y a,* Rodin, and the night; Guston paints pictures of junk, ashtrays, wheels, and cherries. Surprisingly, the rubble shines like a face.

Guston and Jackson Pollock were best friends in high school, expelled together for publishing a paper criticizing the school's emphasis on sports over art. Guston, along with Barnett Newman, was among the celebrated "New York School" of painters in the 1950s; he was lifelong friends with Willem de Kooning. But he remained outside the spotlight compared to his more charismatic contemporaries. He stood in the midst of one of the greatest moments in American painting, at the climax of Abstract Expressionism, and opted out, returning to figuration at the very moment when painting had purged itself of everything figurative.

Historically, Guston and Levinas have been marginalized in their fields (though they are becoming less so), working on projects that fell outside the driving debates of their time.[2] Certainly, Guston is not an "outsider" artist and Levinas not a fringe philosopher, but they are difficult to situate in a coherent history, as both of them return to ideas that had seemingly been surmounted and dispensed with. In Guston this was a return to narration, objects, and the human figure at a moment when these were associated with the death of painting. In Levinas it was the return to ethics, sensibility, and the human at a time when philosophers were concerned with the sociopolitical commitment of art, with truth and propositional language. In both cases, the recuperation of abandoned themes provoked criticism: Guston's painting was considered to be regressive while Levinas's work was unphilosophical.

Guston offers a visual analog of the descent from the universal to the particular: a move (in James's terms) toward "the turbid, restless, lower world" (PU 218) or (in Levinas's language) to "the life underlying the gaze" (GDT 27). Guston asks in paint something Levinas asked in writing, namely whether "proper names, in the middle of all these common names and common-places—can resist the dissolution of meaning and help us to speak."[3] Guston unashamedly makes everything personal, capitalizing all his names. His human figures have the blunt expression of his bottles and cars, even when the figure is his wife, Musa, her eyes welling over with tears. Like Van Gogh, Guston piled on his paint with thick strokes, making his objects solid and matte. He found a way of turning his hand to the things closest to him, painting Richard Nixon, hooded Klansmen, his watch, his brushes, his wife, with a radical equality. His paintings have a way of showing how the merest things defiantly resist their own disappearance. Though he didn't know it, he was painting *il y a*.

Sometimes the resistance looks heroic, as in one of Guston's last paintings, *Wheel* (figure 1), painted in 1979, a year before he died. A giant wheel rises impressively out of a red sea, announcing, "I am a Wheel!" But at the same time it's murmuring, "I'm just a wheel." The announcement is all bravado and an admission of insignificance. It's a wheel out of play, adrift on the sea like flotsam, the wheel of ship that has no boat to steer. Squared-off, it can't roll or turn, yet it bobs there with a stubborn, awkward persistence. If heroic, it's a melancholy, human variety of heroism—to be a wheel coming up or sinking down like the sun, to find oneself spinning, to try to say, at the end of the day, what a thing, what anything, is—to try to play a part, or to say who you are.

3. The Brutality of the World

In the 1950s Guston painted critically acclaimed abstract expressionist work, made up of densely packed, amorphous brushstrokes—like *Dial* (figure 2), completed in 1956. Guston is interesting in relation to a Levinasian/Jamesian minimalism and a radically empirical trajectory because of the shift in his paintings—his move through and then away from abstract expressionism after 1968. This shift is important but not as stark as it might appear or is sometimes described.[4] Guston began with figuration, with the cartoon drawings of his childhood heroes: George Herriman, who created Krazy

FIGURE 1.
Philip Guston. *Wheel*, 1979. Oil on canvas.
48 × 60 inches / 121.9 × 152.4 cm.
Private Collection. *Permission granted by
The McKee Gallery, New York, N.Y.*

Kat, and Bud Fischer of Mutt and Jeff. His earliest paintings were the massive
Works Progress Administration murals he made in New York starting in
1935, which took their lead from Max Beckman and Fernand Léger. From
beginning to end there is a consistency to his color and mark. His late work
finds itself, as if he has pulled something elemental out of the dashes, specks,
and scribbles that make up the eerily beautiful abstract paintings he began
making around 1941. When he returns to his first pictures of objects in the
1960s, he gets organized, concrete, and close. He rediscovers the weight of
things. This bears some similarity to the evolution of de Kooning, whose last
paintings can make you feel as if you are inhabiting a brushstroke. De Kooning remained the model abstract expressionist to the end, but both Guston

FIGURE 2.
Philip Guston. *Dial,* 1956. Oil on canvas.
72 × 76 inches / 182.9 × 193 cm.
Whitney Museum of American Art.
*Permission granted from the Whitney Museum
of American Art, New York, N.Y.*

and de Kooning closed in, getting more intimate, making the painting a part
of an increasingly dense space the viewer inhabits, rather than opening some
infinitely distant space.

Guston moved from high modernism and the purity of paint in itself toward figuration and things. Dumb things. He seized on ashtrays, shoes, sand-
wiches—the majestic junk of the world. In his memoir of Guston, Ross Feld
wrote: "Painting after painting offers us plain things with the deadpan capacity
to hold history: a hood, an overcoat, a bottle, a shoe, a pyramid, a bug, a wheel,

a patched-up sphere, a teacup, a suitcase."[5] His late work is like Husserl's mantra in response to Kant: "To the things themselves!" He goes back to the things, but he goes back to them with a sense of rubble, ruin, and sweetness at once. The majority of Guston's late paintings focus on objects, but without the quiet or remove of a "still-life," without what Levinas criticized as "that calm possession, that pagan enrootedness that characterizes all Heidegger's mention of things—whether it is a bridge, or a pitcher, or a pair of shoes."[6] Guston's objects appear rough with something more like the fever and pitch of comic books and newspaper photos. A heavy-soled shoe reads like the cartoon "POW!" or "SPLAT!" There is a toughness to Guston's tenderness that can hit you, as one recent critic described it, like a "bracing smack."[7]

This is not surprising, since the late paintings also self-consciously respond to a time overwhelmingly defined by violence and war. It may be this visceral point of contact, the contact of war, that makes Levinas and Guston seem so much a part of their time, and relevant to our own time. For Guston it was the war at home, the Civil Rights Movement of the 1960s and the war abroad, in Vietnam, which prefigured his return to figuration. In a 1977 interview, Guston looked back on his self-imposed distancing from Abstract Expressionism, explaining:

> So when the 1960's came along I was feeling split, schizophrenic. The war, what was happening to America, the brutality of the world. What kind of man am I, sitting at home, reading magazines, going into a frustrated fury about everything—and then going into my studio to adjust a red to a blue. I wanted to be complete again, as I was when I was a kid . . . Wanted to be whole between what I thought and what I felt.[8]

"The brutality of the world." To Guston, something felt empty about Abstract Expressionism and all the purity of paint in relation to a real and brutal world, to the world of people and things. Levinas also wrote critically about modern art of the same era that it "speaks of nothing but the adventure of art itself; it strives to be pure painting, pure music."[9] In the quest for purity, art can lose its contact with the impure world we actually inhabit. Worried about that point of contact, Guston offered a Levinasian analysis: "There is something ridiculous and miserly in the myth we inherit from abstract art—that painting is autonomous, pure and for itself. . . . Painting is 'impure.' It is the adjustment of impurities which forces painting's continuity."[10] Guston expressed his return to figuration as wanting "to be whole" between what he thought and what he felt. As a kid he started drawing soon after his father, a traveling salesman, hanged himself. Then Guston drew in a small closet in his house by the light of a single light bulb (which reappears, hanging, in many of his late paintings). The "brutality of the world" is not a singular event. It takes on different shapes, different faces. It comes at different times. Later Guston drew hooded Klansmen driving cars, playing cards, eating, and painting with cigars wedged between their fingers—the imagery blunt and brutal. Later still he painted piles of legs and feet, giant square-ish heads with a single bulging red eye—the remains of the day's wars. Through it all there were paintings to be made, and one can hear in Guston's pictures an Emersonian willfulness to bear on: "Doubt not, O poet, but persist. . . . Stand there balked, dumb, estuttering and stammering, hissed and hooted, stand and strive. . . . Nothing walks, or creeps, or grows, or exists, which must not in turn arise and walk before him as exponent of his meaning."[11]

4. Heaven-Bound

In 1970, with challenges to Modernism in full swing and painting itself entering a crisis, Guston exhibited his new paintings at the Marlborough Gallery in New York. The paintings showed hooded figures, some of the hoods splattered with blood, driving cartoon cars through cityscapes or huddled together in kitchens, dens or studios (figure 3). Describing this work, Guston said: "The KKK has haunted me since I was a boy in L.A. In those years they were there mostly to break strikes, and I drew and painted pictures of conspiracies and floggings, cruelty and evil."[12] If the early drawings expressed something of "cruelty and evil," the new paintings expressed something banal and just bad—which turned out to be much more unsettling. The exhibit, panned by most critics, was met with wonder and disgust.

Guston's late figurative paintings presented something extraordinary. Foremost, it was extraordinary that a critically celebrated abstract expressionist *could develop* in this direction. In fact, most critics characterized Guston's new work as a regression.[13] Guston describes feeling isolated by the critics, but also by his own community, admitting: "my painter friends in New York would come up to me and say, 'Now what did you want to do that for?' It seemed to depress a lot of people. It was as though I had left the Church."[14] The question on everyone's mind seemed to be how abstraction could bring about such blunt

FIGURE 3.
Philip Guston. *Riding Around*, 1969. Oil on canvas.
54 × 79 inches / 137.2 × 200.7 cm.
Private Collection. *Permission granted by*
The McKee Gallery, New York, N.Y.

and artless figuration. The art world was saturated with the majesty of Rothko, Pollock, and de Kooning and rapidly moving toward the flat, sharp imagery of Warhol. Guston did not fit in. It had to be a mistake—the work of a depressed, frustrated painter who couldn't compete—who gave up on painting. Of course, these late works are also now the most famous of Guston's paintings—the work in which he charted new territory. Still, that hasn't dissuaded contemporary critics from describing Guston's late work as "the art of a bitter Jewish survivor," his "breakthrough [as] a breakdown," and his return to figuration as "the American artist's fallback position."[15]

This kind of criticism reflects a prevalent, if unspoken, Platonic ideal: there is a stairway one climbs, from particular to universal, from the love of beautiful bodies to the love of beauty in itself. It is meant to be a one-way climb, ever higher and heaven-bound. First you paint a cup, then a figure, but later (when you're really serious) you leave the *things* behind and begin to adjust a red to a blue. This was the legacy of Mondriaan, who moved from his astonishing trees and dunes toward the famous (and also astonishing) chicklet grids of reds, yellows, and blues. At base, however, it is just Diotima's powerful myth in the *Symposium:* "Beginning from beautiful things to move ever onwards for the sake of that beauty, as though using ascending steps."[16] Abstract Expressionism was supposed to "move ever onwards." Even if it was never clear where "on-wards" could lead, there was a fervent, almost religious belief that things were progressing, that painting was relevant again.

What Guston showed the New York art world in 1970 was that there is another way of moving. He broke with the cycle of art's ironic reply to its own legacy, forgoing Pop and every movement. He broke with his own suc-cesses, his own familiar imagery and palette. He used everything for paint-ing, a quotation from Dickens, a figure from Rubens, a Picasso leg, a shell, a two by four, rusty nails. He was a scavenger for whom nothing was off limits. Everything had to be painted; nothing had to be beautiful.

Guston's trajectory was Platonic in its own right, but it took its lead from the *Republic*'s myth of the cave, where the ascent culminates in a descent. In *Republic* book VII, Socrates describes an unwilling prisoner "dragged . . . by force along the rough, steep, upward way . . . into the light of the sun."[17] Initially the light is blinding, and it is painful for the prisoner to open her eyes. Once accustomed to the bright light of day, she dreads returning to the cave where she will be forced to grope again before her eyes adjust to the dark. But Socrates insists that the ones who leave the cave must also return. He sends the prisoner back, concluding: "You must go down, each in his turn, into the common dwelling of the others and get habituated along with them to seeing dark things."[18]

Guston went back down. His first imagery came directly out of the "dark things" of his time, starting with the Ku Klux Klan. It turned out that the dark things were also the common things—and Guston painted all of them. Arthur Danto wrote of Guston's movement: "It is one thing to aspire to the sublime. It is another to bring into art the preoccupations of a man with ordinary appetites, who worries about love and eating too much, and how to give up smoking, and not just about being evil but being bad."[19] This descent made, and continues to make, critics uneasy. How can you go back without going backward, without giving up or regressing? What happens, especially to the critics, if there is no progression, no hierarchy? What if there is no pinnacle, no peak or point or top—just this revolution up and down, this circular rotation? And what if in the end we don't find ourselves blinded or enlightened by some stunning beauty, but sent back to the cave to be surrounded by old things: papers, brushes, a cup, an ashtray, a pile of junk—dark things, and the pictures we've made in their wakes?

5. Transdescendence

What does it mean to progress? Is progress always an ascent or an overcoming? These are questions about the trajectory of art but they are also questions about the trajectory of life—about trajectories generally. James and Levinas show the value of a movement that doesn't tend in the direction of a final summit. The universe, James insisted, is essentially pluralistic and "chaotic": "no single type of relation runs through all the experiences that compose it" (ERE 46). Faced with so much multiplicity, with the incomprehensible sense of infinite faces, one has to find myriad ways of moving. Following the death of his son, Emerson wrote about being interrupted and suddenly stalled in the midst of life, asking: "Where do we find ourselves?" He answered: "We wake and find ourselves on a stair; there are stairs below us, which we seem to have ascended; there are stairs above us, many a one, which go upward and out of sight."[20] The world, which once seemed navigable and whole, becomes suddenly fractured, comprised of spaces both deeper and higher than one imagined possible. The stairs one thought one was climbing lead both up and down, and it is not always clear which way one is going. We don't always end up where we were heading. We rarely arrive where we thought we would. What if there is no heaven or overarching truth? What if there are no universals and no solid ground? Is there a way of describing this possibility without being condemned as a pessimist, a relativist, an atheist, or a nihilist? Might there be something profoundly optimistic and hopeful in the idea that no end is final, that no word is the last word?

This is something Levinas and James tried to think through and Guston tried to paint through. Perhaps if we consider reconciling Diotima's myth of ascent with Socrates' myth of descending back down into the cave we start to see an early picture of another way of moving. Both myths are about the difficult roads toward education and a certain art of *turning*, of learning to turn from the dark to the light and from the light to the dark. In the *Republic,* Socrates explains:

> The instrument with which each learns—just as an eye is not able to turn toward the light from the dark without the whole body—must be turned around from that which *is coming into being* together with the whole soul until it is able to endure looking at that which *is* and the brightest part of that which *is.* . . . There would, therefore . . . be an art of this turning around.[21]

Socrates stresses the whole-bodied revolution required for turning around. It will take the entire body and the whole soul. Turning, therefore, is not as simple as turning one's head, one lifting one's eyes. The prisoners leaving the cave find an arduous path leading upward and out of view. And just when they think they have arrived, they learn that the same path stretches treacherously back into the shadows. The journey upward was only the first stage of an infinite climb. There is never a definitive, final turn; the educational process Socrates describes is never complete. Learning is never as simple as ascending steps from the sensible to the intelligible. Things get in the way. The road is not always smooth or open. As Levinas discovered, life is "an ill-paved road" (*une route mal pavée*) and we are "jolted about by instants each of which is a beginning all over again" (EE 13 / EaE 34). The living space of the world is not an empty form or container waiting to be filled. The spaces one inhabits are cluttered and require navigating in many directions, making infinite turns.

In order to become educated in the ups and downs, the light and darkness of experience, one has to learn the "art" of "turning around." This is an art—a creative potential—of rebounding or of being able to pivot on a new center of gravity. It is a way of giving oneself over to a new claim and being able to begin again. The prisoner Socrates describes may exert all of his physical and psychic energy making his heroic ascent to the sun, but none of it matters if he arrives outside the cave without the capacity of turning around again from the light to the dark, the last day to the next day, from one source of light to another.

Turning around is the movement Levinas and James articulate and Guston illustrates. James's pluralism entails recognizing multiple centers of significance, each with its own worth. This means giving up the pretension of an overview and surrendering every theory that "hangs in the air of speculation and touches not the earth of life."[22] James was adamant that philosophy was perpetually at risk of becoming inhumane and losing touch with "the eeriness of the world, the mischief and the manyness" (PU 21). The basic gesture of James's radical empiricism is, therefore, a grounding revolution toward particulars in all their complex obscurity. Levinas invokes Jean Wahl's "transdescendence" (*transdescendance*) (LR 137) to describe the movement of art, but also to describe the possibility of transcending transcendence, a movement that delves deeper into life and more intimately toward the human. Levinas seizes on Wahl's idea that there is not only an above (*en haut*) and beyond (*au delà*), but also a deepening down below (*en bas*). Providing an additional, immanent directionality for transcendence allowed for a secular concept of transcendence that Wahl vigorously defended in the 1930s.[23] Levinas did not initially embrace the notion of multiple trancendences inclining in various directions. But by the time he was writing *Totality and Infinity* thirty years later, Levinas underscored his debt to Wahl's notion of multi-directional transcendence, noting that he had "drawn much inspiration from the themes evoked" in "Sur l'idée de la transcendance," in Wahl's *Existence humaine et transcendence* (TI 35 n. 2). Following Wahl, Levinas urges us to turn toward a complicated depth—an infinite abyss, "the hollow of no-place" (HO 7)—that he names a face.

James, Levinas, and Guston enact "transdescendence," renouncing the overview and turning around to what is closest, most opaque, impure, and the most difficult to see. Rather than leading above or beyond the world, "transdescendence" plants one deeper within it. Wahl himself insisted that this was not an idea about *falling,* not a descent "from the absolute to the relative," as if a diminishment from authenticity to inauthenticity.[24] In his 1955 review of Wahl's treatise on metaphysics, "Jean Wahl and Feeling," Levinas asked, "will the philosopher have the strength finally to transcend transcendence, and to fall valiantly into immanence, without letting the value of his effort toward transcendence be lost?"[25] Will the philosopher have the courage to return to the cave—to the sensible, dark, and opaque world of people and things? Will the philosopher be able to turn around without seeing this turn as a defeat, a failure or retreat? Will she be "able to endure looking at that which *is*"?

It's not always easy to endure looking. Sometimes it's almost unbearable. We'd rather climb the steps or descend into the cave—to be on one side or the other, to be anywhere but in the midst. Sometimes you see things you don't want to see, as in *Republic,* with the bodies Leontius saw outside the city walls: "for a while he struggled and covered his face. But finally, overpowered . . . he

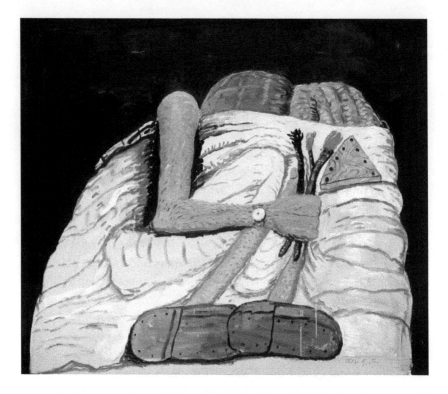

FIGURE 4.
Philip Guston. *Couple in Bed,* 1977. Oil on canvas.
81 × 94¼ inches / 205.7 × 240 cm.
Art Institute of Chicago. *Permission granted by*
The McKee Gallery, New York, N.Y.

opened his eyes wide, ran toward the corpses and said: 'Look you damned wretches, take your fill of the . . . sight.'"[26] Sometimes turning and looking can look like Guston's painting *Couple in Bed* from 1977 (figure 4). Painted after his wife Musa suffered a stroke from which she would never fully recover and three years before the heart attack that killed him, the painting shows Guston together with her in bed, his shoes and hairy legs sticking out from under the cover and their heads melded like two small hills, one red and one yellow, at the crest of the sheet. One of Guston's arms lays across his body, wearing a faceless watch, his hand gripping three paintbrushes. Next to the brushes lies a wedge of wood, bolted or screwed into Musa. Everything in the painting is frail—the brushes Guston is gripping as if they were the last things standing in the world, Musa's tiny body barely rising under the sheet. Their heads are close but distinctly apart. This is what infinite distance and restlessness look like. But also what heaven on earth looks like. It is what it looks like to come home at the end of the day to the person you love and try to sleep—to be up all night with all of your baggage sitting there with you, on you. To grip what you can and face what you can't.

6. Sea Change

Too real, too unreal, too much, the dense feeling of *il y a*. Guston put into paint the *il y a* Levinas puts into words, even though they never crossed paths in their lives. Guston read Blanchot, Beckett, Benjamin—he seemed to read everything—but he never, as far as I know, found Levinas. Still, Guston from 1913–1980, and Levinas from 1906–1995, shared a considerable length of time on earth. Both of them dealt with a certainty uncoupled from truth and uncoupled from beauty; both appealed to the reality of emotion. Both of them thought about shreds, remains, desertion, the closing in of fear, and the ways people cling to things, to each other and to the stuff of their life. They showed, in their own ways, that something persists. Something comes out of nothing. It has an awkward beauty, a dim truth, and a minimal hope.

They never met, but Guston, like Levinas, was interested in the idea of art as allegory, not "a poor man's symbol" but "an ambiguous commerce with reality in which reality does not refer to itself but to its reflection, its shadow" (LR 135). Sometime in 1977 Guston began enthusiastically describing his own pictures as allegories, to the dismay of his close friend and best critic Ross Feld, who initially found the whole concept of allegory simplistic and un-modern. Guston's oversized heads and eyeballs, his shoes and hoods read like disjointed pieces of a strange narrative. Feld wondered why Guston bothered pointing out something so obvious about his paintings and why he wanted to emphasize the same narrative element most critics were busy condemning. In his memoir of Guston, *Guston in Time,* Feld revises his take on allegory and acknowledges: "Whereas a symbol generally pointed to something else, some kernel that might eventually explode into something limitless . . . melancholy allegory opened nothing. Its vision was trained unsparingly on objects that seemed to have *stunned* reality into a temporary stasis."[27] The inconsolable sadness and simultaneous affirmation in Guston's

late works have to do with this sense of "temporary stasis" Feld describes—
the way that the imagery points to something, or tells some story, but the
way that the *something* and the story are also nothing really, and especially
nothing recognizably majestic or impressively metaphysical. If the images
act like signposts, then they point nowhere, or they point back at themselves.
These paintings offer a picture of what *here and now* feels like. It's sometimes
goofy, comic, sad, tragic, boring, sweet, still, black, red, pink.[28]

People, like Feld, who knew Guston, knew he was fascinated by the idea
of melancholy allegory and that his paintings had this in mind. Two things
hung above Guston's worktable in his studio in Woodstock: a hand-lettered
quotation from Dickens and a print of Dürer's *Melancholia*. In *The Origin of
German Tragic Drama*, Walter Benjamin spends a good deal of time describing
Dürer's etching and its symbols of allegory, the "ancient emblems" around
which "the theory of melancholy became crystallized."[29] It is easy to imagine
Guston reading Benjamin's analysis of the etching, looking up from his own
table at the image and then maybe across the room at a new painting like *Riding Around* and getting excited. Guston must have felt he was onto something
and that Benjamin had connected some of the dots before him. Benjamin's
constellation of terms (baroque, allegory, and melancholy) had a special gravity for Guston. They resonated with something Guston was not able, by himself, to put his finger on, correlating terms that made sense out of his own
preoccupation with junk, narratives, and ruins.

Hannah Arendt, in her preface to Benjamin's *Illuminations* talks about
ruins and describes Benjamin's writing as "something which may not be
unique but is certainly quite rare: this gift of *thinking poetically*."[30] She concludes her remarks:

> What guides [Benjamin's] thinking is the conviction that although the liv-
> ing is subject to the ruin of time, the process of decay is at the same time a
> process of crystallization, that in the depths of the sea, into which sinks and
> is dissolved what was once alive, some things suffer a "sea change" and
> survive in new crystallized forms and shapes that remain immune to the
> elements, as though they waited only for the pearl diver who one day will
> come down to them and bring them up into the world of the living—as
> "thought fragments," as something "rich and strange," and perhaps even as
> everlasting *Urphänomene*.[31]

Ruins sometimes crystallize like the grit that suffers a "sea change,"
becoming a luminous pearl. Arendt underscores the hopeful vision at the

bottom of Benjamin's thinking, a revelatory, illuminated, and lasting kernel recovered from history's leveling tide.

The image of a pearl at the bottom of the sea relates to Benjamin's own affection for the baroque (from *barroco* meaning "imperfect pearl"), a style characterized by excessive ornamentation and irregularity. Benjamin sees the pearl in the baroque's imperfection—in the baroque's nearly perfect failure to mean anything by its own extravagant gesture to try to mean everything. The baroque's failure to perfectly fail relates to Benjamin's vision of what we can hope to express given the blunt, imprecise tools for expression we have at our disposal. The baroque, in its allegorical frenzy, highlights a chaotic slippage between language and meaning. Baroque is all over the place. Yet in being all over the place it is a truer expression of life in its luminous imperfection. The baroque offers an imperfect pearl: luminosity without perfection.

Such shimmering light differs from the clarity and beauty that Benjamin reserves for what he calls the classical "symbol." An allegory is less elegant and less concise than a symbol. It remains incapable of succinctly pointing or naming since "any person, any object, any relationship could mean absolutely anything else" (OGTD 175). Compared to the "symbol" Benjamin describes as reflecting the classical ideals of "clarity, brevity, grace and beauty" (OGTD 164), allegory is messy and complicated. It has no way of lighting up all at once, no way of being revelatory like a symbol. Instead, allegory expresses ambiguously in the form of a narrative riddled with detours. Benjamin writes: "Allegory declares itself to be beyond beauty. Allegories are, in the realm of thoughts, what ruins are in the realm of things" (OGTD 178). These are the fallen, crumbling stories, the rubble that shines like a face.

The messy narrative jumble, "beyond beauty," gives allegory a special relation with ordinary language and life as it is lived historically. A poverty or weakness in language forces it towards allegory—towards a way of staging expression in many directions, to account for multiple threads of significance at once. Benjamin arrives at the conclusion that allegory is important as a form of expression that can mirror life's complexity, overflowing itself and tending toward a visual chaos irreducible to any single image.

Allegorical expression—fluid, messy, and plural—is an instance of the "saying," poetic dimension of language. In allowing multiple possibilities for meaning to coexist without canceling one another, allegory is also related to one of the central goals of radical empiricism: to leave room for obscurity and plurality by abandoning the "*all*-form" in favor of the "*each*-form" (PU 34). The shift from "all" to "each" entails giving up totalizing theories and finding ways of attending to idiosyncratic, finite, and impure meanings. James admitted that, in comparison with the majesty of the "*all*-form," the truths of the "*each*-form" would look like "poor scraps [and] mere crumbling successes" (PU 341). Yet James, Guston, Levinas, and Benjamin embrace populated and cluttered landscapes of meaning and move away from purity in all its forms. Each of them emphasizes the haunting traces that seep through every image, the "fringes" of experience and the ambiguous echoes of every face. Writing to Ross Feld about one of his new paintings, Guston said:

> Here in this new picture there is "nothing" to see—except multitudes of masses, that go on forever—in the mind. There is no plane—at all. You could mingle with this crowd, move into it, submerge yourself in it—be part of it. You would hear voices, murmurs, weeping.[32]

Populations overflow the picture, faces crowd in. Guston's paintings evoke the city, the subway, and the streets, Whitman crossing Brooklyn Ferry, Plato's dense cave, Levinas's peopled night. Guston knew that if there was any way of showing the commotion of life, it would have to be another way than by shining a light brightly on one place. James articulated the same insight by incessantly pointing out the overabundance of life beyond every concept we might form of it, writing: "Reality, life, experience, concreteness, immediacy, use what word you will, exceeds our logic, overflows and surrounds it" (PU 212). There is no revelatory lighting—no eternal shining beauty. The lack of any revelatory symbol goes together with the absence of any consoling icon. There is no permanent radiance, just an infinite number of compounding lights burning in our midst.

7. Poetically Certain

In the last pages of *Otherwise Than Being or Beyond Essence*, Levinas poses the following questions: "Can openness have another sense than that of the accessibility of entities through open doors or windows? Can openness have another signification than that of disclosure?" (OB 178–79). Rather than a view, this kind of opening would provide a pervasive sense of something that refuses to become the object of focus. Looking into it would be like trying to see through a thick fog. Merleau-Ponty also thought about a quasi-opening and wondered whether Cubism's shattered forms could teach us about a mode of visibility where we glimpse things indirectly, between cross-sections "like a face in the reeds."[33] Merleau-Ponty describes a visibility by virtue of invisibility, as if the only way for some things to appear at all is to appear as hidden.

The problem is that sometimes the things closest to us are the most hidden, the most opaque, dense and impossible to see. Levinas is ultimately concerned with a more radical opacity than a screen of reeds. James, Levinas, and Guston show that the living space of the world is not transparent, and not everything comes to light. They refute the idea that art has anything to do with a permanent, illuminated, truth, yet they show that art has everything to do with another kind of certainty: a "more instinctual passional propensity" (TT 186) or a "poetic certainty" that might help us turn around to the things and people near us, helping us to navigate without being able to see clearly, through the clutter and the dark.

Levinas used the phrase, "poetically certain," in a short paper he read at a 1966 meeting of the Jeunesse Littéraire de France in memory of Max Picard. Picard was a Swiss writer and philosopher with whom Levinas corresponded periodically. In his address, Levinas explicitly invokes Picard's late work, *The World of Silence* (1952), but Picard published several texts that resonated with Levinas's concerns in the years leading up to and following the war, including *The Human Face* (1930), *The Flight From God* (1934), and *Hitler in Ourselves* (1948). Levinas begins his talk by admitting, "I never met [Picard], but have the impression of having seen his face" (PN 94). He continues: "To me, to speak of Max Picard is almost like invoking an *apparition,* but one that is *strangely real.* That is perhaps the very definition of poetic experience" (PN 94).

"Poetic experience" becomes a guiding thread of Levinas's meditation. Picard was, for Levinas, a vivid presence through the exchange of postcards, letters, and published texts, despite the fact that the two men never crossed paths. They knew each other through their words, through meetings that felt "incomparably acute" (PN 94) in the delivery of a distinctive voice via a seemingly mute page. The strangely intimate presence from a distance leads Levinas to wonder about the nature of this kind of encounter, to wonder how, from his words alone, Picard's "whole self was there in person, facing yours" (PN 94). How did Picard's works deliver his face? Distant and invisible, yet *"strangely real,"* Levinas's correspondence with Picard becomes a living illustration of the proximity Levinas elsewhere seems to reserve for the privileged contact of arriving face to face.

What is the relationship between the soberly ethical straightforwardness of the face to face and the ephemeral poignancy of poetic experience, between the face and a page, a voice and a word? These are questions raised by Picard's work, which Levinas describes as "poetic analysis," adding: "His reading of faces and the world is not always conceptually justifiable, nor phenomenologically convincing. It is poetically certain" (PN 96). These lines might lead one to conclude that Picard's analyses are somehow less rigorous or less truthful than more standard philosophical argumentation. His work is *merely* poetic, beautiful but jejune. But Levinas contests the supposed hierarchy of the clear and distinct over the obscure and opaque, insisting that multiple kinds of value and sources of significance in the world remain irreducible to any overarching, indelible truth.[34] Concepts and theories undoubtedly account for some things, but they cannot accommodate the non-epistemic experiences of transience and vulnerability Levinas associates with the erosive saying of *il y a* and the interruptive expression of a living face. This is not to suggest that a face is a poem, or that poetic certainty translates into ethical certitude. It is only to point out that insofar as anything certain exists at all, it exists provisionally within a narrow register that remains eternally open to revision by the advent of yet another certainty.

Poetic certainty is at odds with conceptualization and with phenomenology, at odds with thought and intentional analysis. Yet, to the degree that it is at odds with attempts to justify or reflect, poetic certainty comes closer to life in its temporal, living complexity. Levinas suggests that reading Picard's work helps one feel more alive, even as it frustrates attempts to judge or to argue. Reflecting on the significance of Picard's "unjustifiable poetry," "on the hither side of the coherent discourse of philosophers," Levinas rhetorically asks: "Are not the fundamental theses on which systems will later rest first imperiously woven like poems . . . ?" (PN 96). These lines recall Levinas's 1947 efforts to articulate a sense (*sens*) prior to and distinct from any settled meaning, "something which is not in its turn an object or a name, which is unnameable and can only appear in poetry" (*il y a quelque chose qui n'est pas, á son tour, un objet, un nom; qui est innommable et ne peut apparaître que par la poésie*) [EE 51 / EaE 91]. Later he warns against "the deafness of hearing only nouns in language" (OB 41). The nominal buckles under the pressures of a verbal, moving force. Something pre-systematic and pre-conceptual animates life beyond anything given, igniting and burning through meaning with a nomadic, poetic sense.

Nothing sturdy crystallizes or accumulates from such bare sense. Instead, instances of poetic certainty complicate, rupture or erode the foundations of accepted truths. This type of certainty is relevant to Guston's pictures, none of which are realistic in the sense of trying to faithfully replicate or represent familiar objects, but all of which have their own distinctive realities. His paintings—wrenching, lonely, sad, funny, arrogant, shy—elicit a mood and can feel like a long exhausting walk, an exuberant cry. Moving among broken bits of the world and witnessing an infinite number of possibilities, pictures and connections, Guston seized on the fragments without claiming recourse to any overarching ideality or sense of a whole. Things were in parts, and the parts were infinitely significant. Talking to a group of art students in 1978 he confessed,

> I must have done hundreds of paintings of shoes, books, hands, buildings and cars, just everyday objects. And the more I did the more mysterious these objects became. The visible world, I think, is abstract and mysterious enough, I don't think one needs to depart from it in order to make art . . . I have a large collection of rusty railroad nails, and they lie around on the table as paper weights. They're big huge nails, and I just nailed one in to a piece of wood. I thought, how would it look *if*. That's a very powerful 'If.'[35]

Guston's paintings awaken a powerful *If* and an ambiguous *il y a:* the sense that things are not as neat or as clear as they once seemed, that the most mundane objects are suddenly dense with possibility, that nothing is resolved. This parallels Levinas's sense of Max Picard's writings—the sudden animation of a thought that becomes viscerally present in its strange, insistent idiosyncrasy, words leaping from the page. These are not descriptions of experiences that are sources of anything as robust as *knowledge;* they are more like intrusions of nonsense into the world of sense, moments when things suddenly flare and sting with an excess of significance. James identified such moments with "the more primitive flux of sensational life" (PU 282), a non-conceptual intimacy with vivid, living realities. Facing a Guston painting, one can have the feeling that *this* is hunger, love, or fatigue. The imagery might look ridiculous, perhaps like a cartoon, but it nonetheless feels *"strangely real"* (PN 94). It's staring back in a form one never imagined, from under Guston's sheet where he and Musa lie.

8. The Expression of Ruins

Appearing only once in Levinas's discourse, the phrase "poetically certain" could be construed as of marginal importance. It might be read as a way of grouping Picard together with other philosophical "poets" Levinas wrote about in the 1960s: Celan, Kierkegaard, Wahl, and Blanchot among them. Yet the phrase could also be applied to the effects of Levinas's own writing as he became increasingly concerned with unsaying the said and finding a style of philosophizing that could enact the essential openness of ethics. The phrase is therefore instructive, not only for expressing the ambiguous reality of Guston's paintings, but for interpreting Levinas and noticing the dramatic, increasing difficulty he had in isolating art from ethics, *il y a* from a face.[36]

Poetic certainty works as an alternative to authenticity and is relevant, perhaps crucial, to ethics insofar as it rekindles meaning in the very moments when one is left in the dark without recognizable patterns, rules or benchmarks. Poetic certainty operates at a sensible level of experience that is tied to emotional responsiveness and the subject's capacity to be moved and exposed; here, certainty is never theoretical or dialectical. In Levinas's language, this is the level of saying which is irreducible to anything said, "a stammering infancy of discourse" (PN 40), a contact or immersion destined to eventual articulation, but as yet undefined. To find oneself opened or made vulnerable by a work of art is not to discover the ethical basis of the self, but it is a reminder that vulnerability takes many forms, that the self comes undone and awakens multiple times in many ways. Levinas is highly sensitive to the dangers of making ethics aesthetic—as if ethics were something from which one might disengage, or gawk at from a distance. But there is an even greater danger in leaving ethics without any emotional impact (or as James put it, without "personal support"), producing a theory that bears no connection with the living feel and unsystematic complexity of life.[37]

Designating art as derivative, merely subjective, or emotive (as opposed to the "objective" truth of brute facts and sure knowledge) misconstrues the intricacy and value of aesthetic experience, a pervasive experience with its own dignity and indeed, as Gadamer insisted, its own truth.[38] Levinas, though he retained an ambivalence about art and a distrust of the seductive lure of beauty, also wrote about the worth of many kinds of truths and saw in modernity a *hopeful* transition: "The end of a certain *intelligibility* but the dawning of a new

one. . . . [the] coming to a close [of] a rationality tied *exclusively* to . . . truth in
the form of unchanging identities . . . complete, perfect" (PN 4–5). Years before, James expressed a similar hope for a transition away from absolutes,
which aimed at "cleaning up the litter with which the world apparently is
filled" (PU 45), and toward life in its sensible tangle. James anticipated a transition that Levinas subsequently lived. The ruptures of the twentieth century
carried with them the challenge to re-conceive meaning outside the paradigms
of a resolution or a happy end.[39] Truth, if the word could be retained, would
henceforth have to include the non-identical, the fragmentary, and the marred.
In addition to new models of truth, Levinas also noted the critical importance
of allowing for many kinds of "facts," obliquely invoking Wahl's "transdescendence" as he proclaimed: "Alongside the mathematization of facts, by tracing
them upward to the level of form, there is the *schematization* (in the Kantian
sense) of intelligibles by the descent into sensibility. Formal, pure concepts,
when put to the test in the concrete, the impure, resonate (or reason) differently, and take on new meanings."[40] Plunged back into the adulterated flux of
life, concepts lose their pristine luster; the Platonic forms deform. Rather than
interpreting this descent as degenerative or as the nihilistic abdication of any
possibility for meaning, Levinas saw the birth of new, more intimate and deli-
cate registers of meaning, each of them kindling their own precarious sense.
Without a doubt, multiplicity can breed ambiguity and confusion, but confusion can breed questions that provoke greater subtlety and new dimensions of
understanding.[41] Simone de Beauvoir, despite her disputes with Levinas, defended the "positive value of ambiguity," even as she recognized the deep-
seated resistance to allowing ambiguity to contaminate ethics. "As long as
there have been men and they have lived," she urged, "they have all felt [the]
tragic ambiguity of their condition, but as long as there have been philosophers
and they have thought, most of them tried to mask it."[42] For philosophy to resonate with both life and thought, it will have to extend beyond the bounds of
cool analysis and the production of ever more static theories. This may require
increasingly experimental, creative ways of thinking and writing and an openness to reason that refuses to conform to the dominant models of rationality.

Throughout these pages I have argued for the minimalism and radical empiricism of Levinas's ethics, an ethics devoted to sociality and plurality and

devoid of abstract principles. I have also argued that hearing this aspect of Levinas's philosophy requires listening to the distinctive quality of his voice as he gives it to us in his syntax, rhythms, images, and examples.

Levinas and James, despite their significantly different personalities, share a commitment to the human and the mere, the fleeting and the fragmentary. Both of them ask us to reevaluate our preconceptions about meaning and to recalibrate our expectations about what ethics is or includes. Ultimately, they insist that ethics is much less lofty and secure than anything that might be inscribed in stone or put into practice in the same way across every situation, time after time. An ethical *theory* devoid of nuance and sensitivity to particularities poses its own dangers and leads to its own violence. Of course, the lure of such a picture of ethics remains immensely powerful, not least because it promises stability and encourages the picture of moral progress toward an ideal ethical state, a vision of overcoming and perfectibility that finds deep anchorage in the human psyche. Neither Levinas nor James would argue that one cannot improve, change, or lead an increasingly good life, but both of them remind us that *progress,* whatever it might mean, cannot be a rectilinear, one-way ascent (however arduous) toward the absolute. The lessons learned today may be useless tomorrow, requiring not simply the elaboration of a rule already in place, but the radical rethinking of every rule. True ruptures—what Kierkegaard would call *ordeals*—require unpredictable, unpracticed response. As James noted in characteristically practical terms, "every real dilemma is in literal strictness a unique situation; and the exact combination of ideals realized and ideals disappointed which each decision creates is always a universe without precedent."[43] In Levinas's language, "unique situations" impose an ethical responsibility to relinquish one's self-assured defenses in order to stay awake to the interruption of new faces. In addition to climbing toward the bright light at the mouth of the cave, we also have to learn how to descend into the dark and move among the shadows. This version of ethics provides a more realistic account of what it means to move and to live in a densely populated landscape rife with ambiguities, endless ups and downs.

Relinquishing the Hegelian model of a march toward the ideal, we inherit a much less concise, less elegant portrait of ethics. We are also left without archetypes and idols that might stand for all time—yet this is not to lose anything that we actually possessed in the first place. Through the dimmer illumination and chaotic staging, a host of genuine sources of significance nonetheless persist. Some of them are faces interrupting every order, contesting the circumscription of ethics within any single frame. Some are impure, awkward or opaque works like Guston's paintings, contesting the dominant trends and art historical models with a steady murmur of protest, saying *no* to the stark alternatives between abstraction and figuration, saying *history is not yet written,* saying *il y a.*[44]

This chapter began with Guston and the rupture of Modernism's quest to render painting pure. Guston exemplifies a swerve in the trajectory of painting, or rather a *volte-face* toward the opaque and the disheveled and a renunciation of beauty and sublimity as the only—or the best—artistic ideals. Art, like ethics, is perpetually tempted by the powerful paradigm of progressive overcoming, the majestic sweep of the new surpassing the old. But Guston, like Levinas and James, shows that progress need not preclude particularity or commit one to the service of an impersonal historical movement or an abstract ideal.

Guston's paintings are visual instances of a radically empirical phenomenology. They illustrate the precarious balancing act between sense and nonsense, description and evasion, the "saying" and the "said," that is also at work in Levinas's late texts. They exemplify a focus on the human that is not the focus on any simple, recognizable, beautiful or pacifying representation. They show us life in its living ambiguity, in its densely populated and complicated landscapes—cluttered and overwhelming, deserted and alien. Guston helps us look at Levinas and see his descriptions as visually urgent, helping us to encounter imagery by other means than through some myopic gaze that claims to encompass "the whole." Conversely, seeing Guston in light of Levinas's incessant invocation of the neglected and the abandoned reveals the ethical force of Guston's pictures and his own focus on a fragmented, distorted, and crumbling world that is perpetually threatened by violence and war. Guston gives us another way of thinking about a world in pieces and the tenuous, ever-shifting connections that holding things in relation. His pictures show a minimal but critical resistance to violence, the anti-heroism of a merely human capacity to continue working—digging through the rubble, groping on the canvas, and facing things one at a time— a resistance that is the minimal work and hope of ethics.

Neither James nor Levinas gives us a coherent ethical theory or an archetypal aesthetic model; Guston does not give us realistic pictures. They give us something else. The value of their projects might best be described in terms of the feeling they each inspire that without clarity, truth, form, and beauty, there

FIGURE 5.
Philip Guston. *Entrance*, 1979. Oil on canvas.
68 × 80 inches / 172.7 × 203.2 cm.
Centre George Pompidou. *Permission granted by*
The McKee Gallery, New York, N.Y.

is still meaningful expression—even if it is expression in ruins. Their works attest to the fact that progress might be indefinite, incremental, and discrete—a series of detours that never leads to any final destination, but a series of detours that still leaves open and alive the ongoing labor of both art and ethics. The image of this alternative version of progress is not a linear path but a deepening spiral, an ongoing revolution. They also show the insufficiency of any single work to be the only or the final work. In this sense, they each lend something to one another and leave open spaces for future, ongoing work. Levinas and James help us glean the ethical importance of the fragmentary in Guston's pictures, and Guston helps us hear the literary and poetic ambiguities of Levinas's and James's texts. We need them all—and then we need to put down our books and seek out *in life* the pictures that sit flatly on the page, the faces we still cannot imagine. Life can look surreal—real *beyond* real. An image can strike a chord; a face can ring out. This doesn't last, but it leaves a wake of sound, a ringing trace in which life is lived. And just as suddenly things revert—the world intervenes, *il y a* returns, possibility turns into impossibility, impossibility to possibility—another interruption, infinite ends, and another face—one more beginning.

AFTERWORD

i.

To come all this way and arrive at the mere expression of ruins is to arrive with very little in one's hands. Poems, paintings, and the "passional" have none of the solidity of axiomatic truths or first principles—so what remains? Is this all we're left with—insomnia, a face shifting expressions in a horizon-less close-up, phenomenology failing to give us the things themselves (but nonetheless failing *to fail*)—the pluralist and chaotic mixture James called "radical empiricism," fragments that don't organize into any lasting whole, a sense of life that exceeds all our efforts to speak or describe—Guston's paintings of junk, the un-heroic hope of *il y a* returning to bring something out of nothing—is that all? Temporary definitions and pervasive ambiguities, imperfect pearls and flickering lights—is that all?

Perhaps.

Near the beginning of "The Origin of the Work of Art," Heidegger describes soldiers packing poems in their backpacks as they head off for war.[1] His remark comes in a line of examples through which he demonstrates the familiarity of works of art and the way they can be like mere things or equipment. A painting can hang on the wall, "like a rifle or a hat."[2] Yet he doesn't ask *why* the soldiers pack poems. Why does Levinas recall Baudelaire when he is being held in a labor camp in France, in 1945? Why does he spend his lifetime writing about the ambiguous and nonetheless meaningful expression of the human face during a century in which it has also been the face of atomic desolations, truly global wars, multiple genocides, and torture? Poems, paintings, and films are not the "hard truth"—yet they, like human faces, are also the real stuff of life. They provide encounters that can weaken universals and reintroduce details, messy and particular, into scenes where such details have been overlooked and damage has been called, simply, "collateral." In the trenches in World War I, Max Beckmann carried a small notebook and a few drawing materials in his pack. Crouching in the dirt, he wrote: "Every so often the thunder of canons sounds in the distance. I sit alone, as I so often do. Ugh, this unending void whose foreground we constantly have to fill with stuff of some sort or another in order not to notice its horrifying depth."[3] Beckmann returned from the war to make paintings of figures outlined in heavy black. In painting, he kept the void at bay, drawing an unmistakable boundary around every human form—holding the dark to the edge.

ii.

Levinas might have contested the trajectory of this book, which began with ethical insomnia and arrives at a painting by Philip Guston. James, although likely to have been more forgiving, also worried about the seductive and potentially anaesthetizing threat of art early in his career.[4] But unlike Levinas, James was himself a painter and increasingly emphasized the role of art in moral education, culminating in his poetry- and literature-riddled *Talks to Teachers on Psychology: And to Students on Some of Life's Ideals.* Both James and Levinas openly blurred the lines between ethics and aesthetics in their own texts, providing philosophy with alternative models of writing and new modes of discourse. Levinas, in particular, leaves us with complicated, unfinished work. The ongoing debates about how best to situate or describe him—whether he should to be categorized as a phenomenologist, an ethicist, a theologian; a post-structuralist, a modernist, a classicist; "a Jew, a Greek"—underscore the complexity of his legacy and the unique anxiety he produces among philosophers of various types. It is unclear to which tradition Levinas most belongs. This makes it difficult to employ him in any particular battle over philosophical territory or to claim him as one's own. While some see this as proof of Levinas's philosophical irrelevance, I see it as a welcome challenge to philosophical categories, an invitation to new ways of thinking, and the opening of new frontiers. Levinas's work is one place to begin thinking about the future of philosophy and to ask whether the future will be determined by the arguments, positions, and divisions of the past—or whether it might move in unforeseen, unexpected, chaotic, creative, and pluralistic directions.

My goal has been to defend Levinas's notion of ethical responsibility as both philosophically convincing and relevant in our own time, while at the same time contesting interpretations of his ethics that depict it as being impersonal, impractical or anti-aesthetic. This has involved deflating some expectations about what Levinas promises or delivers and venturing suggestions that move beyond the letter of his texts. It has also involved recalibrating his most recognizable terms and phrases. I realize that for those who see Levinas as a prophet and stand in awe of his work, my text may seem irreverent. Conversely, for those who see Levinas as an incomprehensible mystic my work may seem effusive. I hope that a healthy dose of irreverence mixed with genuine admiration might help us get to work on Levinas in ways that move beyond defense and attack, praise and insult—helping us see Levinas as neither angel nor beast so that we might work with him on a more minimal, practical, and indeed, human scale. He made this human scale the focus of his life's work; the interpersonal is the very interval which inspired and guided his thought.

I have not attempted to describe, systematically or comprehensively, Levinas's project as a whole, to pay him undo homage or to defend him from every attack. Neither have I attempted a sweeping investigation of James that might take into account every subtlety and tension in his philosophy. I have argued that such attempts would be self-defeating from the beginning, since Levinas's and James's works are characterized, in both form and content, by a deliberate and chaotic pluralism that is resistant to summation or reduction. The aesthetic dimension of their prose plays a crucial role in deflecting efforts to simplify their thought. Reading them requires a hermeneutic sensitivity to their style and imagery, to their distinctive voices and art. Their texts thereby demonstrate the futility of making any hard and fast separation between content and form or between ethics and art. In particular, Levinas's slippage between *il y a* and a face shows the impossibility of any stark differentiation, while his poetic prose illustrates the necessity of honing an ear for the transcendence of words that is integral to hearing the "saying" of others.

Instead of comprehensive overviews, I have tried to expose an instructive convergence of French and American thought through the intersection of

Levinas and James (with an additional bridge provided by Bergson). The correspondence between James and Bergson stands as one example of the dynamic connection and promising interchange between America and France in the decades preceding a Continental/Analytic divide.[5] Seeing the influence of these thinkers on Levinas might help us recapture that spirit and envision new possibilities for the deployment of both phenomenology and pragmatism. The relationship between Levinas and James, in particular, helps to change how we read Levinas's imagery, reminding us of the centrality of bodily, lived experience in his work, which in turn evinces the pragmatic minimalism of his ethics. This intersection also helps emphasize the ethical implications of James's radical empiricism, demonstrating the ongoing and underappreciated relevance of his philosophy for contemporary ethical debates. Seen in light of Jamesian pluralism, we find that Levinas is not an impractical, mystical thinker of passivity, but a pragmatic and minimalist thinker of the interhuman. The radically empirical dimension of his thought changes his lineage in the history of philosophy and shows the way forward to a pragmatic phenomenology that takes cues from both Levinas and James—showing the way to more creative, pluralistic modes of engagement and philosophizing.

In the process of comparing Levinas's radical phenomenology with James's radical empiricism, I have moved from the trauma that is definitive of the displaced subject in the first chapter toward the myriad sources of hope, including poetry and painting, that are definitive of a pluralistic, social world. These sources are "faces," very broadly construed—sites of humanization. They are destabilizing interruptions, but also instances of buoyancy through which life feels more urgent, full, or alive. Responding to such instances with careful, nonviolent attention and staying awake to their indeterminate possibilities is a way of being human and becoming increasingly humane. Of course, aesthetic sensitivity does not simply translate into ethical vigilance. But Levinas and James invite us to expand our conceptions of attentiveness and widen our sense of significance so that we might become increasingly sensitive to and responsible for others. As James stressed: "We ought, all of us, to realize each other in this intense, pathetic, and important way" (TT 267). Faces provide incessant reminders that the world includes more than any single perspective, thought, or experience might encompass, reminders of the surplus of sociality over solitude. Every face is a new chance and a new risk. The more we widen the possibilities for the face to face—moving (as Levinas insists) from literal faces, to the nape of a neck, to Rodin's chiseled arm, and then (beyond Levinas) to the "face" of words, of paintings, landscapes, and animals—the more chance and risk the world contains. One becomes more or less alive to the world depending on one's ability to be impacted by and exposed to life in its precarious and multifarious forms, to hear the call of faces even when—or perhaps especially when—one cannot discern any familiar face.

The hyperbole of Levinas's nearly baroque language and traumatic imagery might seem glaringly at odds with any variety of minimalism, but pointing out the mere and the ordinary requires an extraordinary method. James knew this, as he injected his writing with metaphoric imagery, literary references, and poetic expression—at the same time worrying that his readers might find his texts "too bottomless and romantic."[6] More recently, Stanley Cavell discovered the paradox of trying to show the banal and the prevalent, realizing that his own "quest [for] the ordinary" entailed "romantic orientations and transgressions" in order to arrive at "a perception of the weirdness, or surrealism, of what we call, accept, adapt to, as the usual, the real."[7] This was also something Guston discovered, using every trick up his sleeve, every color at his disposal to paint a sandwich or a shoe.

The things closest to us recede into the background of our routines, while the things most distant seem impossibly foreign and far off. Succumbing to this polarizing alternative between the near and the far, the real and the unreal, can become a way of excusing oneself from the tasks at hand no less than those on the horizon, the former because they are too mundane to be concerned with and the later because they are too far in the future to require immediate work. The tendency to miss the ordinary because it is too close and to privilege the extraordinary because it seems foreign enough to be entirely separate (thereby requiring nothing of us) mirrors the tendency to reserve ethics for a crisis, for life and death situations. A fixation on the exceptional is the basis of most thought experiments and "moral philosophical" puzzles that ask one to imagine shocking scenarios: whether to save one child on the train tracks if it means killing all the passengers in an oncoming train, etc.[8] This is very unlikely to occur in anyone's life, and if such a crisis were to arise, it would be infinitely more complicated than any thought experiment could anticipate. Every experience and every ethical crisis is, as James expressed it, "a unique situation." For James, this means that ethics must be "ready to revise its conclusions from day to day" and that books about ethics should "more ally themselves with a literature which is confessedly tentative and suggestive rather than dogmatic."[9] It is the nature of tragedy to rupture the imaginable with the sudden appearance of the unimaginable; it is, therefore, futile to spend one's life preparing for tragedy. Nevertheless, such "preparation" grips the imagination and allows one to bracket more immediate duties or problems in order to focus on an impending crisis. Entertaining the risk of future, mythic disasters can have a strangely consoling, even liberating effect.[10]

Minimalist ethics requires both more and less than an extravagant ethics based on hypothetical puzzles or future catastrophes. It requires more because it entails paying ongoing attention to the present moment in all its complexity and conflicting demands. Attending to the barrage of daily life can be exhausting and often unsatisfying as one discovers an endless parade of faces requiring response, and as one realizes that the work of ethics will never be done. It requires less, because it does not ask for heroic self-sacrifice or ultimate decisions that will instantaneously alter or affect the course of one's own life or the lives of others. Nothing dramatic happens if one fails to hold the door. No one dies if one fails to say "hello." Yet the cumulative, long-term effects of such failures—one by one, day after day—erode the fragile fabric of civil humanity and can lead, imperceptibly and suddenly, to widespread blindness, egotism, violence, and brutality. Daily instances of turning away deaden one to new faces, letting the world fall increasingly silent and wane more lifeless.

iii.

No single face is the last irruption of humanity in the world. Yet there are particular faces one might remember or recall with unique clarity or frequency. Others recede and change. Not one of them will be the last one. Many of them will remain images, faces seen in the newspaper, a movie, on the web or on television. Some of them will be the ones we can't imagine because we can't forget them. All of them, intimate and distant, will make up a loose, shifting world that is never the whole world.

We can give up the whole without giving up anything, since the *whole* was nothing to begin with. It has been philosophy's pretension to see things from on high and to discover for them "solving names," to use James's phrase.[11] Levinas and James ask us to give up this fixation on the end and the summit; but it is hard to learn how to give things up. This is one reason for reading

Levinas and James. They give us fragments, and compared to any grand theory or complete narrative, their fragments look like ruins. How does one move amid ruins?

Levinas gives us some practical advice. In "Nameless" (originally published in 1966 as "Honneur sans Drapeau") he writes that there are "three truths that are transmissible and necessary to the new generation" (PN 120), a generation postdating World War II. These "truths" are (1) the reality that, "to live humanly we need infinitely fewer things," (2) the conviction that "in crucial times, when the perishability of so many values is revealed, all human dignity consists in believing in their return," and (3) the necessity of teaching "the new generations the strength necessary to be strong in isolation." Elaborating this third truth, he insists we must revive "the memory of those who, non-Jews and Jews, without even knowing or seeing one another, found a way to behave amidst total chaos as if the world had not fallen apart" (PN 121). In the midst of the most brutal times, these are the instances of individuals who found a way, despite everything, to behave decently. Paul Steinberg remembers such acts of decency in his memoir of life in Auschwitz, noting in particular a group of Czech laborers who tossed their lunches into the car of a passing train packed with Jewish prisoners. "To those workers and their descendents," Steinberg writes, "I dedicate these lines, for that unstinting generosity towards their fellowmen who had suffered utter barbarity. I could feel their warmth come down to us with their bread."[12]

Levinas leaves many things undone; we should not underestimate what there is to do. But we should also not feel overwhelmed by being responsible for everything, because this "everything" is limited by the time which we have. In most cases, what we can do or accomplish will be less than ideal. Yet Levinas argues that precisely this is the margin of ethics, the margin of the human. Ethics works at the level of the ordinary—and Levinas insists all along that it can be summed up by the two words, "After you." It's surprising how hard it is to leave the "you" unqualified—to leave this minimal ambiguity. It is surprising how hard it is to leave that opening open to every face.

iv.

In the preface I suggested that reading Levinas is timely. I want to close with a few more suggestions about why we should read Levinas together with

James today. I don't think Levinas delivers the promise I saw when I first read *Totality and Infinity,* but I was looking for too much then. Both Levinas and James can seem like poor or insufficient resources against all-embracing theories that say how to live and how to behave. Their work deals with the level of the person and the personal. They have nothing to say about a definitive worldview beyond saying that in principle there can be no such thing, no ultimate coherence bringing all the pieces together. We live in a loose and shifting environment of different meanings that do not and cannot coalesce. Ethics as Levinas describes it is just an ability to move among shifting pieces without attempting to wedge them together or break them further apart. The basic phenomenological gesture of Levinas's work entails a return—but to a *person,* as she is, in all her opaque complexity.

Levinas has often been criticized for failing to describe how we move from the interpersonal realm between two people (face to face) to the realm where there are more than two (justice and the third party [*le tiers*]).[13] One criticism stems from Levinas's own political views concerning Israel and Palestine, with particular emphasis placed on his infamous 1982 radio interview, "Ethics and Politics," where he seemed "evasive" when asked about responsibility in light of the massacre of Palestinian refugees at the camps at Sabra and Shalita that took place just two weeks prior, in September 1982.[14] Concerns about this aspect of Levinas revolve around questioning whether *every* other has a face and whether Levinas was himself able to embody, or to *face,* the ethical responsibility he articulated. Another criticism of Levinas is that the situation he focuses on is relatively simple compared to the populous world of politics, the world we actually inhabit. This claim goes: it's easy enough to respond to *one* other person, but such radical responsibility falls apart when there are many others. The attention to particularity is unsustainable. When there are many faces, doesn't one have to look through them to see the greater good?

This is a serious criticism, one that exposes a limitation of Levinas's ethics. There is no neat story about how to weigh conflicting demands or how to deal with competing faces. Levinas's ethics is the beginning of a conversation that will inevitably need elaboration into morality and politics—a "saying" that tends toward a "said." And yet, morality and politics do not replace or negate the necessity of ethics, which challenges every system with personal idiosyncrasies and individual, ambiguous *sens.* In the age of globalization we are confronted with many more faces, and with this comes the sobering reality that actions taken on behalf of one group frequently, if not always, work against the interests of another group. The world has become smaller, and various actions or inactions in one part of the planet reverberate more strongly across a globe of interconnected economies, conflicts, markets, and resources. The ability to communicate across vast distances has enabled a global network with many advantages, but it has also enabled and exacerbated predominantly faceless interaction: instant messaging, email, texting, social networking sites, and lives lived in the virtual realities of *Second Life,* video games, and online chatrooms. One can, with these tools, live a social life devoid of human contact—an increasingly disembodied, fantastic, and ultimately solitary existence.

In this atmosphere, reading Levinas and James can return us to the significance of living interaction with actual (not virtual) others. The reminder of flesh and blood need not be a techno-phobic or anachronistic return to a simpler, distant time—a dream of a world gone by. Instead, it can be the injection of living complexity, interaction, and healthy ambiguity into potentially alienating routines and practices that allow us to avoid others (other people, other animals, other places) or to meet them only on our own terms. Philosophically, the aspects I have highlighted in Levinas's and James's thought—the personal, the pragmatic, and the poetic—reanimate the contours of a discipline that is perpetually at risk of falling out of touch with life. The separation of philosophy and life was one of James's primary concerns as he decried "a certain insincerity in our philosophic discussions" (P 11) and pleaded for more openness and tolerance. This included tolerance for increasingly creative methods of writing philosophy, and for the philosophical significance of things like religious and aesthetic experience, that might defy rationalization and categorization. Outside of philosophy, the personal, the pragmatic, and the poetic are uniquely demanding facets of life, requiring work that cannot be exhaustively learned or automatically enacted. The world still requires personal intervention, creativity, and expression—despite a host of tools at our disposal for quickly sorting through, digesting, and dealing with information.

This is why, despite the lack of a political theory that one might wish to extract from Levinas's ethics, there is a practical mandate coincident with his focus on the face—a mandate to expose oneself bodily to the world, to leave the safe confines of one's home and go out into the midst of crowds. It is also a mandate to turn around to those who are close, to begin where you are and work from there. Reflecting on the distinctively Jewish aspects of a commitment to the here and now, Levinas offered: "One can choose utopia. On the other hand . . . one can choose not to flee the conditions from which one's work draws its meaning and remain here below. And that means choosing ethical action." He continued: "This action does not tackle the Whole in a global and magical way, but grapples with the particular" (DF 100). James also emphasized the degree to which the particular demands attention, even if it looks insignificant relative to a more global picture. Unlike Levinas, James verbalized a political counterpart to his radical empiricism, calling it "democratic" insofar as it allows room for multiple perspectives and sees things from the ground up rather than the top down. James was, however, critical of any blanket endorsement of a political system or theory, insisting that "democracy, liberty, etc., dwindle when realized in their sordid particulars" (PU 341). Similarly, Levinas asked: "Do not [ideas] run the perpetual risk of alienation in the purely political game? Can democracy and the 'rights of man' divorce themselves without danger from their prophetic and ethical depths?" (BV xv). The ideal may be well and good, but put to the test in concrete cases, things become infinitely more complicated. Practically speaking, this is one reason why exporting democracy will always be problematic and prone to failure. The political counterpart to a pluralistic ethics that remains at the level of the particular and the face to face is, roughly, the sort of grass roots politics that focuses on working from the ground up, taking responsibility for and within a confined community. It is a form of politics that is not so defined by intimacy that it can't accommodate more than two people at a time—and yet, it retains a sense of intimacy and scale without which policy becomes radically indifferent to particularity.

Levinas does not show the simplistic clarity of the face to face but its essential, complex ambiguity. It is, therefore, not a question of moving from a simple situation toward an increasingly complex one. It is a question of two complexities: the complexity of the personal and the complexity of the impersonal. Both require navigation. Both require focus. Faces are lights in the dark, but the dark is very dark, and nothing is simple, not even the face closest and most intimate to you—the one you think you have known forever. Nothing is simple, and Levinas turns us back to that essential lack of simplicity in the very place where we are most apt to take simplicity for granted.

At the end of each day comes another night; out of the dark of each night dawns a new day. The world lacks closure. Faces personally attest to that infinite opening. *Il y a* interrupts with the impersonal transcendence of transcendence, the sometimes devastating and sometimes saving surprise of "more." There is a rupture of a new singularity after the last singularity; a new heart beats after the last pulse of a weathered heart. Each one is incomparable and incomparably worthy. As Bergson taught, "All moments count. None of them has the right to set itself up as a moment that represents or dominates the others" (CE 332). The only way to proceed among an infinite number of infinities, an infinite number of faces rising all around us, is to proceed, as much as we can, particularly, one at a time, from *this* to *this* without getting ahead of ourselves, without ever getting (as Hegel nobly tried to lead us) from *this* to *that*. Perhaps thought tends toward "solving names," but life includes tendencies that are less precise and distinct than we can sum up in any name. Levinas looked to the shadows, while James focused on the fringes trailing indefinitely at the edge of every experience. The ambiguity that might seem suspect or even threatening to some is also the source of opening that allows philosophy to resonate more deeply with experience, with emotion, with art, and with life.

In challenging us to be more sensitized to and tolerant of life in multiple forms, Levinas and James ask us to seek ways of living in greater intimacy with one another and our world. Accepting this challenge entails subjecting oneself to the risks inherent in any intimate relation. Such risks can be substantial. But foregoing the challenge means missing the adventure, the heights and depths that imbue life with, in James's words, "sensational tang" (PP 2: 712). To hold onto a narrow vision of philosophy, of what it can accomplish, what it might be or what it might yet become, is to risk missing the novel, idiosyncratic, and creative ways thought is capable of moving in tandem with a perpetually moving world. Incrementally, carefully, philosophy can proceed with less rigidity and with more vulnerability—becoming further exposed to the pluralities and intricacies that challenge every theory with another surprising jolt of life.

NOTES

Preface

1. Levinas opens his preface to *Totality and Infinity* with this line: "Everyone will readily agree that it is of the highest importance to know whether we are not duped by morality" (TI 21).

2. One of the most glaring examples of the critical seizure of *Totality and Infinity* comes in Alain Badiou's *Ethics*. In the first note to his second chapter, Badiou cites *Totality and Infinity* and follows the citation with the decisive line: "This is [Levinas's] major work." Badiou's subsequent critique suffers from his lack of engagement with any of Levinas's other works. Alain Badiou, *Ethics: An Essay on the Understanding of Evil*, trans. Peter Hallward (London and New York: Verso, 2001), 29.

3. This is not to suggest that important work has not been done relative to each text. In particular, Bettina Bergo, Fabio Ciaramelli, Simon Critchley, John Drabinski, Jean Greisch, and Adriaan Peperzak (among others, but exemplary for their detailed analyses) have extensively investigated *Otherwise Than Being or Beyond Essence,* while Robert Bernasconi both introduced the English translation and argued for the importance of *Existence and Existents.*

4. Bettina Bergo provides a helpful overview of four different conceptions of the transition from *Totality and Infinity* to *Otherwise Than Being or Beyond Essence,* detailing the positions of Sephan Stasser, Étienne Feron, Fabio Ciaramelli, and Adriaan Peperzak. See Bettina Bergo, *Levinas Between Ethics and Politics: For the Beauty that Adorns the Earth* (Dordrecht: Kluwer, 1999), 134–47.

5. As Michael Morgan writes, *Otherwise Than Being or Beyond Essence* is emblematic of "philosophical growth and development and not as a fundamental reorientation or rejection of earlier views." Michael L. Morgan, *Discovering Levinas* (Cambridge: Cambridge University Press, 2007), xvii.

6. This is similar to the hope Hilary Putnam finds in John Dewey, calling it "a strategic optimism . . . we badly need in the present time." It is also bears comparison to the "prophetic pragmatism" Cornell West describes as navigating between "Sisyphean pessimism and utopian perfectionism." Hilary Putnam, *Ethics Without On-*

tology (Cambridge, Mass.: Harvard University Press, 2006), 11; and Cornell West, *The American Evasion of Philosophy: A Genealogy of Pragmatism* (Madison: University of Wisconsin Press, 1989), 215.

7. "(We) say, before an open door, 'After you, sir!' It is an original 'After you, sir!' that I have tried to describe." Emmanuel Levinas, *Ethics and Infinity: Conversations with Philippe Nemo,* trans. Richard A. Cohen (Pittsburgh: Duquesne University Press, 1985), 89.

8. Derrida famously asserts Levinas's empiricism at the close of "Violence and Metaphysics," claiming that he "totally renews empiricism, and inverses it by revealing it to itself as metaphysics" (VM 151). Robert Bernasconi, contesting Theodore De Boer's transcendental reading of the face, has also written about the complex intertwining of the transcendental and the empirical in *Totality and Infinity,* arguing: "Levinas does not choose between them or attempt to reconcile them. They remain irreducible moments of the logically absurd structure of the *anterior posteriori*." See Robert Bernasconi, "Re-Reading *Totality and Infinity*," in *The Question of the Other,* ed. Alreen B. Dallery and Charles E. Scott (Albany: State University of New York Press, 1989), 31–32. Additionally, John Llewelyn describes and defends what he calls (borrowing from Rosenzweig) the "absolute empiricism" of *Totality and Infinity.* See John Llewelyn, *Emmanuel Levinas: The Genealogy of Ethics* (London: Routledge, 1995), 112–15. I am indebted to all of this previous work, yet in following a link with James's radical empiricism I suggest a version of Levinasian empiricism that has been left, as yet, unconsidered.

9. The link has not been examined before. But one should note that Henry Samuel Levinson, in his introduction to *A Pluralistic Universe,* writes that "James makes way for an account of the ethical and spiritual life that prefigures contemporary works like Emmanuel Levinas's *Totality and Infinity*" (PU xii). Similarly, in the introduction to *Totality and Infinity,* John Wilde writes: "The radical empiricists who, since the time of William James, have doubted that the methods of transcendental idealism fit the patterns of experience, will find much supporting evidence in this work" (TI 12). These are fruitful suggestions, but neither Levinson nor Wilde elaborates the connection.

10. Jacques Derrida, *Adieu to Emmanuel Levinas,* trans. Pascale-Anne Brault and Michael Naas (Stanford: Stanford University Press, 1999), 12.

11. Sandra B. Rosenthal and Patrick L. Bourgeois, *Pragmatism and Phenomenology: A Philosophic Encounter* (Amsterdam: B. R. Grüner, 1980), 4.

12. This is the gist of Rorty's criticism: what Levinas describes is not "ethics" in any meaningful (i.e., *practical*) sense of the term. See Richard Rorty, "Response to Simon Critchley," in Mouffe, ed., *Deconstruction and Pragmatism,* 41–46.

13. Notable exceptions include Richard Bernstein and Hilary Putnam, who have each made Levinas the subject of significant work.

14. Dominique Janicaud, "The Theological Turn of French Phenomenology," trans. Bernard G. Prusak, in *Phenomenology and the "Theological Turn": The French Debate* (New York: Fordham University Press, 2000).

15. Bettina Bergo surveys several new directions in Levinas scholarship in the preface to the recent paperback edition of her *Levinas Between Ethics and Politics,* ix–xli. Peter Atterton and Matthew Calarco have also collected an impressive array of "third wave" essays that explore the socio-political implications of Levinas's work and its fu-

ture implications. See *Radicalizing Levinas,* ed. Peter Atterton and Matthew Calarco (Albany: State University of New York Press, forthcoming).

1. Insomnia

The epigraph is from "The Boast of Quietness," trans. Stephen Kessler (© 1999 by Maria Kodama), from Jorge Luis Borges, *Selected Poems,* ed. Alexander Coleman (New York and London: Penguin, 2000). Used by permission of Viking Penguin.

1. Levinas's critique of Heidegger centers almost exclusively on *Being and Time,* and therefore emphasizes (and critiques) Dasein's *"Being-free for* the freedom of choosing itself and taking hold of itself" (BT 232). This notion of freedom leads immediately into Heidegger's accounts of anxiety and authenticity: "Authenticity brings Dasein face to face with its *Being-free for . . .* the authenticity of its Being" (BT 232). For Levinas's own account of "finite freedom," see OB 121–29 and GDT 176–79. For one detailed account of Heidegger and Levinas in relation, see Tina Chanter, *Time, Death, and the Feminine: Levinas with Heidegger* (Stanford: Stanford University Press, 2001).

2. Keats explains "negative capability" as "when a man is capable of being in uncertainties, Mysteries, doubts, without any irritable reaching after fact and reason." John Keats, letter to George and Tom Keats, 21/27 December 1817, included in *Selected Letters of John Keats,* ed. Grant Scott (Cambridge, Mass.: Harvard University Press, 2002), 60.

3. Critchley concludes: "In short, the Levinasian subject is a traumatic neurotic." Simon Critchley, *Infinitely Demanding: Ethics of Commitment, Politics of Resistance* (London and New York: Verso, 2007), 61. While acknowledging Levinas's own suspicion of psychoanalysis, Critchley advances a reading of Levinasian subjectivity in light of Freud's late theory of the death-drive, and more recently, in terms of Lacan. See his "The Original Traumatism: Levinas and Psychoanalysis," in Simon Critchley, *Ethics, Politics, Subjectivity: Essays on Derrida, Levinas and Contemporary French Thought* (London and New York: Verso, 1999), 183–97.

4. Gilles Deleuze, *The Fold: Leibniz and the Baroque,* trans. Tom Conley (Minneapolis: University of Minnesota Press, 1993), 5.

5. Jean-Paul Sartre and Benny Lévy, *Hope Now: The 1980 Interviews,* trans. Adrian van den Hoven (Chicago: University of Chicago Press, 1996), 71.

6. Ibid., 68.

7. See, for example, Taylor's concern about a "forgetting of self which aspires beyond human powers." Charles Taylor, *Sources of the Self: The Making of the Modern Identity* (Cambridge: Cambridge University Press, 1989), 533 n. 66.

8. Paul Davies, who has done tremendous work on the structure of Levinas's prose, explains that this turning "determines [*Otherwise Than Being*'s] tropes, prefigures its figures. Think of the extraordinary syntax, the series of names (substitution, obsession, responsibility, trauma, psychosis, hostage, one-for-the-other, etc.), each replaced and interrupted by the others before it can harden into a theme, a definition, or a term." Davies insists that the method of writing Levinas employs enacts the ethical responsibility he describes. But he also questions the difficulty of Levinas's language and thereby the responsibility, asking: "If, from the first, Levinas's 'ethics' can be written as an 'ethical empiricism,' written with reference to the real, the non-philosophical, the empirical, then how are we to begin to justify the extraordinary difficulty of

his language?" Paul Davies, "On Resorting to an Ethical Language," in *Ethics as First Philosophy: The Significance of Emmanuel Levinas for Philosophy, Literature and Religion,* ed. Adriaan T. Peperzak (New York and London: Routledge, 1995), 96, 103.

9. Insomnia is one Levinas's obsessions, from his 1935 essay "On Escape" (*De l'évasion*) through to his 1976 lecture "In Praise of Insomnia" (GDT 207–212).

10. Levinas, "God and Philosophy," OGM 59.

11. Levinas, "From Consciousness to Wakefulness," OGM 25.

12. In ¶54 of his Fifth Meditation, Husserl describes the "experience of someone else" in terms of "an associatively awakened system of manifold appearances." He goes on to explain: "Every successful understanding of what occurs in others has the effect of opening up new associations and new possibilities of understanding; and conversely, since every pairing association is reciprocal, every such understanding uncovers my own psychic life in its similarity and difference." Edmund Husserl, *Cartesian Meditations: An Introduction to Phenomenology,* trans. Dorion Cairns (Dordrecht: Kluwer, 1950), 120.

13. Critchley uses the image of a spiral to describe Levinas's prose: "The language of *Otherwise Than Being* . . . performs a kind of spiraling movement, between the inevitable language of the ontological Said and the attempt to unsay that Said in order to locate the ethical Saying within it." Simon Critchley, *The Ethics of Deconstruction: Derrida and Levinas* (Edinburgh: Edinburgh University Press, 1992), 8.

14. Jean-François Lyotard, "Levinas' Logic," in *Face to Face with Levinas,* ed. Richard A. Cohen (Albany: State University of New York Press, 1986), 117.

15. Elisabeth Weber discusses the traumatic structure of *Otherwise Than Being or Beyond Essence,* arguing that Levinas's metaphors, superlatives, and repetitions "stand for a wound, a scar, a trauma . . . [and] carry into the text the trace of a real that left many of those who survived it insane, and left others tormented for the rest of their lives." Alternatively, Paul Ricoeur is critical of the traumatic nature of Levinas's prose, and describes his language as *"verbal terrorism."* See Elisabeth Weber, "The Notion of Persecution in Levinas's *Otherwise Than Being or Beyond Essence,*" in Peperzak, ed., *Ethics as First Philosophy,* 72; and Paul Ricoeur, "Otherwise: A Reading of Emmanuel Levinas's *Otherwise than Being or Beyond Essence,*" in *Yale French Studies* 104: *Encounters with Levinas* (2003), 93.

16. Edith Wyschogrod, *Emmanuel Levinas: The Problem of Ethical Metaphysics* (New York: Fordham University Press, 2000), xiv.

17. One can link a non-linear way of reading and writing to various modernist tendencies in poetry and literature, specifically to the influence of Maurice Blanchot (which I discuss in chapter 5) and to Levinas's reading of the Talmud (both the tradition of reading *aloud* and proceeding right to left). In the introduction to his *Nine Talmudic Readings,* Levinas emphasizes the unique demands placed on the readers of the Talmud, explaining: "The pages of the Talmud, mischievous, laconic in their ironic or dry formulations, but in love with the possible, register an oral tradition and a teaching which came to be written down accidentally." In terms that could function as a description of a strategy for reading his own ethical texts, he continues: "It is important to bring [the pages of the Talmud] back to their life of dialogue or polemic in which multiple, though not arbitrary, meanings arise and buzz in each saying" (NTR 4).

18. The saying and the said feature centrally in *Otherwise Than Being or Beyond Essence,* but Levinas foreshadows his later work when he invokes these terms in the

preface to *Totality and Infinity*. There he writes that the "word by way of preface . . . belongs to the very essence of language, which consists in continually undoing its phrase by the foreword or the exegesis, in unsaying the said, in attempting to restate without ceremonies what has already been ill understood in the inevitable ceremonial in which the said delights" (TI 30).

19. Georges Bataille, "From Existentialism to the Primacy of Economy," in Robbins, *Altered Reading*, 160.

20. *Insomnia*, dir. Christopher Nolan (Alcon Entertainment, 2002).

21. Levinas, "From the Carefree Deficiency," OGM 47.

22. Freud also characterizes *angst* in terms of an intellectual power. In *Beyond the Pleasure Principle* he distinguishes anxiety from "fright," noting that "there is something about anxiety that protects its subject against fright and so against fright-neuroses." In this picture, anxiety shields the mind from trauma. Sigmund Freud, *Beyond the Pleasure Principle*, ed. and trans. James Strachey (New York and London: W. W. Norton, 1961), 11.

23. Aristotle explains, "one element in the soul is irrational and one has a rational principle. . . . Of the irrational element one division seems to be widely distributed, and vegetative in its nature, I mean that which causes nutrition and growth." Aristotle, *The Nicomachean Ethics*, trans. Sir David Ross (New York: Oxford University Press, 1991), 30 (1102b).

24. See sec. III, chap. C, § 4 of TI: "Time and the Will: Patience," where Levinas considers "the suffering called physical" (TI 238).

25. This is a point that Critchley emphasizes; see *Infinitely Demanding*, 60–61.

26. Levinas, "Is Ontology Fundamental?" EN 4.

27. Despite the dominance of dark imagery in his texts, Levinas also invokes *happiness, love,* and *joy* as examples of the sensible commingling of the physical and the psychological, or the complexity of what it means to *be* a body. See (for example) TI 143–151, and OB 79, 120.

28. Levinas was reading Proust in the early 1940s, and this description echoes significant passages in *Swann's Way*. See for instance Marcel Proust, *Swann's Way*, trans. Lydia Davis (London: Penguin, 2004), 32–33. Thanks to David Dusenbury for bringing this connection to my attention.

29. Levinas elaborates, "The concept of the 'there is' represents the phenomenon of absolutely impersonal being. 'There is' posits the simple fact of being without objects, being in complete silence, in utter non-thought, in every manner of retreat from existence. 'Il y a' in the sense of 'il pleut,' 'il fait beau'" (IRB 212).

30. Henry James, *The Beast in the Jungle and Other Stories* (New York: Dover, 1993), 39.

31. Ibid., 71.

32. Ibid., 69.

33. Rainer Maria Rilke, "*Orpheus. Eurydice. Hermes,*" in *The Selected Poetry of Rainer Maria Rilke,* trans. Stephen Mitchell (New York: Vintage, 1989), 227.

34. Levinas, "Philosophy and Transcendence," AT 20.

35. Bergson explains, "If I want to mix a glass of sugar and water, I must, willy nilly, wait until the sugar melts. This little fact is big with meaning. For here the time I have to wait is not that mathematical time which would apply equally well to the entire history of the material world. . . . It coincides with my impatience, that is to say, with a certain portion of my own duration, which I cannot protract or contract as I like" (CE 9–10).

36. James Joyce, "The Dead," in *Dubliners* (New York: Penguin Books, 1967), 225.

37. Levinas, "From Consciousness to Wakefulness," GCM 32.

38. Levinas's focus on breath at the end of *Otherwise Than Being or Beyond Essence* stands as another indication of the centrality of the body in his later text. It also signals an important coincidence with James's conviction that "consciousness" is inseparable from the bodily experience of breathing: "the stream of thinking . . . is only a careless name for what, when scrutinized, reveals itself to consist chiefly of the stream of my breathing. The 'I think' which Kant said must be able to accompany all my objects, is the 'I breathe' which actually does accompany them" ("Does Consciousness Exist?" ERE 37). Later, James writes: "*Âme, vie, soufflé, qui saurait bien les distinguer exactement?*" ("La Notion de Conscience," ERE 221). I return to this coincidence between Levinas and James in chapter 3.

39. Ralph Waldo Emerson, "Circles," in *The Portable Emerson,* ed. Carl Bode with Malcolm Cowley (New York: Penguin, 1981), 228.

40. James, "The Energies of Men," in WWJ 671, 672. For a recent investigation of the centrality of "energy" to James's moral philosophy, see Sergio Franzese, *The Ethics of Energy: William James's Moral Philosophy in Focus* (Frankfurt: Ontos Verlag, 2008).

41. Hannah Arendt, *Men in Dark Times* (Orlando: Harcourt, Brace, 1968), ix.

42. In a 1981 dialogue with Richard Kearney, Levinas said: "I always make a clear distinction, in what I write, between philosophical and confessional texts. I do not deny that they may ultimately have a common source of inspiration. I simply state that it is necessary to draw a line of demarcation between them as distinct methods of exegesis, as separate languages." See Richard Kearney, *States of Mind: Dialogues with Contemporary Thinkers on the European Mind* (Manchester: Manchester University Press, 1995), 184.

43. This thought coincides with Richard Bernstein's thesis in his paper "Evil and the Temptation of Theodicy," that "the primary thrust of Levinas's thought is to be understood as his response to the horror of evil that has erupted in the twentieth century." See Richard J. Bernstein, "Evil and the Temptation of Theodicy," in *The Cambridge Companion to Levinas,* ed. Simon Critchley and Robert Bernasconi (Cambridge: Cambridge University Press, 2002); see also R. Clifton Spargo, *Vigilant Memory: Emmanuel Levinas, the Holocaust, and the Unjust Death* (Baltimore: Johns Hopkins University Press, 2006).

44. Wallace Stevens, "Sunday Morning," in *The Collected Poems of Wallace Stevens* (New York: Vintage, 1990), 67. (© 1954 by Wallace Stevens, renewed in 1982 by Holly Stevens. Used by permission of Alfred A. Knopf, a division of Random House, Inc.)

45. Levinas in conversation with Kearney, *States of Mind,* 188.

46. Georges Bataille, in a letter to René Char, also invoked cracks in the wall. Considering the failure of action unique to literature and the power of a certain powerlessness, he admits: "We who write are well aware that humanity could easily do without the images we create"; and continues: "This silence and darkness, however, prepare the muffled crack and tremulous glimmering of fresh thunderstorms; they prepare *the return* of a sovereign conduct that cannot be harnessed to the downward pull of self-interest." Seeing humanity in the silence and darkness, the desert and the rubble, he offers a Levinasian admission: "Let me affirm that I honestly know nothing about what I am, or what my fellow men are, or what the world we live in might be . . . I am clinging in my astonished helplessness to a cord. I do not know if I love the

night. Perhaps I do, for fragile human beauty moves me in that disquieting way only when I understand that the night from whence it comes, and into which it goes, is unfathomable. How I *love* the distant outline that men have ceaselessly left of themselves in this darkness! . . . Humanity, sordid or tender, and always *astray,* even in its miseries, its stupidity, and crimes, presents an intoxicating defiance . . . Humanity is most touching in its inanity when night grows filthier, when the horror of night turns its creatures into a vast heap of rubbish." Georges Bataille, "Letter to René Char on the Incompatibilities of the Writer," trans. Christopher Carsten, in *Yale French Studies* 78: *On Bataille* (1990): 35–37; originally published in *Botthege Oscure,* May 1950.

2. Faces

1. Levinas, "Place and Utopia," DF 100.
2. Levinas, "Meaning and Sense," BPW 57.
3. Edmund Husserl, *The Idea of Phenomenology,* trans. William P. Alston and George Nakhnikian (Dordrecht: Kluwer, 1990), 14–15. In his notes preceding the lectures, Husserl expressed his quest for phenomenological *clarity,* writing: "I want to come face to face with the essence of the possibility of that reaching [of cognition toward the transcendent]. I want to make it given to me in an act of 'seeing'" (4). This passage is instructive for sensing how Levinas will critique Husserl's emphases on vision, his notion of the transcendent, and his conception of coming "face to face."
4. Derrida describes Levinas's distance from Husserl and Heidegger in terms of a double, increasingly bloody patricide: "The respectful, moderate reproach directed against Husserl in a Heideggerian style will soon become the main charge of an indictment this time directed against Heidegger, and made with a violence that will not cease to grow" (VM 88).
5. In the same lecture, Levinas devotes significant time to applauding Bergson and claiming him as a critical ally, noting: "Bergson is an essential step in the movement which puts in question the framework of a spirituality borrowed from knowledge and therefore from the privileged and primary signification of presence, being, and ontology." Levinas, "Transcendence and Intelligibility," BPW 154. I will say more about Bergson's relationship with James and influence on Levinas in the next chapter.
6. Levinas, "Transcendence and Intelligibility," BPW 153.
7. Levinas, "The Other, Utopia and Justice," EN 227. Levinas's interest in the "concrete" reflected a general philosophical obsession of the times but was also fueled by the influential teachings of Jean Wahl, whose *Vers le concret* appeared in 1930 (with the first two chapters focusing on William James).
8. Levinas, "Dying For . . . ," EN 211.
9. The problem Levinas sees in Heidegger's description of being-with lies in the distinction Heidegger draws between the average, everyday "*they-self*" (das Man-Selbst) and "the *authentic Self*—that is, the Self which has been taken hold of in its own way" (BT 167). This is coincident with Levinas's critique that Heidegger remains tied to an individualistic, solipsistic account of meaning, particularly in his descriptions of being-toward-death ("*the they does not permit us the courage for anxiety in the face of death*" [BT 298]) and Heidegger's own reiteration of the "face to face" in division II, part I as a trope for the auto-confrontation of a being with her "ownmost possibility": "Dasein . . . brought face to face with itself as delivered over to that possibil-

ity which is not to be outstripped . . ." (BT 298). Or later: "Dasein . . . brought face to face with its own uncanniness . . ." (BT 342).

10. Heidegger defends his fundamental ontology and explains, "the truth of Being as the clearing itself remains concealed for metaphysics." He goes on: "Forgetting the truth of Being in favor of the pressing throng of beings unthought in their essence is what ensnarement [*Verfallen*] means in *Being and Time*." See "Letter on Humanism," in Martin Heidegger, *Basic Writings: from* Being and Time *(1927) to* The Task of Thinking *(1964)*, rev. edition, ed. David Ferrell Krell (San Francisco: HarperCollins, 1993), 235.

11. James uses this phrase to describe the "primitive quest" of metaphysics: "The world has always appeared to the natural mind as a kind of enigma, of which the key must be sought in the shape of some illuminating or power-bringing word or name. That word names the universe's *principle,* and to possess it is, after a fashion, to possess the universe itself. 'God,' 'Matter,' 'Reason,' 'the Absolute,' 'Energy' are so many solving names. You can rest when you have them. You are at the end of your metaphysical quest" (P 52).

12. Levinas's urban emphasis is also one-sided, since he does not have much of a sense of natural, less populated landscapes, thus raising the issue of his relationship to environmental ethics. This is something John Sallis and John Llewelyn (among others) consider; see Sallis's "Levinas and the Elemental," and Llewelyn's "Toward a More Democratic Ecological Order with Levinas," both in Atterton and Calarco, eds., *Radicalizing Levinas,* 137–49, 150–77.

13. *The Prelude* IV.338–39, in William Wordsworth, *The Prelude or Growth of a Poet's Mind,* ed. Ernest De Selincourt (New York: Oxford University Press, 1970), 62.

14. Walt Whitman, "Crossing Brooklyn Ferry," sec. I, in *Whitman,* ed. Richard Wilbur (New York: Dell, 1959), 164.

15. Heidegger, *Basic Writings,* 248; Levinas, "Humanism and An-Archy" and "Without Identity," HO 45, 58.

16. Heidegger, *Basic Writings,* 248, 247.

17. Levinasian humanism prioritizes human beings and might thereby reflect a troubling anthropocentrism. In this sense, Heidegger's humanism is more closely linked with a progressive environmentalism. Given their difference, it seems critical to follow both lines of thought, all the while trying to think the difference or non-difference between the death of a person, the death of a pet, a wild animal, a plant, a building, and a place.

18. Levinas's response (29 January 1962) to a letter from José Etcheveria, BPW 31.

19. After the publication of Victor Farías's *Heidegger et le nazisme* in 1987, there was renewed debate about the moral implications of Heidegger's philosophy, and particularly of *Being and Time*. Levinas seemed generally unsurprised by Farías's book, feeling that it failed to uncover anything new. For Levinas, *Being and Time* remained a touchstone of phenomenology; he maintained: "The essential thing is the work itself, or, at least, *Sein und Zeit,* which remains one of the greatest books in the history of philosophy, even for those who reject or dispute it" (EN 225).

20. As I emphasized in chapter 1, Levinas's work centers on a radicalizing of subjectivity as non-identical, plural, and unstable. Already in his 1935 article "On Escape" (first published in *Recherches philosophiques*), Levinas underscored the myth of the "self-sufficency" of the "I" (*le moi*), claiming: "This conception of the 'I' as self-sufficient is one of the essential marks of the bourgeois spirit and its philosophy" (OE 50).

He continued: "In this reference to himself [*soi-même*], man perceives a type of duality. His identity with himself loses the character of a logical or tautological form; it takes on a dramatic form . . ." (OE 55).

21. *Leaves of Grass,* in Walt Whitman, *Complete Poetry and Collected Prose,* ed. Justin Kaplan (New York: Library of America, 1982), 125–26. It is for his open and exuberant sense of the world's plurality that James identified Whitman as the archetype of "healthy-mindedness," as one who exudes "his own love of comrades . . . gladness that he and they exist" (VRE 84).

22. Diane Perpich, *The Ethics of Emmanuel Levinas* (Stanford: Stanford University Press, 2008), 54.

23. Heidegger is the direct inspiration for this transformation of seemingly ordinary expressions (*Sorge, Stimmung, Angst*) into technical and quasi-technical philosophical vocabulary—a dismantling of the distinctions between the ordinary and the extraordinary that reveals a disruptive metaphorical and poetic dimension of language. One could also think about Wittgenstein's use of "games" and Gadamer's invocation of "play" along these lines. Colin Davis notes that the "fraught combination of ordinary language with paradox . . . places [Levinas's key notions] right at the edge . . . of intelligibility." See Colin Davis, *Levinas: An Introduction* (Notre Dame: University of Notre Dame Press, 1996), 136.

24. Bernhard Waldenfels, "Levinas and the Face of the Other," in Critchley and Bernasconi, eds., *Cambridge Companion to Levinas,* 63.

25. Ibid., 64.

26. Further complicating things, Levinas uses "a bare arm sculpted by Rodin" (EN 231–32) in the same interview to describe the expansive possibilities for a "face." I return to this example and the relationship between ethics and art, in chapter 5. For a nuanced discussion of Levinas's relationship with Grossman's novel, see Morgan, *Discovering Levinas,* chap. 1.

27. Maurice Merleau-Ponty, *The Visible and the Invisible,* trans. Alphonso Lingis (Evanston: Northwestern University Press, 1964), 141, 147–48.

28. The literature on this topic is vast and rapidly growing. The seminal text is John Llewelyn, *The Middle Voice of Ecological Conscience: A Chiasmic Reading of Responsibility in the Neighborhood of Levinas, Heidegger and Others* (New York: St. Martin's Press, 1991). See also Llewelyn's article (which reappears in a slightly revised version as the third chapter of his book), "Am I Obsessed by Bobby? (Humanism of the Other Animal)," in *Re-Reading Levinas,* ed. Robert Bernasconi and Simon Critchley (Bloomington: Indiana University Press, 1991). Other work includes: David Wood, "Some Questions for My Levinasian Friends," in *Addressing Levinas,* ed. Eric Sean Nelson, Antje Kapust, and Kent Still (Evanston: Northwestern University Press, 2005); Matthew Calarco, *Zoographies: The Question of the Animal from Heidegger to Derrida* (New York: Columbia University Press, 2008); and *Animal Philosophy: Essential Readings in Continental Thought,* ed. Matthew Calarco and Peter Atterton (London and New York: Continuum, 2004).

29. Bergson elaborates: "The new is ever up-springing . . . the causes here, unique in their kind, are part of the effect, have come into existence with it, and are determined by it as much as they determine it—this we can feel within ourselves and also divine, by a kind of sympathy, outside ourselves, but we cannot think it, in the strict sense of the word, nor express it in terms of pure understanding" (CE 8, 180).

30. Judith Butler, *Precarious Life: The Powers of Mourning and Violence* (London and New York: Verso, 2006), 134.

31. James, "The Moral Philosopher and the Moral Life," WWJ 625.

32. This is a similar reduction to what Merleau-Ponty cites as Descartes' "attempt and failure" in the *Dioptrics*: "The Cartesian model of vision is modeled after the sense of touch." Both Levinas and Merleau-Ponty critique the Cartesian model of sensibility for being reductive and the Cartesian model of space for occluding the dimension of depth. See Merleau-Ponty's "Eye and Mind," in Maurice Merleau-Ponty et al., *The Merleau-Ponty Aesthetics Reader: Philosophy and Painting,* ed. Galen A. Johnson and Michael B. Smith (Evanston: Northwestern University Press, 1993), 130-31.

33. Levinas alludes to taste and hunger in *Totality and Infinity:* "To recognize the Other is to recognize a hunger" (TI 75), and particularly in sec. II, chap. B where he discusses "enjoyment," writing: "Heidegger does not take the relation of enjoyment into consideration . . . *Dasein* in Heidegger is never hungry" (TI 134). In *Otherwise Than Being or Beyond Essence,* however, hunger—now the radically embodied form of *desire*—takes center stage as the *interruption* of egoist enjoyment, the traumatic "bread from one's mouth" reiterated as the concretion of substitution throughout the later text.

34. Diane Perpich questions the degree to which one can differentiate the face and the body in Levinas's thought: "It is unclear whether it is the face that undoes and 'ruins' representation or whether the conditions for this undoing are already there before the face-to-face encounter in the sensuous existing of the lived body." Perpich, *Ethics of Emmanuel Levinas,* 64. Bernhard Waldenfels also insists that "Levinas's ethics are rooted in a phenomenology of the body, close to that of Husserl, Sartre, and Merleau-Ponty, even when he goes his own way." Waldenfels, "Levinas and the Face of the Other," 65. Christian Diehm also adopts a view of the face as inseparable from a body, but goes even further, writing: "By situating the ethical demand of the other in the body we are forced to recognize that there is an incredible multiplicity of ethical demands emanating from an incredible multiplicity of sources. And it is not immediately obvious which demands are to be met, or can be met. But what we must understand is that it is not simply the other person who claims us. Every body is the other." See Christian Diehm, "Facing Nature: Levinas Beyond the Human," in *Emmanuel Levinas: Critical Assessments,* 4 vols., ed. Claire Elise Katz (London and New York: Routledge, 2004), vol. 4, 185; see also Rosalyn Diprose, *Corporeal Generosity: On Giving with Nietzsche, Merleau-Ponty, and Levinas* (Albany: State University of New York Press, 2002).

35. This means that the "human" is not a closed or articulate category—it is never clear precisely *what* the human means. Levinas insists: "The alterity of the Other does not depend on any quality that would distinguish him from me, for a distinction of this nature would precisely imply between us that community of genus which already nullifies alterity" (TI 194).

36. Levinas explains the way in which a face produces height and depth: "The relation with the Other alone introduces a dimension of transcendence, and leads us to a relation totally different from experience in the sensible sense of the term, relative and egoist" (TI 193).

37. Janicaud identifies *Totality and Infinity* as the critical point where phenomenology turns into theology, identifying Levinas with "the rupture of immanent phenomenality" and "the disaster or catastrophe of abandoning the phenomenon." See Janicaud, "Theological Turn of French Phenomenology," 31.

38. Samuel Beckett, *Nohow On: Three Novels* (New York: Grove Press, 1996), 89.

39. Edward S. Casey, *The World at a Glance* (Bloomington: Indiana University Press, 2006), 438.

40. Levinas, "Humanism and An-archy," HO 52.

41. Levinas, "Without Identity," HO 63.

42. Richard Cohen's introduction to *Humanism of the Other* (HO xxix). For a comprehensive account of the Davos affair and an investigation of Levinas's prewar writing in its connection with Heideggerian ontology, see Jesse Sims's unpublished doctoral dissertation, "Reconfiguring Ontology: Transcendence, Subjectivity, and Being in Levinas's Early Philosophy" (New School for Social Research, New York City, May 2009), pp. 197–277.

43. Heidegger, *Basic Writings,* 234.

44. Critiquing the face's lack of context, Terry Eagleton writes: "Levinas seems not to recognize that to strip the subject of its social context is to render it more abstract rather than more immediate, and thus more akin to the bloodless Enlightenment subject he detests." Terry Eagleton, *Trouble with Strangers: A Study of Ethics* (Oxford: Wiley-Blackwell, 2009), 227. I consider the face's unique kind of abstraction in a section on close-ups, later in this chapter.

45. Ludwig Wittgenstein, *Philosophical Investigations,* trans. G. E. M. Anscombe (New York: Macmillan, 1953), par. 19.

46. Levinas notes: "The Heideggerian *es gibt* is a generosity. This is the great theme of the later Heidegger; being gives itself anonymously. But like an abundance, like a diffuse goodness. On the contrary, [*il y a*] is unbearable in its indifference. Not an anguish but a horror, the horror of the unceasing, of a monotony deprived of meaning" (IRB 45).

47. Levinas, "Transcendence and Intelligibility," BPW 152.

48. Maurice Merleau-Ponty, "Indirect Language and the Voices of Silence," in *Signs,* trans. Richard C. McCleary (Evanston: Northwestern University Press, 1964), 46.

49. "Meaning and Sense" incorporates, verbatim, significant parts of Levinas's 1963 essay, "La trace d'lautre." The original passage reads: "si la signifiance de la trace consiste à signifier sans faire apparaître, si elle établit une relation avec l'illéité—relation qui, personelle et éthique,—qui, obligation,—ne dévoile pas—si, par consequent la trace n'appartient pas à la comprehension de l'"appariaître' et du 'se dissimuler,'—on pourrait, du moins, s'en approcher par une autre voie en situant cette signifiance à partir de la phenomenology qu'elle interrompt" (EDHH 278).

50. Robbins, *Altered Reading,* 28.

51. Levinas's notion of the trace relates intimately to Derrida's discussion of erasure and trace in *Of Grammatology* (originally published in French in 1967). Derrida insists that we can only use metaphysical terms (like *experience*) "under erasure" (*sous rature*), and he describes the "trace" as "not only the disappearance of an origin . . . [the trace also] means that the origin did not even disappear, that it was never constituted except reciprocally by a nonorigin, the trace, which thus becomes the origin of the origin." Derrida credits Levinas as integral to this formulation, stressing, "I relate this concept of the *trace* to what is at the center of the latest work of Emmanuel Levinas and his critique of ontology." Jacques Derrida, *Of Grammatology,* trans. Gayatri Chakravorty Spivak (Baltimore: Johns Hopkins University Press, 1997), 61, 70.

52. John Drabinski pays careful attention to this feature of Levinas's though in his *Sensibility and Singularity: The Problem of Phenomenology in Levinas* (New York: State University of New York Press, 2001). Drabinski, emphasizing the degree to which Levinas carries on Husserl's project through a redirection of the phenomenological method,

offers a meticulous reading of Levinas in light of Husserl; for the discussion of *sens* see chap. 1, esp. 25ff. In "Violence and Metaphysics" Derrida also notes Levinas's preoccupation with *sens,* and relates this to Hegel's focus on the word *Sinn;* see VM 99.

53. Drabinski, *Sensibility and Singularity,* 25.

54. Gilles Deleuze, *Cinema I: The Movement-Image,* trans. Hugh Tomlinson and Barbara Habberjam (Minneapolis: University of Minnesota Press, 2006), 87–88.

55. Ibid., 88.

56. Levinas translates vulnerability into the biblical prohibition "Thou shall not kill." He explains, "Thou shall not kill does not signify merely the interdiction against plunging a knife into the breast of the neighbor. Of course, it signifies that, too. But so many ways of being comport a way of crushing the other" (IRB 53).

57. See Levinas, "Philosophy and Awakening," EN 83–85.

58. Levinas, "God and Philosophy," BPW 133.

59. In *Altered Reading,* Jill Robbins notes that Lévy-Bruhl was "a strong influence on the generation of Levinas's teachers" (87) and traces that influence in some detail. See *Altered Reading,* chap. 5, esp. 86–90, and her introduction, p. xxi.

60. Levinas, "Lévy-Bruhl and Contemporary Philosophy," EN 47.

61. For example, Levinas writes that "the face . . . commands a gathering—or a proximity . . . it commands a thinking that is more ancient and more aware than knowledge or experience." Emmanuel Levinas, "Beyond Intentionality," trans. Kathleen McLaughlin, in *Philosophy in France Today,* ed. Alan Montefiore (Cambridge: Cambridge University Press, 1983), 106.

62. Feminists frequently criticize Levinas's use of the term *il,* along with other terms such as "son" and "fraternity," particularly in *Totality and Infinity.* These issues have been well articulated by Luce Irigaray, Stella Sandford, Claire Katz, Tina Chanter, and Diane Perpich—among others. Without diminishing these critiques or apologizing for Levinas, the use of *il* and *illeity* strike me as necessary to Levinas's sense of the proximity between *il* and *il y a.* For those who want to replace *il* with *elle*—you are left without the critical (audible) slippage. The priority of *il* in the French language is another story, and in English we are perhaps overly reactive to this issue given the neutrality of the indefinite articles in our own language.

63. Levinas's shift from the perspective of Macbeth to Banquo is emblematic of a larger shift across his work as he gains distance from the war: from the stifling thought of imprisonment and escape which is definitive of *Existence and Existents,* to the thought of survival and the un-dead lives of victims which dominates *Otherwise Than Being or Beyond Essence.*

64. William Shakespeare, *Macbeth,* in *The Complete Oxford Shakespeare,* ed. Stanley Wells and Gary Taylor (Oxford: Oxford University Press, 1986), 1311; act I, scene 3, ll. 77–80.

65. Badiou, *Ethics,* 22.

66. Levinas, "Transcendence and Intelligibility," BPW 158.

3. Experience

1. Heidegger, *Basic Writings,* 248.

2. Derrida compares Levinas's thought with empiricism in the final pages of "Violence and Metaphysics," writing that "the true name of the renunciation of the con-

cept, of the a prioris and the transcendent horizons of language is *empiricism*" (WD 151). Derrida criticizes empiricism for denying the transcendent power of language. Contrary to Derrida, Dominique Janicaud accuses Levinas of not being empirical enough in "The Theological Turn of French Phenomenology." Caught between a rock and a hard place, Levinas cannot satisfy either Derrida's quest to overcome dualistic hierarchies between empiricism and metaphysics or Janicaud's effort to restore phenomenology to Husserl's "return to the things themselves!" An investigation of Derrida's and Janicaud's understandings of empiricism goes beyond my scope here, but in holding Levinas next to James, I am suggesting an empiricism that neither Derrida nor Janicaud has considered.

3. See Jankélévitch's notion of forgiveness as "un-livable real life experience" in Vladimir Jankélévitch, *Forgiveness,* trans. Andrew Kelley (Chicago: University of Chicago Press, 2005), 120. See also Jankélévitch, *Le Je-ne-sais-quoi et le presque-rien* (Paris: Presses Universitaires de France, 1957).

4. See David Hume, particularly section II of *An Enquiry Concerning Human Understanding* (New York: Prometheus Books, 1988).

5. There are, of course, notable exceptions. Sandra B. Rosenthal has compared aspects of Levinas with George Herbert Meade (and others). See her article, "A Time for Being Ethical: Levinas and Pragmatism," *The Journal of Speculative Philosophy* 17, no. 3 (2003): 192–203. See also Simon Critchley, "Deconstruction or Pragmatism—Is Derrida a Private Ironist or a Public Liberal?" in Mouffe, ed., *Deconstruction and Pragmatism,* 19–40; Claire Elise Katz, "'The Presence of the Other is a Presence That Teaches': Levinas, Pragmatism, and Pedagogy," *Journal of Jewish Thought and Philosophy* 14, nos. 1–2 (2006): 91–108; and Joshua James Shaw, *Emmanuel Levinas on the Priority of Ethics: Putting Ethics First* (Amherst, N.Y.: Cambria, 2008).

6. Arthur Lovejoy famously identified "thirteen pragmatisms," and James himself expressed increasing ambivalence about the term. In a 1907 letter to Dickinson Miller, James called "pragmatism" "a most unlucky word" (LWJ 295), and in a 1908 letter to Theodore Flournoy he wrote: "The general blanket-word pragmatism covers so many different opinions, that it naturally arouses irritation to see it flourished as a revolutionary flag" (LWJ 300). See Arthur O. Lovejoy, *The Thirteen Pragmatisms and Other Essays* (Baltimore: Johns Hopkins University Press, 1963).

7. Richard J. Bernstein, "Pragmatism, Pluralism and the Healing of Wounds," in *Pragmatism: A Reader,* ed. Louis Menand (New York: Vintage, 1997), 387–89.

8. Janicaud singles out *Totality and Infinity* as the critical point at which phenomenology turned into theology, and calls this "the disaster or catastrophe of abandoning the phenomenon." Janicaud, "The Theological Turn of French Phenomenology," 31.

9. Ibid., 67.

10. Ibid., 65.

11. Robert Bernasconi notes the importance of *Existence and Existents* in his foreword to the English translation, and also notes the lack of audience for the work: "Emmanuel Levinas could with some justice have said of *Existence and Existents,* as David Hume said of his *Treatise of Human Nature,* that it 'fell dead born from the press'" (EE vii).

12. Bernasconi underscores the significance of Levinas's critique of Heidegger in this early work, calling it: "One of the boldest instances of one thinker finding his voice by turning to a description of experience in order to contest the vision of another thinker.

The fact that it has taken so long for readers to recognize that already in this book a deci-sive contestation of Heidegger—perhaps *the* decisive contestation of Heidegger—was taking place does not make it any less true that it happened here" (EE xv).

13. Wittgenstein, *Philosophical Investigations*, pars. 2, 3e.

14. For a historical account of Levinas's influences (both those he claimed for him-self and those he did not) and the religious and philosophical precursors to his ethics, see Samuel Moyn's *Origins of the Other: Emmanuel Levinas Between Revelation and Ethics* (Ithaca: Cornell University Press, 2005).

15. Levinas did have access to some books while in captivity. He recalls reading Hegel, and "Plenty of things I had not had the time to read before: more Proust than ever, the authors of the eighteenth century, Diderot, Rousseau, and then random au-thors" (IRB 41).

16. In an interview with François Poirié in 1986, Levinas responded to a question about how he became interested in philosophy with the following answer: "I think that it was first of all my readings in Russian, specifically Pushkin, Lermontov, and Dostoevsky, and above all Dostoevsky. The Russian novel, the novel of Dostoevsky and Tolstoy, seemed to me very preoccupied with fundamental things. Books shot through with anxiety—with an essential, religious anxiety—but readable as the search for the meaning of life" (IRB 28).

17. Husserl was particularly influenced by the chapter on "The Stream of Thought" in volume I of the *Principles* and began reading the text in its entirety shortly after its publication in 1890, as he prepared for his 1891 lecture course on psychology. For one account of the depth of this influence, see John Wild, *The Radical Empiricism of Wil-liam James* (New York: Doubleday, 1969). Also see Johannes Linschoten, *On the Way Toward a Phenomenological Psychology: the Psychology of William James* (Pittsburgh: Duquesne University Press, 1968); Bruce Wilshire, *William James and Phenomenology* (Bloomington: Indiana University Press, 1968); and Richard Cobb-Stevens, *James and Husserl: The Foundations of Meaning* (The Hague: Martinus Nijhoff, 1974).

18. Edmund Husserl, "Persönliche Aufzeichnungen," ed. W. Biemel, *Philosophical and Phenomenological Research* 16, no. 13 (1956), 295. Quoted and translated by Rich-ard Cobb-Stevens in *James and Husserl*, 41.

19. Herbert Spiegelberg and Karl Schuhmann, *The Phenomenological Movement: A Historical Introduction* (Dordrecht: Kluwer, 1994), 101.

20. Wahl invited Levinas to give a series of lectures at his Collège Philosophique in 1947, following the publication of *Existence and Existents*. Remembering Wahl after his death, Levinas described him as "the life force of the academic, extra-academic and even, to a degree, anti-academic philosophy necessary to a great culture." Later in his eulogy, Levinas mentions Wahl's fascination with James (the only other explicit mention of James in Levinas's published work), and cites a passage from *The Varieties of Religious Experience*. See "Jean Wahl: Neither Having nor Being," in OS 67. The ref-erence to James appears on p. 75.

21. Ralph Barton Perry writes, "Without doubt the most important philosophical and personal attachment of James's later years was that which he formed with Henri Bergson." Ralph Barton Perry, *The Thought and Character of William James* (Cam-bridge, Mass.: Harvard University Press, 1948), 338.

22. Moyn, explaining that Bergson's *The Two Sources of Morality and Religion* did not appear until 1932, following a twenty-five year silence, adds: "if Bergson influ-

enced Levinas, it is through his general theory of perception and knowledge, rather than because of any rigorous distinction between things and people or the development of this distinction into a moral theory." Moyn, *Origins of the Other*, 38.

23. For one account of Bergson's influence on Levinas, see Richard Cohen, *Ethics, Exegesis, and Philosophy: Interpretation After Levinas* (Cambridge: Cambridge University Press, 2001), 27–52. Replying to François Poirié's question about Bergson's influence, Levinas responded: "You must realize, at the time of which I am speaking, that it to say, from 1924 to 1930, during the first years of my studies in France, that [Bergsonism] *was* philosophy, taught as the new philosophy, and I remained very faithful to this sensation of novelty . . ." (IRB 31).

24. Marcus P. Ford identifies James as a postmodernist, insisting that "James' break with the modern worldview is embodied in his proposals for a postmodern science, a postmodern view of God and ethics, and a postmodern alternative to war." See David Ray Griffin, John B. Cobb, Jr., Marcus P. Ford, Pete A. Y. Gunter, and Peter Ochs, *Founders of Constructive Postmodern Philosophy: Peirce, James, Bergson, Whitehead, and Hartshorne* (Albany: State University of New York Press, 1992), 126.

25. James, letter to Bergson of 14 December 1902. LWJ 179.

26. For a detailed discussion of the influence of evolutionism on nineteenth-century thought see Philip P. Wiener, *Evolution and the Foundations of Pragmatism* (Cambridge, Mass.: Harvard University Press, 1949). See also chapter 9, "The Personal Equation in Science: William James's Psychological and Moral Uses of Darwinian Theory," in Robert J. Richards, *Darwin and the Emergence of Evolutionary Theories of Mind and Behavior* (Chicago: University of Chicago Press, 1989).

27. In his 1906 lecture on "The Dilemma in Philosophy," James put the problem this way: "For a hundred and fifty years past the progress of science has seemed to mean the enlargement of the material universe and the diminution of man's importance. The result is what one may call the growth of naturalistic or positivistic feeling. Man is no lawgiver to nature, he is an absorber. She it is who stands firm; he it is who must accommodate himself. Let him record truth, inhuman though it be, and submit to it!" (P 15).

28. This does not amount to a simplistic mantra to believe whatever one wants, whenever one wants. Instead, in his famous 1896 address, "The Will to Believe," James insisted that "our passional nature" is "a normal element in making up our minds" (WWJ 723), and in particularly fraught or complex situations (particularly when moral questions arise), "this influence must be regarded both as an inevitable and as a lawful determinant of our choice" (WWJ 728). James's point is that belief infiltrates thought at varying thresholds; in cases when we are struck with intensely "living options which the intellect and the individual cannot by itself resolve" (WWJ 734), we had better proceed in whatever way we can. Inaction in such cases is itself a form of action.

29. I follow John McDermott in this: "The 'psychology,' 'will to believe,' radical empiricism,' and 'pragmatism' are of a piece in [James's] philosophy." See John McDermott, "Person, Process and the Risk of Belief," WWJ xxxiii.

30. In describing the strategy of his ethical writing at the end of *Otherwise Than Being or Beyond Essence*, Levinas writes: "Our philosophical discourse does not pass from one term to the other by searching the 'subjective' horizons of what shows itself, but embraces *conjunctions* of elements in which concepts as presence or subject break up" (OB 184). My emphasis on "conjunctions" in this citation could be read in light of

James's stress on "conjunctive relations" (ERE 44) as a radically empiricist strategy to glimpse the "saying" in its living, non-static complexity.

31. Such a tendency relates to the substitution of an *idea* about sensation for the sensation itself—an exchange that dulls and deadens the living vibrancy of sensible experience. See James's chapter on sensation in PP 2: 1–43, and my discussion of this issue in the section on "faces" in chapter 2.

32. Bergson, "Villa Montmorency, 6 January 1903," KW 357.

33. James, letter to Bergson from London, 4 October 1908, LWJ 315.

34. Several commentators have noted that James was more widely embraced in France than Bergson ever was in America, where there grew a fierce urgency in establishing a purely *American* philosophy. Kennan Ferguson explains: "The severing of Bergson's and James's thought, so thoroughly reinforced in the United States, occurred only minimally in France. But as extensive as Bergson's influences were at the beginning of the century, the memory and study of his thought nonetheless slowly disappeared from the scene of Continental philosophy. The Bergson-James connection—indeed, the entire *fin de siècle* period of substantial overlap between American and French thought—thus became obscured by the equally important differences which predated this connection and developed from it." Kennan Ferguson, *William James: Politics in the Pluriverse* (Lanham, Md.: Rowman & Littlefield, 2007), 67.

35. Levinas in dialogue with Richard Kearney in Kearney, *States of Mind,* 179.

36. Levinas, "The Other, Utopia and Justice," EN 224.

37. Levinas, "Foreword," PN 3.

38. Deleuze describes Bergsonian duration in terms of a constitutive surplus, writing: "Duration is not merely lived experience; it is also experience enlarged or even gone beyond; it is already a condition of experience." Gilles Deleuze, *Bergsonism,* trans. H. Tomlinson and B. Habberjam (New York: Zone Books, 2002), 37.

39. See Bergson, "Introduction to Metaphysics," KW 281.

40. Ibid., 282.

41. Levinas recounts this list—with a rationale for each of his choices—in a 1989 interview with Christoph von Wolzogen that is reprinted in IRB 154.

42. The lack of new material and a slowing of Bergson scholarship was exacerbated by at least two factors. The first was the death of many of Bergson's students in World War I. The second was the revelation after Bergson's death, in 1941, that he had forbidden the publication of any posthumous papers in his will. His wife destroyed all of his unpublished work. There is, as a result, no Bergson archive as there is with Husserl, Heidegger, and Merleau-Ponty—and, more recently, Levinas and Derrida.

43. John Dewey makes a similar criticism of Bergson. In "The Need for a Recovery of Philosophy," Dewey writes about the necessity of a shift in philosophy that is not simply an abrupt turn away from traditional issues, but a "surrender [of] all pretension to be peculiarly concerned with ultimate reality, or with reality as a complete (i.e., completed) whole: with the *real* object." He then mentions Bergson directly: "So vitally a contemporary thinker as Bergson . . . does not find it in his heart to abandon the counterpart identification of philosophy with search for the truly Real; and hence finds it necessary to substitute an ultimate and absolute flux for an ultimate and absolute permanence. Thus his great empirical services in calling attention to the fundamental importance of considerations of time for problems of life and mind get com-

promised with a mystic, non-empirical 'Intuition.'" John Dewey, "The Need for a Recovery in Philosophy," in Menand, ed., *Pragmatism: A Reader,* 219–32.

44. This Bergsonian theme bears resemblance to Stanley Cavell's sense of "moral perfectionism" with its emphasis on the self and the future—Heideggerian emphases that Levinas ultimately contests. I return to this issue in chapter 4.

45. Charles Baudelaire, *The Flowers of Evil,* trans. William Aggeler (Fresno: Academy Library Guild, 1954).

46. Ibid.

47. See "Reality and its Shadow," LR 137ff.

48. Itching is particularly acute example of this phenomenon. See for instance, Atul Gawande's article, "The Itch. Its mysterious power may be a clue to a new theory about brains and bodies," in *The New Yorker,* 30 June 2008.

49. James thinks this example is decisive, and writes: "This case seems to me to contain in miniature form the data for an entire psychology of volition" (PP, 2:525).

50. James discusses "passivity" in the context of the four characteristics of "mysticism" the *Varieties of Religious Experience.* He explains, "the mystic feels as if his own will were in abeyance and indeed sometimes as if he were grasped and held by a superior power" (VRE 303). Despite the similarities between this language and Levinas's description of ethical subjectivity, Levinas would contest the association of passivity (in the radical sense he intends) with mysticism of any kind: "The ethical relation, the face to face, cuts across every relation one could call mystical" (TI 202). James provides a more Levinasian description of passivity in his lecture on "healthy mindedness," writing: "Something must give way, a native hardness must break down and liquefy; and this event . . . is frequently sudden and automatic, and leaves the Subject an impression that he has been wrought by an external power" (VRE 96).

51. Levinas ends *Otherwise than Being or Beyond Essence* with an image of breath and the necessity of what he calls "a futher deep breathing" (*Un plus loin—une respiration profonde*) (OB 180 / AE 277) to underscore sensibility's priority over consciousness.

52. In his lecture, "Hegel and his Method," James explains the simultaneous grandeur and sterility of Hegel's dialectic. He critiques the irrationality of the Hegelian *absolute* and defends a pluralistic empiricism as a philosophy of "eaches" that are "at any rate real enough to have made themselves at least *appear* to every one, whereas the absolute has as yet appeared immediately to only a few mystics, and indeed to them very ambiguously" (PU 129).

53. Martin Heidegger, "Building, Dwelling, Thinking," in *Poetry, Language, Thought,* trans. Michael Hofstadter (New York: Harper & Row, 1971), 157.

54. Samuel Beckett, *Endgame* (New York: Grove Press, 1958), 82.

55. Levinas, "Is Ontology Fundamental?" EN 3–4.

56. These are situations where nothing adds up, disrupting the Hegelian dialectic driven *forward* by negation. Howard Caygill notes this disruption and calls Levinas's description of limit situations "a deflationary reversion . . . deflating the opening move of Hegel's *Phenomenology of Spirit,* which departs from the indication of 'this' or 'that' toward a universal or abstract notion of something." Levinas describes a situation of being stalled at sense-certainty, stalled at "this." Howard Caygill, *Levinas and the Political* (London: Routledge, 2002), 54.

57. The suggestion that every soul is "cracked" to some degree runs counter to Cavell's assertion that "on James's account, it does not seem imaginable that *everyone*

might be subject to this condition"—namely, the condition of the "sick soul." Cavell reads this as a refusal on James's part to take skepticism seriously. See Stanley Cavell, "What's the Use of Calling Emerson a Pragmatist?" in *The Revival of Pragmatism,* ed. Morris Dickstein (Chapel Hill: Duke University Press, 1999), 78.

58. In his introduction to *The Writings of William James,* John McDermott suggests that this passage is closely linked to passages from James's diaries from 1870, a year identified with his "Crisis" texts and his suicidal tendencies. In the chapter on "The Sick Soul," in *The Varieties of Religious Experience,* James tells us he will have to draw from personal experience: "Since these experiences of melancholia are in the first instance absolutely private and individual, I can now help myself out with personal documents" (VRE 122). In a letter to Frank Abauzit, who translated *The Varieties of Religious Experience* into French, James openly admitted "the document . . . is my own case—acute neurasthenic attack with phobia. I naturally disguised the *provenance!*" VRE, appendix VI, 508.

59. Jean Wahl, *Vers le concret* (Paris: J. Vrin, 1932), 92. My translation.

60. James, "The Moral Philosopher and the Moral Life," WWJ 625.

61. Ibid., 619.

62. Levinas, "Hermeneutics and the Beyond," EN 70.

63. In his essay "Place and Utopia," Levinas links the emphasis on the *here and now* with a specifically Jewish sensibility, explaining: "If Judaism is attached to the here below, it is not because it does not have the imagination to conceive of a supernatural order, or because matter represents some sort of absolute for it; but because the first light of conscience is lit for it on a path that leads from man to his neighbor" (DF 100).

64. James, "The Moral Philosopher and the Moral Life," WWJ 611.

65. Sartre, "About Man," an interview with Benny Lévy in Sartre, *Hope Now,* 68.

66. Ruth Anna Putnam, "Some of Life's Ideals," in *The Cambridge Companion to William James,* ed. Ruth Anna Putnam (Cambridge: Cambridge University Press, 1997), 295.

4. Emotion

The lines (in the epigraph) from "Since feeling is first" © 1926, 1954, © 1991 by the Trustees for the E. E. Cummings Trust; © 1985 by George James Firmage from E. E. Cummings, *Complete Poems: 1904–1962,* ed. George J. Firmage. Used by permission of Liveright Publishing Corporation.

1. In a letter to his father in 1867, James made this point clear, writing: "I can understand now no more than ever the world-wide gulf you put between 'Head' and 'Heart'; to me they are inextricably entangled together, and seem to grow from a common stem" (LWJ 1: 97).

2. James, letter to Shadworth H. Hodgson, 12 September 1886. LWJ 1: 257.

3. Levinas, "Philosophy, Justice, Love," IRB 175.

4. Levinas, "Intention, Event, and the Other," IRB 145.

5. See Hilary Putnam, "Levinas and Judaism," in Critchley and Bernasconi, eds., *Cambridge Companion to Levinas,* 33–62.

6. Stanley Cavell, *Conditions Handsome and Unhandsome: The Constitution of Emersonian Perfectionism* (Chicago: University of Chicago Press, 1990), xxii.

7. In the *Crisis,* Husserl notes: "W. James was alone, as far as I know, in becoming aware of the phenomena of horizon—under the title of 'fringes'—but how could he in-

quire into it without the phenomenologically acquired understanding of intentional objectivity and of implication?" Edmund Husserl, *The Crisis of European Sciences and Transcendental Phenomenology*, trans. David Carr (Evanston: Northwestern University Press, 1970), 264.

8. James anticipates criticism of his imagery, asking: "Does not every sudden shock, appearance of a new object, or change in a sensation, create a real interruption. . . . Do not such interruptions smite us every hour of our lives, and have we the right, in their presence, still to call our consciousness a continuous stream?" (PP 1: 240).

9. Levinas, "Alterity and Transcendence," AT 139, 140.

10. In his 1986 interview, "Being-Toward-Death," Levinas said: "I am very cautious with this word [experience]. Experience is knowledge. The presence of the other touches me ('touches,' as in *je suis touché,* is better because then I am actually passive). I am concerned" (IRB 136).

11. One classic example of the ambiguity surrounding emotion is Kant's well-known focus on the priority of reason and the universality of the moral law "in its purity and genuineness," and his subsequent insistence in the third *Critique* on the feelings of the beautiful and the sublime: "an emotion that seems to be no sport." The feeling of the sublime signals the dawn of the paradigmatically moral feeling of respect, and Kant adds: "we say of a man who remains unaffected in the presence of what we consider sublime, that he has no *feeling.*" If such a human being were a possibility (and Kant doubts that she is), we would be hard-pressed to recognize her as *human.* Immanuel Kant, *The Critique of Judgement,* trans. James Creed Meredith (Oxford: Clarendon Press, 1952), 91, 116.

12. Feminist philosophy makes contesting this hierarchy one of its central goals and has done much to complicate hard and fast distinctions between emotion and reason. One example is Carol Gilligan's suggestion of an ethics of care to supplement an ethics of right. See Carol Gilligan, *In a Different Voice: Psychological Theory and Women's Development* (Cambridge, Mass.: Harvard University Press, 1993). One could also look to Simone de Beauvoir, Simone Weil, Luce Irigaray, Julia Kristeva, Eva Kittay, and Melanie Klein for alternative accounts of emotional engagement, development, and ethical sensibility. I consider one account provided by Cora Diamond at the close of this chapter.

13. Aristotle, *Rhetoric,* in *Aristotle: Selected Works,* ed. Hippocrates G. Apostle (Grinnell, Iowa: Peripatetic Press, 1991), 1378a.

14. Martha Nussbaum, *Love's Knowledge* (New York: Oxford University Press, 1990), 40.

15. Ibid., 42.

16. Ronald de Sousa (like Nussbaum and others) refuses the either/or paradigm of emotions as rational or irrational, writing: "It is largely thanks to our emotions that we are neither angels, beasts, nor even machines, but something of all three." Ronald de Sousa, *The Rationality of Emotion* (Cambridge, Mass.: MIT Press, 1987), 4.

17. In his lengthy letter to Bergson on 13 June 1907, James credits *Creative Evolution* with "inflicting an irrecoverable death-wound upon Intellectualism." He goes on to proclaim: "I thank heaven that I have lived to this date—that I have witnessed the Russo-Japanese War, and seen Bergson's new book appear—the two great modern turning-points of history and of thought!" (LWJ 2: 294).

18. David Hume, *A Treatise of Human Nature,* 2 vols., ed. David Fate Norton and Mary J. Norton (Oxford: Oxford University Press, 2007), vol. 1, 266.

19. I am focusing on "feeling" rather than "emotion" because of the greater philosophical nuance in James's concern with feeling in his late work, particularly following his 1895–1896 seminar on "The Feelings." I follow David Lamberth is viewing this course as setting the stage for the views that were later collected as James's *Essays in Radical Empiricism*. See David C. Lamberth, *William James and the Metaphysics of Experience* (Cambridge: Cambridge University Press, 1999), 82ff.; see also Lamberth's "James' Varieties Reconsidered: Radical Empiricism, the Extra-Marginal and Conversion," in *The American Journal of Theology and Philosophy* 15, no. 3 (1994): 257–67.

20. Harvey Cormier describes the interpenetration of facts and values in relation to James's conception of truth as "a struggle—the struggle of the thinker or believer to develop a body of beliefs that can satisfy her. Pragmatism understands truth as what results when thinkers try to decide, under pressure of experience, what it's best to think." Harvey J. Cormier, *The Truth is What Works: William James, Pragmatism, and the Seed of Death* (New York: Rowan & Littlefield, 2001), 17. Gerald Meyers calls this "*subjective* pragmatism." Gerald E. Myers, *William James: His Life and Thought* (New Haven: Yale University Press, 1986), 298. See also Hilary Putnam, "James's Theory of Truth," in *The Cambridge Companion to William James,* ed. Ruth Anna Putnam (Cambridge: Cambridge University Press, 1997), 166–85.

21. Ruth Anna Putnam is a strong defender of this aspect of James, stressing the moral dimension of James's thought and underscoring his conviction that "we choose our philosophical views . . . on passional grounds"; see her "The Moral Impulse," in Dickstein, ed., *Revival of Pragmatism,* 62. James Conant also defends the positive value of the "passional" dimension of James's philosophy—and philosophy more generally. See Conant, "The James/Royce Dispute and the Development of James's 'Solution,'" in Ruth Anna Putnam, ed., *Cambridge Companion to William James,* 208ff.

22. "Life is always worth living," writes James, "if one have such responsive sensibilities. But we of the highly educated classes (so called) have most of us got far, far away from Nature. We are trained to seek the choice, the rare, the exquisite exclusively, and to overlook the common. We are stuffed with abstract conceptions, and glib with verbalities and verbosities; and in the culture of these higher functions the peculiar sources of joy connected with our simpler functions often dry up, and we grow stone-cold and insensible to life's more elementary and general goods and joys" (TT 257).

23. One should note James's mistrust of Rousseau and the degree to which James insisted on the coincidence of emotion and *action*. James warns: "There is no more contemptible type of human character than that of the nerveless sentimentalist and dreamer, who spends his life in a weltering sea of sensibility and emotion, but who never does a manly deed. Rousseau, inflaming all the mothers of France, by his eloquence, to follow Nature and nurse their babies themselves, while he sends his own children to the foundling hospital, is the classical example of what I mean" (PP 1: 125).

24. In "The Perception of Reality" in the *Principles,* James urges: ". . . what we need is practical reality, reality for ourselves; and, to have that, an object must not only appear, but it must appear both *interesting* and *important.* . . . *reality means simply relation to our emotional and active life*" (PP 2: 295).

25. In his biography of William James, Robert Richardson notes that James re-titled his "The Psychology of Belief" as "The Perception of Reality," demonstrating his view that the two topics were interchangeable and showing a transition from a more scientific, detached outlook reflected in the earlier title to a more personal and artistic out-

look characteristic of James's later thought. See Robert D. Richardson, *William James: In the Maelstrom of American Modernism* (Boston: Houghton-Mifflin, 2006), 289ff.

26. On 21 October 1865, James wrote home to his parents: "I left the party up at Sao Paulo on the 20th of last month . . . having gone up two rivers, the Içá and Jutay. . . . On the whole it was a most original month, and one which from its strangeness I shall remember to my dying day . . ." (LWJ 1: 67).

27. For one contemporary account of neural plasticity, see the profile of behavioral neurologist Vilayanur S. Ramachandran in "Brain Games," by John Colapinto, *The New Yorker*, 11 May 2009.

28. The Lang-James theory of emotion emphasizes the physical component of emotional response, the degree to which sadness intensifies when one cries, fear when one runs, etc. James lamented the oversimplification of this theory into a *causal* theory of feeling, criticizing the "enthusiasts" who claim "we feel sorry because we weep, we feel afraid because we run." James, "The Gospel of Relaxation," in TT 199. For a contemporary critique of James's account of emotion, see Wilshire, *William James and Phenomenology*, 211–16.

29. James complains: "The trouble with the emotions in psychology is that they are regarded too much as absolutely individual things. So long as they are set down as so many eternal and sacred psychic entities, like the old immutable species in natural history, so long that all that *can* be done with them is reverently to catalogue their separate characters, point, and effects" (PP 2: 449).

30. Pierre Hadot, *Philosophy as a Way of Life: Spiritual Exercises from Socrates to Foucault*, ed. Arnold I. Davidson, trans. Michael Chase (Oxford: Blackwell, 1995), 84.

31. Robert Richardson suggests James's interest in "relaxation" was first inspired by Annie Payson Call's short book in popular psychology entitled *Power Through Repose*. See Richardson, *William James*, 310ff.

32. This is the gist of Hilary Putnam's critique of Levinas's "one-sidedness." See his "Levinas and Judaism," in Critchley and Bernasconi, eds., *Cambridge Companion to Levinas*, 55–58.

33. In "The Energies of Men," James insists: "To relax, to say to ourselves . . . 'Peace!' 'Be still!' is sometimes a great achievement of inner work" (WWJ 673). He goes on to describe the ways in which "spiritual exercises" (WWJ 679) and "Hatha Yoga, Raja Yoga, and Karma Yoga" (WWJ 679) in particular might contribute to the work of relaxation.

34. Very close to Levinas on this issue, James describes the Self as a bodily *position*, explaining: "Where the body is is 'here;' when the body acts is 'now' . . ." He continues: "The body is the storm center, the origin of co-ordinates, the constant place of stress in all that experience-train. . . . The word 'I,' then, is primarily a noun of position, just like 'this' and 'here'" (ERE 170 n.).

35. In *Otherwise Than Being or Beyond Essence*, Levinas explains substitution in terms that recall the etymology of hypostasis—the physical gravity of a pillar supporting a roof. He writes: "Impassively undergoing the weight of the other, thereby called to uniqueness, subjectivity no longer belongs to the order where the alternative of activity and passivity retains its meaning. . . . It is as though the unity and uniqueness of the ego were already the hold on itself of the gravity of the other" (OB 118).

36. The reference to poetry is striking in this line. The destabilizing power of poetry is one of Levinas's alternatives to Heideggerian truth and authenticity, something I discuss in chapter 5.

37. Bruce Wilshire has linked this idea to James's phenomenological/anticipatory ideas of intentionality and *Lebenswelt,* noting: "It is as if the Self were blasted open and distributed across the face of the lived-world." Wilshire, *William James and Phenomenology,* 125.

38. Jean Améry, *At the Mind's Limits,* trans. Sidney Rosenfeld and Stella P. Rosenfeld (Bloomington: Indiana University Press, 1980), 22.

39. Levinas, "Philosophy and Awakening," EN 86.

40. Ibid., 88.

41. Ibid., 88.

42. In a conversation with the journal *Autrement* in 1988, Levinas talked about the slippage between the impersonal and the personal in terms of "a subtle ambiguity," saying: "The self, the *I,* cannot limit itself to the incomparable uniqueness of each one, which is expressed in the face of each one. Behind the unique singularities, one must perceive the individuals of a *genus* . . . There is a subtle ambiguity of the individual and the unique, the personal and the absolute, the mask and the face" (EN 229). This "subtle ambiguity"—the intermingling trace of *il y a*—acts as an abstracting force on the "uniqueness of each one," ultimately making it possible to compare, condemn, and judge, thus making room for justice.

43. Plato, *Timaeus,* in *Plato: The Collected Dialogues,* ed. Edith Hamilton and Huntington Cairns (Princeton: Princeton University Press, 1989), 19 b–c.

44. Foucault, defending the "care of the self," advocates practices in reading, writing, meditation, and introspection to facilitate the subject's deeper return to herself and better acquaintance with and insulation of her own soul. See Michel Foucault, *The Care of the Self: The History of Sexuality,* vol. 3, trans. R. Hurley (New York: Vintage, 1988), 50–51.

45. In a 17 September 1867 letter to Oliver Wendell Holmes, James expressed a view of solitude strikingly similar to Levinas's, writing: "a tedious egotism seems to be the only mental plant that flourishes in sickness and solitude . . ." (LWJ 1: 99).

46. Levinas's image of the ladder recalls and relates to Wittgenstein's claim in the *Tractatus* (6.54): "My propositions are elucidatory in this way: he who understands me finally recognizes them as senseless, when he has climbed out through them, on them, over them. (He must so to speak throw away the ladder, after he has climbed up on it.)" Ludwig Wittgenstein, *Tractatus Logico-Philosophicus,* trans. C. K. Ogden (London: Routledge, 1992), 189.

47. John Drabinski describes this in terms of a break with idealism, explaining: "Levinas will abandon the dominant form of intentionality in idealism: the intentionality set out from the ego. For Levinas, ethics will always be a relation and a sense that is constituted otherwise than idealism." Drabinski, *Sensibility and Singularity,* 25.

48. In "Philosophy and Awakening," Levinas credits Husserl's "intersubjective reduction" with glimpsing the possibility of situating the meaning of the subjective in the subjection to others. Focusing on the notion of "intersubjectivity" in the fourth and fifth of his *Cartesian Meditations,* Levinas writes: "Husserl's theory of the Intersubjective Reduction describes the astonishing or traumatizing . . . possibility of a sobering up in which the *I,* facing the Other, is freed from itself, and awakens from dogmatic slumber" (EN 86–87).

49. Rousseau identifies pity as "the only Natural virtue," describing it as "a disposition suited to beings as weak and as subject to so many ills as we are." Jean-Jacques

Rousseau, "Discourse on the Origin and the Foundations of Inequality Among Men," in *The Discourses and Other Early Political Writings,* ed. and trans. Victor Gourevitch (Cambridge: Cambridge University Press, 2000), 152.

50. In "Peace and Proximity," Levinas explains: "The thought that is awake to the face of the other human is not a thought of . . . a representation, but straightaway a thought for . . . a nonindifference for the other, upsetting the equilibrium of the steady and impassive soul of knowledge" (BPW 67).

51. Levinas, "Jean Wahl and Feeling," EN 114–15.

52. Levinas, "Philosophy and Awakening," EN 86.

53. In book E of the *Politics,* Aristotle describes intimacy (private relationships, trust, and friendship) as forces that will corrode a tyranny. The rule of the tyrant depends upon destroying the relationships between individuals—making neighbor suspect neighbor. Yet a fearful, trustless population also becomes the greatest threat against the tyrant himself—and so Aristotle adds physical and psychological abuse to the list of a tyrant's methods of keeping his subjects incapable of individual or collective action.

54. Levinas makes this clear in "Philosophy and Awakening," writing that "the substantive, the nameable, the entity and the Same—so essential to the structure of re-presentation and of truth as the truth of presence—remain the privileged and primordial terms of consciousness [in Husserlian phenomenology]. But above all, phenomenology itself isolates these structures by a reflection that is an inner perception and in which the descriptive process 'synchronizes' the flux of consciousness into knowledge" (EN 81).

55. This is the frustration Hilary Putnum attributes to "moral legislators": those who want definite, universal rules and balk at an essential vagueness which they "have . . . an enormous difficulty in accommodating." Putnam, *Ethics Without Ontology,* 33.

56. "Violence of the Face," AT 172. Levinas elaborates: "At no time have I tried to exclude justice—that would be stupid—from the human order. But I have made an attempt to return to justice from what one might call charity, and which appears to me as an unlimited obligation toward the other, and in this sense accession to his *uniqueness* as a person" (AT 175).

57. One can find an impersonal sense of being bound together in Freud, a late-found, minimal optimism in humankind he describes in "The Future of an Illusion": "One of the few gratifying and exalting impressions which mankind can offer is when, in the face of an elemental catastrophe, it forgets the discordancies of its civilization and all its internal difficulties and animosities, and recalls the great common task of preserving itself against the superior power of nature." Sigmund Freud, *The Future of an Illusion,* in *The Freud Reader,* ed. Peter Gay (London: W. W. Norton, 1995), 693.

58. Levinas uses similar terminology, describing the face as a "concrete abstraction torn up from the world, from horizons and conditions" (OB 91).

59. Cora Diamond, "How Many Legs?" in *Value and Understanding: Essays for Peter Winch,* ed. Raimond Gaita (New York: Routledge, 1990), 169.

60. Ibid., 173.

61. For her discussion of Scrooge see section 3 of Cora Diamond, "The Importance of Being Human," in *Human Beings,* ed. David Cockburn (Cambridge: Cambridge University Press, 1991), 35–62.

62. Merleau-Ponty, *The Visible and the Invisible,* 11.

63. Cora Diamond, "Anything but Argument?" in *The Realistic Spirit: Wittgenstein, Philosophy, and the Mind* (Cambridge, Mass.: MIT Press, 1995), 303.

64. Cora Diamond, "The Difficulty of Reality and the Difficulty of Philosophy," in Stanley Cavell, Cora Diamond et al., *Philosophy and Animal Life* (New York: Columbia University Press, 2008), 43–89.

65. One could trace this thought back to Aristotle and his account of early childhood education hinging on imaginative, imitative play that allows for an expanded sense of connectedness with the world and the possibilities for one's own role in it.

66. Emerson, "Experience," in *Portable Emerson*, 275.

67. James, "The Sentiment of Rationality," WWJ 321.

68. Levinas, "The Proximity of the Other," AT 107, 109.

69. Levinas, "The Other, Utopia and Justice," EN 232.

70. Levinas, "Peace and Proximity," BPW 167.

71. Heidegger, "What are Poets For?" in *Poetry, Language, Thought*, 138.

72. Ibid., 128.

5. Poetry

1. I want to warn against any gross simplification that reading Levinas is difficult and reading James is easy. They have very different approaches, but both of them are complex. The danger is that their respective prose styles can lead to hasty judgments about the content of their thought.

2. This is part of Dermot Moran's introductory entry on Levinas, citing him as "perhaps the most deliberately opaque of contemporary European philosophers." Dermot Moran, *Introduction to Phenomenology* (London: Routledge, 2000), 322.

3. James Hoopes, *Community Denied: The Wrong Turn of Pragmatic Liberalism* (Ithaca: Cornell University Press, 1998), 54.

4. James, "The Moral Philosopher and the Moral Life," WWJ 626. In his conclusions to *The Varieties of Religious Experience,* James criticizes prose that is overly sterile or devoid of emotional impact, explaining: "We get a beautiful picture of an express train supposed to be moving, but where in the picture . . . is the energy and the fifty miles an hour?" (VRE 395).

5. Gerald Myers notes: "Readers of James are often struck by his pictorial language; the vividness of his imagery provokes various comparisons to the works of his brother Henry. The image is indispensable for the Jamesian metaphysics, much as it was for Plato's." Myers, *William James*, 317.

6. Despite his vigorous defense of philosophy as "passional vision," James suffered from constant insecurity about his own style of writing and the criticism it often provoked. Prior to the Hibbert Lectures, he confided to Theodore Flournoy his dismay at having to give additional public lectures, admitting: "I find that my free and easy and personal way of writing, especially in 'Pragmatism,' has made me an object of loathing to many respectable academic minds, and I am rather tired of awakening that feeling, which more popular lecturing on my part will probably destine me to increase" (LWJ 2: 300–301).

7. Levinas, "Jacques Derrida: Wholly Otherwise," PN 56.

8. Ibid., 58.

9. Jill Robbins's book, *Altered Reading,* is the best and most thorough investigation of the tension between the form and content of Levinas's prose. Following in the footsteps of Derrida's questions at the end of "Violence and Metaphysics" about whether we are *"first* Jews or *first* Greeks" (VM 153), Robbins concludes: "When Levinas 'says' Abraham, he 'does' Odysseus." This is her way of describing how Levinas circles back into the very tradition he tries to escape. In her case it is not so much the circle of philosophic language that is essentially Greek as much as the circle of language that is essentially *figural.* I am indebted to Robbins's work. I am, however, suggesting a less stark opposition between Levinas's writing about art and his own artful texts, contesting Robbins's characterization of Levinas as "a philosopher who is at pains to exclude the aesthetic." Robbins, *Altered Reading,* 91, 53.

10. For instance, Richard Cohen argues for a stark division between ethics and aesthetics, writing: "The realm of senses is anything if not seductive—tempting, alluring, allusive, multiple, ever on the move, onward, forward, avant-garde. Sirens' calls, rocky coasts, molting selves—adventure! But Levinas will call this . . . the very denial of maturity." Cohen, *Ethics, Exegesis and Philosophy,* 13.

11. Derrida writes: "Certainly, Levinas recommends the good usage of prose which breaks Dionysiac charm or violence, and forbids poetic rapture, but to no avail . . . in *Totality and Infinity* the thematic development is neither purely descriptive nor purely deductive. . . . Because of all these challenges to the commentator and the critic, *Totality and Infinity* is a work of art and not a treatise" (VM 312 n. 7).

12. Derrida links Levinas's prioritization of hearing with Hegel's idealization of hearing and sound in the *Aesthetics:* "Hearing is concerned with the tone, rather than the form and colour of an object, with the vibration of what is corporeal; it requires no process of dissolution, as the sense of smell requires, but merely a trembling of the object" (VM 100).

13. Gary Peters has written about the implications for the priority of the a-rhythmic and non-harmonious on "new music," particularly atonal music and John Cage. See Gary Peters, "The Rhythm of Alterity: Levinas and Aesthetics," *Radical Philosophy* 82 (March/April 1997): 9–16.

14. This is a method of reading that Levinas recommends, particularly in his *Talmudic Readings,* where he insists: "Teachers must bring this aspect out for their students: those who would learn to read must distinguish the literal from the poetic meaning." "Poetry and Resurrection: Notes on Agon," PN 8. For examples of such a method in action see Emmanuel Levinas, *Nine Talmudic Readings,* trans. Annette Aronowicz (Bloomington: Indiana University Press, 1990).

15. Xavier Tilliette commented that Levinas "had certain expressions that hit the nail on the head, yet it was all quite difficult to grasp. His language was certainly interesting, although ultimately it was an artificial language, a bit fantastical, behind which lay Russian, German, and Hebrew. . . . His writing style is also quite unique. It was, at the very least, an *artistic writing.*" Tilliette is quoted by Salomon Malka, in *Emmanuel Levinas: His Life and Legacy,* trans. Michael Kigel and Sonja M. Embree (Pittsburgh: Duquesne University Press, 2006), 152–53.

16. As Hent de Vries notes, Levinas is not only reacting to Heidegger but is also thinking about "the Jewish *Blederverbot,* the prohibition of images, which reduced the work of art to an idol." Hent de Vries, "Instances: Levinas on Art and Truth," in

Philosophy of Religion for a New Century, ed. Jeremiah Hackett and Jerald Wallulis (Dordrecht: Kluwer, 2004), 193.

17. Both Merleau-Ponty and Sartre interpreted Levinas's essay as a personal attack. They published the essay nonetheless, but with a prefatory note outlining the various ways in which Levinas had misinterpreted Sartre. See *Les Temps Modernes* 38 (1948): 769–70.

18. It is worth noting that Levinas provided his own analysis of nausea, three years prior to Sartre, in his 1935 essay, "On Escape." See OE 66ff.

19. Unlike Heidegger's use of Van Gogh's painting and the Greek Temple, Levinas does not use Rodin's sculpture as a visual tool to bring an object into view. The statue resists being an example or an idol/cult object, remaining more profoundly useless than Heidegger allows his examples to be. Hagi Kenaan discusses Heidegger's use of examples in *The Present Personal: Philosophy and the Hidden Face of Language* (New York: Columbia University Press, 2005), 87–124.

20. Levinas's examples in chapter 3 of *Existence and Existents* and "Reality and its Shadow" include (in addition to Rodin): Delacroix, Hugo, Shakespeare, Racine, Blanchot, Mallarmé, Giraudoux, da Vinci, Gogol, Chekhov, Molière, Cervantes, Proust, Dostoyevsky, and Poe. Shakespeare also appears in both texts, but not in the section devoted overtly to art, titled "Exoticism," where Rodin first appears in *Existence and Existents.*

21. Levinas, "Peace and Proximity," BPW 167.

22. Rodin, quoted by William Hale in *The World of Rodin: 1840–1917* (London: Time Life, 1969), 76.

23. Rainer Maria Rilke, *Auguste Rodin,* trans. Daniel Slager (New York: Archipelago, 2004), 45.

24. Recalling his father's complicated relationship with art, Michael Levinas (himself an accomplished composer) identified "a problem that belonged to [Levinas's] time, after the war: that of a work of art or a piece of writing that is not sealed, that is not formalized in an institutional manner, around which there is an enormous question mark or an enormous vertigo of incompleteness." Michael Levinas then cited Giacometti as a contemporary to his father whose work most embodied this ideal. Quoted in Malka, *Emmanuel Levinas,* 264.

25. Levinas's interest in close-ups relates to a difference between vision that sees at a distance and something akin to the "gaze" Jean-Luc Nancy describes as "dissolving vision." See Jean-Luc Nancy, "Painting (and) Presence," in *The Birth to Presence,* trans. Brian Holmes et al. (Stanford: Stanford University Press, 1993), 360. And I will also note here that the close-up of Kelvin's right *ear* toward the end of Andrei Tarkovsky's *Solaris* represents one challenge to the notion of reducing the concept of the close-up to the superficially or narrowly understood face. Thanks to David Dusenbury for reminding me of this particular scene.

26. Gerald L. Bruns, "The Concepts of Art and Poetry in Emmanuel Levinas's Writings," in Critchley and Bernasconi, eds., *Cambridge Companion to Levinas,* 209.

27. Barnett Newman, "The Sublime is Now," in *Art in Theory 1900–2000: An Anthology of Changing Ideas,* ed. Charles Harrison and Paul Wood (Oxford: Blackwell, 1992), 580–82.

28. Kant, *Critique of Judgment,* § 29, 120.

29. See Arthur Danto's "Barnett Newman and the Heroic Sublime" in *The Nation,* 17 June 2002. Also see "Newman: The Instant," in Jean-François Lyotard, *The Inhu-*

man: Reflections on Time, trans. Geoffrey Bennington and Rachel Bowlby (Stanford: Stanford University Press, 1988), 78–88.

30. Hent de Vries rightly points out: "Long before Lyotard, Levinas thought art—both the beautiful and the sublime—as the 'inhuman' (his word) and its temporality as the instant, the split-second of a neither moral nor immoral, hence an-ethical rather than irresponsible evasion." De Vries, "Instances: Levinas on Truth and Art," 204.

31. Plato, *Republic,* trans. Allan Bloom (New York: Basic, 1968), 607b–c.

32. Levinas, "The Transcendence of Words," LR 148.

33. Ibid., 147.

34. Robert Eaglestone, "'Cold Splendor': Levinas's Suspicion of Art," in *Ethical Criticism: Reading after Levinas* (Edinburgh: Edinburgh University Press, 1997), 124.

35. Levinas, "Jean Lacroix: Philosophy and Religion," PN 87.

36. Reflecting on the originality of Wahl's thought, Levinas wrote: "Transcendence is perhaps the essential element of Wahl's teaching—but a transcendence indifferent to hierarchy. A bursting toward the heights or descent toward the depths of the sensible world; trans-ascendance and trans-descendence are purely, and pure, transcendencies" (OS 81).

37. "Reality and its Shadow" reflects an anxiety that softens somewhat over the course of Levinas's later writing. This is something both Jill Robbins and John Llewelyn note. As Levinas gains temporal distance from the Holocaust, he becomes increasingly, though never fully, able to bear imagery. There is a morbid undercurrent to Levinas's prose in "Reality and its Shadow": he is writing about art, but it is impossible to read the essay without feeling that Levinas is unable to see anything but corpses. See Jill Robbins, *Altered Reading,* 40; and John Llewelyn, *Middle Voice of Ecological Conscience,* 98–113.

38. For a detailed investigation of the relationship between Blanchot and Levinas, see Gabriel Riera, *Intrigues: From Being to the Other* (Fordham: Fordham University Press, 2006). Also see Paul Davies, "A Fine Risk: Reading Blanchot Reading Levinas," in Bernasconi and Critchley, eds., *Re-Reading Levinas,* 201–228; and Simon Critchley, *Very Little . . . Almost Nothing: Death, Philosophy, Literature* (London: Routledge, 1997), 31–84.

39. Blanchot, who housed and hid Levinas's wife while Levinas was in captivity during the war, recalled: "It took the misfortune of a disastrous war for our friendship, which could have slackened, to be tightened again. Especially since . . . [Levinas] entrusted me, by a kind of secret request, with the task of watching over his loved ones whom the perils of a detestable politics threatened." Maurice Blanchot, "N'oublie pas," *L'Arche* 373 (May 1988).

40. Levinas, "Dying For . . . ," EN 211.

41. Maurice Blanchot, "The Essential Solitude," in *The Station Hill Blanchot Reader: Fiction and Literary Essays,* ed. George Quasha, trans. Lydia Davis, Paul Auster, and Robert Lamberton (Barrytown, N.Y.: Station Hill Press, 1999), 402.

42. Maurice Blanchot, *The Step Not Beyond,* trans. Lycette Nelson (Albany: State University of New York Press, 1992), 74.

43. Ibid., 75.

44. See Levinas; section 6, "The Trace of the Other," in EDHH, 278–82. In OB, Levinas writes: "The infinite who orders me is neither a cause acting straight on, nor a theme, already dominated, if only retrospectively, by freedom. This detour at a face

and this detour from this detour in the enigma of a trace we have called illeity" (OB 12).

45. Levinas, "The Other, Utopia, Justice," EN 229, 231, 232.

46. In "The Art of Ethics," Wyschogrod writes: "Art and ethics in Levinas's sense can be thought of as fields in which disclosures of formlessness occur: in art, the amorphous power of being; in ethics, the Other who calls me to responsibility." This is right, but there is also a dense physicality and materiality in Levinas's descriptions of art and ethics. Edith Wyschogrod, "The Art of Ethics," in Peperzak, ed., *Ethics as First Philosophy*, 139.

47. Alain Toumayan writes: "Poetry . . . focusing on the materiality, the substance of language as such, turns toward the obscure, threatening, unrevealed and unreveal-able indeterminacy that is prior to and beneath the world." Alain Toumayan, *Encountering the Other: The Artwork and the Problem of Difference in Blanchot and Levinas* (Pittsburgh: Duquesne University Press, 2004), 59. Elisabeth Marie Lovelie compares Blanchot's notion of poetic language with Mallarmé's distinction between *useful* language (*parole brute*) and language that reflects something absent (*parole essentielle*). Lovelie argues: "It is precisely this dualistic ordering that Blanchot . . . challenges. Instead of accepting the opposition, Blanchot shows how both modes bear traces of poetic language." And she adds, it is the "act of destabilization that designates poetic language as a different mode of language." Elisabeth Marie Lovelie, *Literary Silences in Pascal, Rousseau and Beckett* (Oxford: Oxford University Press, 2003), 179.

48. Maurice Blanchot, "Literature and the Right to Death," in *Station Hill Blanchot Reader*, 386. Originally published as *La Littérature et le droit à la mort*, in *Faux Pas* (1942).

49. Ibid., 383–84.

50. Maurice Blanchot, "L'Étrange et l'étranger," in *La Nouvelle Revue Français* 70 (1958): 753–83.

51. Levinas, "The Servant and Her Master," LR 156 (PN 147). Here I have opted for Michael Holland's translation in *The Levinas Reader*.

52. Paul de Man refers to the dark space infiltrating language, arguing: "The distinction between literature and philosophy cannot be made in terms of a distinction between aesthetic and epistemological categories. All philosophy is condemned, to the extent that it is dependent on figuration, to be literary and, as the depository of this very problem, all literature is to some extent philosophical." He continues by saying that this interpenetration is so deep that it leads to the "difficult question whether the entire semantic, semiological, and performative field of language can be said to be covered by tropological models, a question which can only be raised after the proliferating and disruptive power of figural language has been fully recognized." Paul de Man, *Aesthetic Ideology*, ed. Andrzej Warminski (Minneapolis and London: University of Minnesota Press, 1996), 50.

53. Blanchot thinks about language's inherent poverty in terms of the inevitable retreat of Eurydice, writing: "If inspiration means that Orpheus fails and Eurydice is lost twice over, if it means the insignificance and void of the night, it also turns Orpheus toward that failure and that insignificance and coerces him, by an irresistible impulse, as though giving up failure were much more serious than giving up success, as though what we call the insignificant, the inessential, the mistaken, could reveal itself—to

someone who accepted the risk and freely gave himself to it—as the source of all authenticity." Maurice Blanchot, "The Gaze of Orpheus," in *Station Hill Blanchot Reader,* 440.

54. Blaise Pascal, *Pensées* (London: Dover, 2003), sec. V, para. 295. Among other places Levinas quotes this line, see the epigraph to OB and "Ethics as First Philosophy," sec. IV, 82 in LR.

55. Blanchot, "Literature and the Right to Death," in *Station Hill Blanchot Reader,* 385.

56. Ibid., 368.

57. Heidegger, "Building, Dwelling, Thinking," in *Poetry, Language, Thought,* 154.

58. The thought of nomadic truth resonates with James's assertion that knowing is "in transit and on its way" (ERE 67). He continues: "The greater part of all our knowledge never gets beyond this virtual stage. It is never completed or nailed down. . . . We live, as it were, upon the front edge of an advancing wave-crest, and our sense of determinate direction in falling forward is all we cover of the future of our path" (ERE 69).

59. Emerson, "Circles," in *Portable Emerson,* 239.

60. Blanchot, "Literature and the Right to Death," in *Station Hill Blanchot Reader,* 360.

61. Georges Bataille, "From Existentialism to the Primacy of Economy," 175.

62. Emily Dickinson, "It was not Death, for I stood up," in *The Poems of Emily Dickinson,* ed. R. W. Franklin (Cambridge: Harvard University Press, 1999), 161. Reprinted by permission of the publishers and the Trustees of Amherst College from *The Poems of Emily Dickinson,* Ralph W. Franklin, ed. (Cambridge, Mass.: Belknap Press of Harvard University Press), © 1998, 1999 by the President and Fellows of Harvard College; © 1951, 1955, 1979, 1983 by the President and Fellows of Harvard College.

63. James, letter to François Pillon, 12 June 1904, LWJ 2: 204.

64. Levinas, "Foreword," PN 3.

65. W. G. Sebald recounts the impression of an officer returning to Hamburg after the air raids at the end of July 1943: "We saw children tidying and raking a front garden. It was so far beyond comprehension that we told other people about it, as if it were some sort of marvel." W. G. Sebald, *On the Natural History of Destruction* (New York: Modern Library, 2004), 42.

6. Painting

The epigraph is from "The Love Song of J. Alfred Prufrock," from T. S. Eliot's *Collected Poems 1909–1962,* © 1936 by Harcourt, Inc., and renewed 1964 by T. S. Eliot, reprinted be permission of Houghton Mifflin Harcourt Publishing Company.

1. Kennan Ferguson, emphasizing the political relevance of Jamesian pluralism, notes: "Before the advent of the state-sponsored twentieth-century horrors of fascism and totalitarianism, James found the rationalization and systemization of the modern world profoundly destructive to humanity." See Ferguson, *William James,* xxii.

2. Guston is now recognized as critical to the development of new kinds of figuration that have erupted in contemporary painting—the interest in cartoons, graphic novels, and graffiti. This can be seen in the work of painters such as Dana Schutz and Amy Sillman, among others. Levinas, as Simon Critchley notes, came into vogue in the 1980s when "questions of ethics, politics, law and democracy were back on the

philosophical and cultural agenda . . . " See Critchley and Bernasconi, eds., *Cambridge Companion to Levinas*, 3.

3. Levinas, "Foreword," PN 4. The importance of proper names is something Rorty writes about in his essay "Heidegger, Kundera, and Dickens," explaining: "In a moral world based on what Kundera calls 'the wisdom of the novel,' moral comparisons and judgments would be made with the help of proper names rather than general terms or general principles." There is a small but significant point of coincidence here between Rorty and Levinas—a sense of the details being more important than the generalities. Richard Rorty, "Heidegger, Kundera, and Dickens," in *Essays on Heidegger and Others: Philosophical Papers, Volume 2* (Cambridge: Cambridge University Press, 1991), 78.

4. Arthur Danto explains: "Becoming an abstract painter was not, so far as I can tell, a momentous choice for Guston in the 1950s. He was part of a New York art world in which it was a natural next move for a gifted and ambitious artist." He goes on to describe the significant influence East Asian philosophy had on Guston in that decade. "Along with John Cage and the composer Morton Feldman . . . [Guston] attended Dr. Suzuki's lectures on Zen Buddhism at Columbia, and he evolved his abstract forms out of the calligraphic doodles he made with quill pen and ink. 'My greatest ideal is Chinese painting,' he wrote in 1978, 'especially Sung painting dating from the tenth or eleventh century.' There is a Sung feeling in the quivering abstractions of the 1950s, as if of natural forms shrouded in mist." Arthur C. Danto, "The Abstract Impressionist: Philip Guston," *The Nation,* 29 December 2003.

5. Ross Feld, *Guston in Time* (New York: Counterpoint, 2003), 15.

6. Levinas, "The Poet's Vision," PN 138.

7. Nicole Krauss, "The First Painter After the Last," *Modern Painting,* Winter 2003.

8. Guston, quoted by Martin Hentschel in his essay, "From the Abstract to the Figurative: Philip Guston's Stony Path" in *Philip Guston: Gemälde 1947–1979* (Bonn: Hatje Cantz, 1999), 52.

9. Levinas, "The Poet's Vision," PN 133.

10. Guston, quoted by his daughter, Musa Mayer, in her *Night Studio: A Memoir of Philip Guston* (New York: Da Capo Press, 1988), 141.

11. Emerson, "The Poet," in *Portable Emerson,* 263.

12. Guston, quoted in Mayer, *Night Studio,* 149. See also Debra Bricker Balken, *Philip Guston's Poor Richard* (Chicago: University of Chicago Press, 2001), 94.

13. It wasn't just the professional critics who were baffled and almost personally insulted by Guston's late work. Several of his close friends found the shift unacceptable and broke off ties with him. (De Kooning was a notable exception.) In Ross Feld's memoir of Guston, *Guston in Time,* he describes gathering in Guston's studio at his Kaddish. Feld describes the composer, Morton Feldman—a once-close friend, but for the better part of a decade, estranged from Guston—seeing Guston's last small paintings hanging on his studio wall. Feldman never understood Guston's return to imagery, and their friendship ended as soon as Guston's abstractions gave way to things. Feld (who was also in the room at the time) quotes Feldman saying, "*Now* I understand what he was getting at!" Feld goes on: "At least for me, hearing him say this was to suffer a kind of existential splinter the philosopher Emmanuel Levinas analogizes insomnia to: hearing and seeing what you don't want to hear and see, the intimate hollowness, the seemingly endless vertigo of time coming at you in waves." Feldman,

writing about Guston years later, never thought of himself as having arrived too late. See Feld, *Guston in Time,* 72.

14. Philip Guston, "Philip Guston Talking," in *Theories and Documents of Contemporary Art: A Sourcebook of Artists' Writings,* ed. Kristine Stiles and Peter Selz (Berkeley and Los Angeles: University of California Press, 1996), 252.

15. Donald Kuspit, "Philip Guston's Self-Doubt," posted to artnet.com: http://www.artnet.com/magazine/features/kuspit/kuspit12-4-03.asp.

16. Plato, *The Symposium and The Phaedrus: Plato's Erotic Dialogues,* trans. with comm. William S. Cobb (New York: State University of New York Press, 1993), 211c.

17. Plato, *Republic,* 516a.

18. Ibid., 520b–c.

19. Danto, "The Abstract Impressionist: Philip Guston."

20. Emerson, "Experience," 266.

21. Plato, *Republic,* 518c–d.

22. James, 30 December 1885 letter to Shadworth H. Hodgson, LWJ 1: 244.

23. See Jean Wahl, *Existence humaine et transcendance* (Neuchâtel: Éditions de la Baconnière, 1944). Samuel Moyn underscores the influence of Wahl's early secular readings of Kierkegaard on Levinas, which Levinas only came to voice in his own way after beginning to question Heidegger's attempts to overcome transcendence post-1933, and more substantially in writings from the 1940s and later. See Moyn, *Origins of the Other,* 164–94.

24. In a discussion with Gabriel Marcel and others, Wahl insisted, "it is not true that I ever use this word [transdescendence] to describe descending from the absolute to the relative." Gabriel Marcel, *Tragic Wisdom and Beyond, including Conversations between Paul Ricoeur and Gabriel Marcel,* trans. Stephen Jolin and Peter McCormick (Evanston: Northwestern University Press, 1973), 60.

25. Levinas, "Jean Wahl and Feeling," PN 116.

26. Plato, *Republic,* 440a.

27. Feld, *Guston in Time,* 14.

28. In her wonderful book about Guston, Dore Ashton thinks about the humanity of his work and notes: "Guston may have learned from Goya that simple areas of dark and light, when kept in human scale, can be even more horrifying than the great *Sturm und Drang* paintings of late Romanticism." Dore Ashton, *A Critical Study of Philip Guston* (Berkeley and Los Angeles: University of California Press, 1976), 189.

29. Walter Benjamin, *The Origin of German Tragic Drama,* trans. Joan Osborne (London and New York: Verso, 1998), 151. All subsequent references will be made in text as OGTD.

30. Arendt's introduction to Walter Benjamin, *Illuminations: Essays and Reflections,* ed. Hannah Arendt, trans. Harry Zohn (New York: Schocken Books, 1968), 50.

31. Ibid., 51.

32. Guston, letter to Ross Feld, reprinted in Feld, *Guston in Time,* 9.

33. "Eye and Mind," in Merleau-Ponty et al., *Merleau-Ponty Aesthetics Reader,* 140.

34. This notion of fallible, plural truths opens Levinas to the same criticism that F. H. Bradley leveled against James: charges of subjectivism and positivism. Neither Levinas nor James is concerned with establishing stable sources of understanding or knowledge. Both move philosophy away from classical epistemological questions. James answered Bradley in this way: "For [the rationalist], intellectual products are most true which, turning their face toward the Absolute, come nearest to symbolizing

its way of uniting the many and the one. For [the radical empiricist], those are most true which most successfully dip back into the finite stream of feeling and grow most easily confluent with some particular wave or wavelet" (ERE 99).

35. Guston, "Philip Guston Talking," 251.

36. William Edelglass also associates the phrase "poetically certain" with Levinas's language in his late work, and insists that "Levinas never lost his distrust of the intoxicating power of poetry. Nevertheless there is a significant shift in his thinking regarding the role of the arts, and in particular to a more generous understanding of the poetic." William Edelglass, "Levinas's Language," *Analecta Husserliana* 85 (2005): 54.

37. James, "The Moral Philosopher and the Moral Life," in WWJ 618.

38. Gadamer articulates his aim in the introduction to *Truth and Method*: ". . . to defend the experience of truth that comes to us through the work of art against the aesthetic theory that lets itself be restricted to a scientific conception of truth." Hans-Georg Gadamer, *Truth and Method,* 2nd rev. edition, trans. Joel Weinsheimer and Donald G. Marshall (London and New York: Continuum, 2000), xxii.

39. This is Richard Bernstein's language. He describes Levinas's contestation of the finality of universals as based in the demand "from the phenomenon of Auschwitz (if we are not duped by morality) that we conceive of the moral law independently of the Happy End." Richard J. Bernstein, *Radical Evil: A Philosophical Interrogation* (Cambridge: Polity Press, 2002), 170.

40. Levinas, "Paul Celan: From Being to Other," PN 175 n. 12.

41. Additional subtlety is not always a welcome complication. James knew this. Realistic about an inevitable resistance to the ambiguity of his pluralism, he acknowledged the pervasive and deeply human instinct "to see everything as yes or no, as black or white" (PU 77).

42. Simone de Beauvoir, *The Ethics of Ambiguity* (New York: Citadel Press, 1976), 7.

43. James, "The Moral Philosopher and the Moral Life," WWJ 626.

44. None of this yields anything that is true for all time, and none of it helps us to judge which faces call out more urgently than others or which works should be exhibited or canonized. Choices have to be made, and Levinas relegates it to the realm of morality and politics to begin the deliberative process of weighing competing particularities. In the meantime, there is meaning without the rigidity of final judgments, and perhaps a more flexible, fallible variety of meaning is the only kind that retains an intimate connection with life.

Afterword

1. Heidegger writes: "If we consider the works in their untouched actuality and do not deceive ourselves, the result is that the works are as naturally present as are things . . . Works of art are shipped like coal on the Ruhr and logs from the Black Forest. During the First World War Hölderlin's hymns were packed in the soldier's knapsack together with cleaning gear." Heidegger, "The Origin of the Work of Art," in *Poetry, Language Thought,* 19.

2. Ibid., 19.

3. Beckmann's diary entry, in Max Beckmann, *Self-Portrait in Words: Collected Writings and Statements, 1903–1950,* ed. Barbara Copeland Buenger (Chicago: University of Chicago Press, 1997), 133.

4. In the chapter on "Habit" in the *Principles of Psychology,* James warns: "Woe to him who can only recognize [Goods] when he thinks them in their pure and abstract form! The habit of excessive novel-reading and theatre-going will produce true monsters in this line" (PP 1: 125).

5. Bruce Wilshire and Ronald Bruzina emphasize the degree to which the Continental/Analytic divide stunts James scholarship, explaining: "Many writers in America persist on dividing our James scholars into 'nativists' and 'foreigners,' i.e., those who discuss James within an exclusively American context, and those who make reference to Continental thought." The essays collected in *Phenomenology: Dialogues and Bridges* challenge this division. Bruce Wilshire and Ronald Bruzina, eds., *Phenomenology: Dialogues and Bridges* (Albany: State University of New York Press, 1982), ix.

6. James, letter to François Pillon, 12 June 1904, LWJ 2: 204.

7. Stanley Cavell, *In Quest of the Ordinary: Lines of Skepticism and Romanticism* (Chicago: University of Chicago Press, 1998), ix, 9. For a recent statement of a similar idea, see Gail Weiss, *Refiguring the Ordinary* (Bloomington: Indiana University Press, 2008).

8. For an account of the history and value of such dilemmas and the intersections of moral psychology, ethics, and behavioral experimentation, see Kwame Anthony Appiah, *Experiments in Ethics* (Cambridge, Mass.: Harvard University Press, 2008).

9. James, "The Moral Philosopher and the Moral Life," WWJ 626, 625.

10. I witnessed such an effect firsthand among rural families in Ohio in the summer of 2004: these families were able to displace their anxiety about jobs and healthcare into the supposedly more pressing, abstract anxiety about the potential for a terrorist attack outside Akron.

11. I have previously cited James's description of the "primitive quest" of metaphysics: "The world has always appeared to the natural mind as a kind of enigma, of which the key must be sought in the shape of some illuminating or power-bringing word or name. That word names the universe's *principle,* and to possess it is, after a fashion, to possess the universe itself. 'God,' 'Matter,' 'Reason,' 'the Absolute,' 'Energy' are so many solving names. You can rest when you have them. You are at the end of your metaphysical quest" (P 52).

12. Paul Steinberg, *Speak You Also: A Survivor's Reckoning,* trans. Linda Coverdale (New York: Metropolitan, 2000), 140.

13. This is the last in a series of interrelated problems that Critchley identifies with regard to Levinas, characterizing this problem as "the *political fate* of Levinasian ethics, namely the vexed problem of Israel." See Simon Critchley, "Five Problems in Levinas's View of Politics and the Sketch of a Solution to Them," *Political Theory* 32, no. 2 (2004): 178. See also Caygill's *Levinas and the Political,* 159–98.

14. "Evasive" is Michael Morgan's characterization. He provides a detailed and nuanced reading of Levinas's Zionism in the penultimate chapter of Morgan, *Discovering Levinas,* 336–414. See also Simon Critchley, "Persecution Before Exploitation: A Non-Jewish Israel," *Parallax* 8, no. 24: *Levinas and Politics,* ed. Charmaine Coyle and Simon Critchley (2002): 71–77.

BIBLIOGRAPHY

Améry, Jean. *At the Mind's Limits.* Trans. Sidney Rosenfeld and Stella P. Rosenfeld. Bloomington: Indiana University Press, 1980.

Appiah, Kwame Anthony. *Experiments in Ethics.* Cambridge, Mass.: Harvard University Press, 2008.

Arendt, Hannah. *Men in Dark Times.* Orlando: Harcourt, Brace, 1968.

Aristotle. *Rhetoric.* In *Aristotle: Selected Works,* ed. Hippocrates G. Apostle. Grinnell, Iowa: Peripatetic Press, 1991.

Ashton, Dore. *A Critical Study of Philip Guston.* Berkeley and Los Angeles: University of California Press, 1976.

Atterton, Peter, and Matthew Calarco, eds. *Radicalizing Levinas.* Albany: State University of New York Press, forthcoming.

Badiou, Alain. *Ethics: An Essay on the Understanding of Evil.* Trans. Peter Hallward. London and New York: Verso, 2001.

Bataille, Georges. "From Existentialism to the Primacy of Economy." Included in Robbins, *Altered Reading.*

———. "Letter to René Char on the Incompatibilities of the Writer." Trans. Christopher Carsten, in *Yale French Studies* 78: *On Bataille* (1990): 35–37.

Baudelaire, Charles. *The Flowers of Evil.* Trans. William Aggeler. Fresno: Academy Library Guild, 1954.

Beckett, Samuel. *Endgame.* New York: Grove Press, 1958.

———. *Nohow On: Three Novels.* New York: Grove Press, 1996.

Beckmann, Max. *Self-Portrait in Words: Collected Writings and Statements, 1903–1950.* Ed. Barbara Copeland Buenger. Chicago: University of Chicago Press, 1997.

Benjamin, Walter. *Illuminations: Essays and Reflections.* Ed. Hannah Arendt. Trans. Harry Zohn. New York: Schocken Books, 1968.

———. *The Origin of German Tragic Drama.* Trans. Joan Osborne. London and New York: Verso, 1998.

Bergo, Bettina. *Levinas Between Ethics and Politics: For the Beauty that Adorns the Earth.* Dordrecht: Kluwer, 1999.

Bernasconi, Robert. "Re-Reading *Totality and Infinity*." In *The Question of the Other,* ed. Alreen B. Dallery and Charles E. Scott. Albany: State University of New York Press, 1989.

———, and Simon Critchley, eds. *Re-Reading Levinas.* Bloomington: Indiana University Press, 1991.

Bernstein, Richard J. "Evil and the Temptation of Theodicy." In Critchley and Bernasconi, eds., *Cambridge Companion to Levinas.*

———. "Pragmatism, Pluralism and the Healing of Wounds." In Menand, ed., *Pragmatism: A Reader.*

———. *Radical Evil: A Philosophical Interrogation.* Cambridge: Polity, 2002.

Blanchot, Maurice. "L'Étrange et l'étranger." *La Nouvelle Revue Français* 70 (1958): 753–83.

———. «N'oublie pas.» *L'Arche* 373 (May 1988).

———. *The Station Hill Blanchot Reader: Fiction and Literary Essays.* Ed. George Quasha. Trans. Lydia Davis, Paul Auster, and Robert Lamberton. Barrytown, N.Y.: Station Hill Press, 1999.

———. *The Step Not Beyond.* Trans. Lycette Nelson. Albany: State University of New York Press, 1992.

Borges, Jorge Luis. *Selected Poems.* Ed. Alexander Coleman. New York and London: Penguin, 2000.

Bricker Balken, Debra. *Philip Guston's Poor Richard.* Chicago: University of Chicago Press, 2001.

Bruns, Gerald L. "The Concepts of Art and Poetry in Emmanuel Levinas's Writings." In Critchley and Bernasconi, eds., *Cambridge Companion to Levinas.*

Butler, Judith. *Precarious Life: The Powers of Mourning and Violence.* London and New York: Verso, 2006.

Calarco, Matthew. *Zoographies: The Question of the Animal from Heidegger to Derrida.* New York: Columbia University Press, 2008.

———, and Peter Atterton, eds. *Animal Philosophy: Essential Readings in Continental Thought.* London and New York: Continuum, 2004.

Casey, Edward S. *The World at a Glance.* Bloomington: Indiana University Press, 2006.

Cavell, Stanley. *Conditions Handsome and Unhandsome: The Constitution of Emersonian Perfectionism.* Chicago: University of Chicago Press, 1990.

———. *In Quest of the Ordinary: Lines of Skepticism and Romanticism.* Chicago: University of Chicago Press, 1998.

———. "What's the Use of Calling Emerson a Pragmatist?" In Dickstein, ed., *Revival of Pragmatism.*

Caygill, Howard. *Levinas and the Political.* London: Routledge, 2002.

Chanter, Tina. *Time, Death, and the Feminine: Levinas with Heidegger.* Stanford: Stanford University Press, 2001.

Cobb-Stevens, Richard. *James and Husserl: The Foundations of Meaning.* The Hague: Martinus Nijhoff, 1974.

Cohen, Richard. *Ethics, Exegesis, and Philosophy: Interpretation After Levinas.* Cambridge: Cambridge University Press, 2001.

Cormier, Harvey J. *The Truth is What Works: William James, Pragmatism, and the Seed of Death.* New York: Rowan & Littlefield, 2001.

Critchley, Simon. "Deconstruction or Pragmatism—Is Derrida a Private Ironist or a Public Liberal?" In Mouffe, ed., *Deconstruction and Pragmatism*.
———. *The Ethics of Deconstruction: Derrida and Levinas*. Edinburgh: Edinburgh University Press, 1992.
———. "Five Problems in Levinas's View of Politics and the Sketch of a Solution to Them." *Political Theory* 32, no. 2 (2004): 172–85.
———. *Infinitely Demanding: Ethics of Commitment, Politics of Resistance*. London and New York: Verso, 2007.
———. "The Original Traumatism: Levinas and Psychoanalysis." In Simon Critchley, *Ethics, Politics, Subjectivity: Essays on Derrida, Levinas and Contemporary French Thought*. London and New York: Verso, 1999.
———. "Persecution Before Exploitation: A Non-Jewish Israel." *Parallax* 8, no. 24: *Levinas and Politics,* ed. Charmaine Coyle and Simon Critchley (2002): 71–77.
———. *Very Little . . . Almost Nothing: Death, Philosophy, Literature*. London: Routledge, 1997.
———, and Robert Bernasconi, eds. *The Cambridge Companion to Levinas*. Cambridge: Cambridge University Press, 2002.
Danto, Arthur C. "The Abstract Impressionist: Philip Guston." *The Nation,* 29 December 2003.
Davies, Paul. "A Fine Risk: Reading Blanchot Reading Levinas." In Bernasconi and Critchley, eds., *Re-Reading Levinas*.
———. "On Resorting to an Ethical Language." In Peperzak, ed., *Ethics as First Philosophy*.
Davis, Colin. *Levinas: An Introduction*. Notre Dame: University of Notre Dame Press, 1996.
de Beauvoir, Simone. *The Ethics of Ambiguity*. New York: Citadel Press, 1976.
Deleuze, Gilles. *Bergsonism*. Trans. H. Tomlinson and B. Habberjam. New York: Zone Books, 2002.
———. *Cinema I: The Movement-Image*. Trans. Hugh Tomlinson and Barbara Habberjam. Minneapolis: University of Minnesota Press, 2006.
———. *The Fold: Leibniz and the Baroque*. Trans. Tom Conley. Minneapolis: University of Minnesota Press, 1993.
de Man, Paul. *Aesthetic Ideology*. Ed. Andrzej Warminski. Minneapolis and London: University of Minnesota Press, 1996.
Derrida, Jacques. *Adieu to Emmanuel Levinas*. Trans. Pascale-Anne Brault and Michael Naas. Stanford: Stanford University Press, 1999.
———. *Of Grammatology*. Trans. Gayatri Chakravorty Spivak. Baltimore: Johns Hopkins University Press, 1997.
de Sousa, Ronald. *The Rationality of Emotion*. Cambridge, Mass.: MIT Press, 1987.
de Vries, Hent. "Instances: Levinas on Art and Truth." In *Philosophy of Religion for a New Century,* ed. Jeremiah Hackett and Jerald Wallulis. Dordrecht: Kluwer, 2004.
Dewey, John. "The Need for a Recovery in Philosophy." In Menand, ed., *Pragmatism: A Reader*.
Diamond, Cora. "Anything but Argument?" in *The Realistic Spirit: Wittgenstein, Philosophy, and the Mind* (Cambridge, Mass.: MIT Press, 1995).
———. "The Difficulty of Reality and the Difficulty of Philosophy." In Stanley Cavell, Cora Diamond et al., *Philosophy and Animal Life*. New York: Columbia University Press, 2008.

———. "How Many Legs?" In *Value and Understanding: Essays for Peter Winch*, ed. Raimond Gaita. New York: Routledge, 1990.

———. "The Importance of Being Human." In *Human Beings*, ed. David Cockburn. Cambridge: Cambridge University Press, 1991.

Dickstein, Morris, ed. *The Revival of Pragmatism*. Chapel Hill: Duke University Press, 1999.

Diehm, Christian. "Facing Nature: Levinas Beyond the Human." In *Emmanuel Levinas: Critical Assessments*, 4 vols., ed. Claire Elise Katz. London and New York: Routledge, 2004.

Diprose, Rosalyn. *Corporeal Generosity: On Giving with Nietzsche, Merleau-Ponty, and Levinas*. Albany: State University of New York Press, 2002.

Drabinski, John. *Sensibility and Singularity: The Problem of Phenomenology in Levinas*. New York: State University of New York Press, 2001.

Eaglestone, Robert. "'Cold Splendor': Levinas's Suspicion of Art." In Robert Eaglestone, *Ethical Criticism: Reading after Levinas*. Edinburgh: Edinburgh University Press, 1997.

Eagleton, Terry. *Trouble with Strangers: A Study of Ethics*. Oxford: Wiley-Blackwell, 2009.

Edelglass, William. "Levinas's Language." *Analecta Husserliana* 85 (2005): 47–62.

Emerson, Ralph Waldo. *The Portable Emerson*. Ed. Carl Bode with Malcolm Cowley. New York: Penguin, 1981.

Feld, Ross. *Guston in Time*. New York: Counterpoint, 2003.

Ferguson, Kennan. *William James: Politics in the Pluriverse*. Lanham, Md.: Rowman & Littlefield, 2007.

Foucault, Michel. *The Care of the Self: The History of Sexuality, vol. 3*. Trans. R. Hurley. New York: Vintage, 1988.

Franzese, Sergio. *The Ethics of Energy: William James's Moral Philosophy in Focus*. Frankfurt: Ontos Verlag, 2008.

Freud, Sigmund. *Beyond the Pleasure Principle*. Ed. and trans. James Strachey. New York and London: W. W. Norton, 1961.

———. *The Future of an Illusion*. In *The Freud Reader*, ed. Peter Gay. New York and London: W. W. Norton, 1995.

Gadamer, Hans-Georg. *Truth and Method*. 2nd rev. edition. Trans. Joel Weinsheimer and Donald G. Marshall. London and New York: Continuum, 2000.

Gilligan, Carol. *In a Different Voice: Psychological Theory and Women's Development*. Cambridge, Mass.: Harvard University Press, 1993.

Griffin, David Ray, John B. Cobb, Jr., Marcus P. Ford, Pete A. Y. Gunter, and Peter Ochs. *Founders of Constructive Postmodern Philosophy: Peirce, James, Bergson, Whitehead, and Hartshorne*. Albany: State University of New York Press, 1992.

Guston, Philip. "Philip Guston Talking." In *Theories and Documents of Contemporary Art: A Sourcebook of Artists' Writings*, ed. Kristine Stiles and Peter Selz. Berkeley and Los Angeles: University of California Press, 1996.

Hadot, Pierre. *Philosophy as a Way of Life: Spiritual Exercises from Socrates to Foucault*. Ed. Arnold I. Davidson. Trans. Michael Chase. Oxford: Blackwell, 1995.

Heidegger, Martin. *Basic Writings: from* Being and Time *(1927) to* The Task of Thinking *(1964)*. Rev. and exp. edition. Ed. David Ferrell Krell. San Francisco: HarperCollins, 1993.

———. *Poetry, Language, Thought*. Trans. Michael Hofstadter. New York: Harper & Row, 1971.

Hentschel, Martin. "From the Abstract to the Figurative: Philip Guston's Stony Path." In *Philip Guston: Gemälde 1947–1979*. Bonn: Hatje Cantz, 1999.

Hoopes, James. *Community Denied: The Wrong Turn of Pragmatic Liberalism*. Ithaca: Cornell University Press, 1998.

Hume, David. *An Enquiry Concerning Human Understanding*. New York: Prometheus, 1988.

———. *A Treatise of Human Nature*. 2 vols. Ed. David Fate Norton and Mary J. Norton. Oxford: Oxford University Press, 2007.

Husserl, Edmund. *Cartesian Meditations: An Introduction to Phenomenology*. Trans. Dorion Cairns. Dordrecht: Kluwer, 1950.

———. *The Crisis of European Sciences and Transcendental Phenomenology*. Trans. David Carr. Evanston: Northwestern University Press, 1970.

———. *The Idea of Phenomenology*. Trans. William P. Alston and George Nakhnikian. Dordrecht: Kluwer, 1990.

———. "Persönliche Aufzeichnungen." Ed. W. Biemel. *Philosophical and Phenomenological Research* 16, no. 13 (1956): 293–302.

James, Henry. *The Beast in the Jungle and Other Stories*. New York: Dover, 1993.

Janicaud, Dominique. "The Theological Turn of French Phenomenology." Trans. Bernard G. Prusak, in *Phenomenology and the "Theological Turn": The French Debate*. New York: Fordham University Press, 2000.

Jankélévitch, Vladimir. *Forgiveness*. Trans. Andrew Kelley. Chicago: University of Chicago Press, 2005.

———. *Le Je-ne-sais-quoi et le presque-rien*. Paris: Presses Universitaires de France, 1957.

Joyce, James. *Dubliners*. New York: Penguin, 1967.

Kant, Immanuel. *The Critique of Judgement*. Trans. James Creed Meredith. Oxford: Clarendon Press, 1952.

Katz, Claire Elise. "'The Presence of the Other is a Presence That Teaches': Levinas, Pragmatism, and Pedagogy." *Journal of Jewish Thought and Philosophy* 14, nos. 1–2 (2006): 91–108.

Kearney, Richard. *States of Mind: Dialogues with Contemporary Thinkers on the European Mind*. Manchester: Manchester University Press, 1995.

Keats, John. *Selected Letters of John Keats*. Ed. Grant Scott. Cambridge, Mass.: Harvard University Press, 2002.

Kenaan, Hagi. *The Present Personal: Philosophy and the Hidden Face of Language*. New York: Columbia University Press, 2005.

Lamberth, David C. "James' Varieties Reconsidered: Radical Empiricism, the Extra-Marginal and Conversion." *The American Journal of Theology and Philosophy* 15, no. 3 (September 1994): 257–67.

———. *William James and the Metaphysics of Experience*. Cambridge: Cambridge University Press, 1999.

Levinas, Emmanuel. "Beyond Intentionality." Trans. Kathleen McLaughlin, in *Philosophy in France Today*, ed. Alan Montefiore. Cambridge: Cambridge University Press, 1983.

———. *Ethics and Infinity: Conversations with Philippe Nemo*. Trans. Richard A. Cohen. Pittsburgh: Duquesne University Press, 1985.

———. *Nine Talmudic Readings*. Trans. Annette Aronowicz. Bloomington: Indiana University Press, 1990.

Linschoten, Johannes. *On the Way Toward a Phenomenological Psychology: The Psychology of William James*. Pittsburgh: Duquesne University Press, 1968.

Llewelyn, John. "Am I Obsessed by Bobby? (Humanism of the Other Animal)." In Bernasconi and Critchley, eds., *Re-Reading Levinas*.

———. *The Middle Voice of Ecological Conscience: A Chiasmic Reading of Responsibility in the Neighborhood of Levinas, Heidegger and Others*. New York: St. Martin's Press, 1991.

———. *Emmanuel Levinas: The Genealogy of Ethics*. London: Routledge, 1995.

Lovejoy, Arthur O. *The Thirteen Pragmatisms and Other Essays*. Baltimore: Johns Hopkins University Press, 1963.

Lovelie, Elisabeth Marie. *Literary Silences in Pascal, Rousseau and Beckett*. Oxford: Oxford University Press, 2003.

Lyotard, Jean-François. "Levinas' Logic." In *Face to Face with Levinas*, ed. Richard A. Cohen. Albany: State University of New York Press, 1986.

———. "Newman: The Instant." In *The Inhuman: Reflections on Time*, trans. Geoffrey Bennington and Rachel Bowlby. Stanford: Stanford University Press, 1988.

Malka, Salomon. *Emmanuel Levinas: His Life and Legacy*. Trans. Michael Kigel and Sonja M. Embree. Pittsburgh: Duquesne University Press, 2006.

Marcel, Gabriel. *Tragic Wisdom and Beyond, including Conversations between Paul Ricoeur and Gabriel Marcel*. Trans. Stephen Jolin and Peter McCormick. Evanston: Northwestern University Press, 1973.

Mayer, Musa. *Night Studio: A Memoir of Philip Guston*. New York: Da Capo Press, 1988.

Menand, Louis, ed. *Pragmatism: A Reader*. New York: Vintage, 1997.

Merleau-Ponty, Maurice. *Signs*. Trans. Richard C. McCleary. Evanston: Northwestern University Press, 1964.

———. *The Visible and the Invisible*. Trans. Alphonso Lingis. Evanston: Northwestern University Press, 1964.

——— et al. *The Merleau-Ponty Aesthetics Reader: Philosophy and Painting*. Ed. Galen A. Johnson and Michael B. Smith. Evanston: Northwestern University Press, 1993.

Moran, Dermot. *Introduction to Phenomenology*. London: Routledge, 2000.

Morgan, Michael L. *Discovering Levinas*. Cambridge: Cambridge University Press, 2007.

Mouffe, Chantal, ed. *Deconstruction and Pragmatism*. London: Routledge, 1996.

Moyn, Samuel. *Origins of the Other: Emmanuel Levinas Between Revelation and Ethics*. Ithaca: Cornell University Press, 2005.

Myers, Gerald E. *William James: His Life and Thought*. New Haven: Yale University Press, 1986.

Nancy, Jean-Luc. "Painting (and) Presence." In *The Birth to Presence*, trans. Brian Holmes et al. Stanford: Stanford University Press, 1993.

Newman, Barnett. "The Sublime is Now." In *Art in Theory 1900–2000: An Anthology of Changing Ideas*, ed. Charles Harrison and Paul Wood. Oxford: Blackwell, 1992.

Nussbaum, Martha. *Love's Knowledge*. New York: Oxford University Press, 1990.

Peperzak, Adriaan T., ed. *Ethics as First Philosophy: The Significance of Emmanuel Levinas for Philosophy, Literature and Religion*. New York and London: Routledge, 1995.

Perpich, Diane. *The Ethics of Emmanuel Levinas*. Stanford: Stanford University Press, 2008.

Perry, Ralph Barton. *The Thought and Character of William James.* Cambridge, Mass.: Harvard University Press, 1948.

Peters, Gary. "The Rhythm of Alterity: Levinas and Aesthetics." *Radical Philosophy* 82 (March/April 1997): 9–16.

Plato. *Republic.* Trans. Allan Bloom. New York: Basic, 1968.

———. *The Symposium and The Phaedrus: Plato's Erotic Dialogues.* Trans. with comm. William S. Cobb. New York: State University of New York Press, 1993.

———. *Timaeus.* In *Plato: The Collected Dialogues,* ed. Edith Hamilton and Huntington Cairns. Princeton: Princeton University Press, 1989.

Putnam, Hilary. *Ethics Without Ontology.* Cambridge, Mass.: Harvard University Press, 2006.

———. "James's Theory of Truth." In Ruth Anna Putnam, ed., *Cambridge Companion to William James.*

———. "Levinas and Judaism." In Critchley and Bernasconi, eds., *Cambridge Companion to Levinas,* 33–62.

Putnam, Ruth Anna. "Some of Life's Ideals." In Ruth Anna Putnam, ed., *Cambridge Companion to William James.*

———, ed. *The Cambridge Companion to William James.* Cambridge: Cambridge University Press, 1997.

Richards, Robert J. *Darwin and the Emergence of Evolutionary Theories of Mind and Behavior.* Chicago: University of Chicago Press, 1989.

Richardson, Robert D. *William James: In the Maelstrom of American Modernism.* Boston: Houghton-Mifflin, 2006.

Ricoeur, Paul. "Otherwise: A Reading of Emmanuel Levinas's *Otherwise than Being or Beyond Essence.*" In *Yale French Studies* 104: *Encounters with Levinas* (2003): 82–99.

Riera, Gabriel. *Intrigues: From Being to the Other.* Fordham: Fordham University Press, 2006.

Rilke, Rainer Maria. *Auguste Rodin.* Trans. Daniel Slager. New York: Archipelago, 2004.

———. *The Selected Poetry of Rainer Maria Rilke.* Trans. Stephen Mitchell. New York: Vintage, 1989.

Robbins, Jill. *Altered Reading: Levinas and Literature.* Chicago: University of Chicago Press, 1999.

Rorty, Richard. "Heidegger, Kundera, and Dickens." In *Essays on Heidegger and Others: Philosophical Papers Volume 2.* Cambridge: Cambridge University Press, 1991.

———. "Response to Simon Critchley." In Mouffe, ed., *Deconstruction and Pragmatism.*

Rosenthal, Sandra B. "A Time for Being Ethical: Levinas and Pragmatism." *The Journal of Speculative Philosophy* 17, no. 3 (2003): 192–203.

———, and Patrick L. Bourgeois. *Pragmatism and Phenomenology: A Philosophic Encounter.* Amsterdam: B. R. Grüner, 1980.

Rousseau, Jean-Jacques. *The Discourses and Other Early Political Writings.* Ed. and trans. Victor Gourevitch. Cambridge: Cambridge University Press, 2000.

Sartre, Jean-Paul, and Benny Lévy. *Hope Now: The 1980 Interviews.* Trans. Adrian van den Hoven. Chicago: University of Chicago Press, 1996.

Shakespeare, William. *Macbeth.* In *The Complete Oxford Shakespeare,* ed. Stanley Wells and Gary Taylor. Oxford: Oxford University Press, 1986.

Shaw, Joshua James. *Emmanuel Levinas on the Priority of Ethics: Putting Ethics First.* Amherst, N.Y.: Cambria, 2008.

Spargo, R. Clifton. *Vigilant Memory: Emmanuel Levinas, the Holocaust, and the Unjust Death.* Baltimore: Johns Hopkins University Press, 2006.

Spiegelberg, Herbert, and Karl Schuhmann. *The Phenomenological Movement: A Historical Introduction.* Dordrecht: Kluwer, 1994.

Steinberg, Paul. *Speak You Also: A Survivor's Reckoning.* Trans. Linda Coverdale. New York: Metropolitan, 2000.

Stevens, Wallace. *The Collected Poems of Wallace Stevens.* New York: Vintage, 1990.

Taylor, Charles. *Sources of the Self: The Making of the Modern Identity.* Cambridge: Cambridge University Press, 1989.

Toumayan, Alain. *Encountering the Other: The Artwork and the Problem of Difference in Blanchot and Levinas.* Pittsburgh: Duquesne University Press, 2004.

Wahl, Jean. *Existence humaine et transcendance.* Neuchâtel: Éditions de la Baconnière, 1944.

———. *Vers le concret.* Paris: J. Vrin, 1932.

Waldenfels, Bernhard. «Levinas and the Face of the Other.» In Critchley and Bernasconi, eds., *Cambridge Companion to Levinas.*

Weber, Elisabeth. "The Notion of Persecution in Levinas's *Otherwise Than Being or Beyond Essence.*" In Peperzak, ed., *Ethics as First Philosophy.*

Weiss, Gail. *Refiguring the Ordinary.* Bloomington: Indiana University Press, 2008.

West, Cornell. *The American Evasion of Philosophy: A Genealogy of Pragmatism.* Madison: University of Wisconsin Press, 1989.

Whitman, Walt. *Complete Poetry and Collected Prose.* Ed. Justin Kaplan. New York: Library of America, 1982.

———. *Whitman.* Ed. Richard Wilbur. New York: Dell, 1959.

Wiener, Philip P. *Evolution and the Foundations of Pragmatism.* Cambridge, Mass.: Harvard University Press, 1949.

Wild, John. *The Radical Empiricism of William James.* New York: Doubleday, 1969.

Wilshire, Bruce. *William James and Phenomenology.* Bloomington: Indiana University Press, 1968.

———, and Ronald Bruzina, eds. *Phenomenology: Dialogues and Bridges.* Albany: State University of New York Press, 1982.

Wittgenstein, Ludwig. *Philosophical Investigations.* Trans. G. E. M. Anscombe. New York: Macmillan, 1953.

———. *Tractatus Logico-Philosophicus.* Trans. C. K. Ogden. London: Routledge, 1992.

Wood, David. «Some Questions for My Levinasian Friends.» In *Addressing Levinas,* ed. Eric Sean Nelson, Antje Kapust, and Kent Still. Evanston: Northwestern University Press, 2005.

Wordsworth, William. *The Prelude or Growth of a Poet's Mind.* Ed. Ernest De Selincourt. New York: Oxford University Press, 1970.

Wyschogrod, Edith. "The Art of Ethics." In Peperzak, ed., *Ethics as First Philosophy.*

———. *Emmanuel Levinas: The Problem of Ethical Metaphysics.* New York: Fordham University Press, 2000.

INDEX

Page numbers in italics refer to illustrations.

Abstract Expressionism: Guston and, 162–64, 168; rise of, 144

abstraction, 59–61

acts: vs. consciousness, 83–84; of decency, 194; ethical, 100

aesthetics, and ethics, xviii–xix, 133–57, 182–83

"After you," xiv–xv, 64, 100, 194

allegory, 175–78

ambiguity: and description, 47; and ethics, 24–28, 183, 197; and knowledge, 85; need for, xviii; non-mystical, 58–59; of subjectivity, 14

American connection with French thought, 162, 190–92, 214n34

American Pragmatism, 66–67

anxiety, 9–13, 15

appearance, 47–48, 55, 60–61

Arendt, Hannah: on Benjamin, 176–77; on illumination, 27

Aristotle: on emotion, 103–104; on friendship, 122, 221n53; and sensibility, 13–14; on the soul, 25–26, 107

art: engaged, 139–40, 147–48; and ethics, 129, 135, 151; and experience, 145–46; hope in, 156–59; Levinas on, xviii–xix, 134, 138, 145–46; modern, 142–45; progress in, 161–62, 170–72, 185; and radical empiricism, 185–89; and trans-

descendence, 173–75; worship of, 146–47

audible, the, privileging of, 55, 129, 134–38

Auschwitz, 194

Badiou, Alain, on "theological turn," 62

Bataille, Georges, on cracks, 203–204n46

Baudelaire, Charles, 80–81, 90, 188

Beast in the Jungle, The (James), 18

Beckmann, Max, 189

Being and Time (Heidegger), 10, 33–38, 50, 206n19

Benjamin, Walter, on allegory, 176–77

Bergson, Henri: on *durée,* 20–21, 75–76; on *élan vital,* 46, 54, 79–81; on emotion, 104; and Heidegger, 79; and James, xv–xvi, 59, 71–72, 75–79, 162, 191; and Levinas, 78–81; on sensible reality, 86; on sympathetic acquaintance, 77

Blanchot, Maurice: on aging, 21; on brilliance, 26–27; Levinas on, 22, 148–53, 156–57; on mourning, 28; on poetry, 149–57; on restlessness, 25; writing style of, 133

blindness, 93–95, 105, 118

body, the: and consciousness, 204n38; emotion and, 107–109; face as, 44,

MEGAN CRAIG is a painter and Assistant Professor
of Philosophy and Art at Stony Brook University,
New York. She earned her Ph.D. at the New School
for Social Research and her B.A. at Yale University.
She teaches and works in the intersection between
ethics and aesthetics, and her paintings have been
exhibited nationally and internationally.

Milton Keynes UK
Ingram Content Group UK Ltd.
UKHW022158250424
441772UK00009B/458

9 780253 222381